GUNFLINT FALLING

Also by Cary J. Griffith
Published by the University of Minnesota Press

Gunflint Burning: Fire in the Boundary Waters

GUNFLINT
FALLING

BLOWDOWN IN THE
BOUNDARY WATERS

CARY J. GRIFFITH

UNIVERSITY OF MINNESOTA PRESS
MINNEAPOLIS
LONDON

Published by the University of Minnesota Press
111 Third Avenue South, Suite 290
Minneapolis, MN 55401-2520
http://www.upress.umn.edu

ISBN 978-1-5179-1556-8 (hc)
ISBN 978-1-5179-1557-5 (pb)

A Cataloging-in-Publication record for this book is available from the
Library of Congress.

Printed in the United States of America on acid-free paper

The University of Minnesota is an equal-opportunity educator and employer.

30 29 28 27 26 25 24 23   10 9 8 7 6 5 4 3 2 1

For the Gunflint Trail Historical Society, the Chik-Wauk Museum and Nature Center, and all of the resorts and residents who have chosen to live and recreate along the Trail. You have helped many learn about and experience one of North America's greatest wilderness areas. Thank you.

CONTENTS

PART III. JULY 5–19: SEARCH, RESCUE, AND ASSESSMENT

PART IV. RECOVERY

MAP OF THE
GUNFLINT BLOWDOWN, 1995

Moving from WSW to ENE, the storm entered the Arrowhead region of northeastern Minnesota in the early afternoon. Here, winds of 80 to 100 mph resulted in injuries to about 60 canoe campers and damage to tens of millions of trees within the 477,000 acres of forest land . . . in the course of leveling a swath 30 miles long and 4 to 12 miles wide.

—*After the Blowdown: A Resource Assessment of the Boundary Waters Canoe Area Wilderness, 1999–2003* (USDA, 2007)

T he map on the next two pages shows the location of several people impacted by the derecho that hit the Boundary Waters Canoe Area Wilderness on July 4, 1999. From west to east, they were:

USFS wilderness ranger Nicole Selmer—leading a group of eight who were working to improve BWCAW portage trails from Mudro Lake to Fourtown Lake

USFS wilderness ranger Pete Weckman—on routine patrol up Moose Lake and points farther north

Camper Lisa Naas—camping on the BWCAW's Lake Polly with four friends

Camper Vicky Brockman—camping on the BWCAW's Alpine Lake with two friends

(continued on page xii)

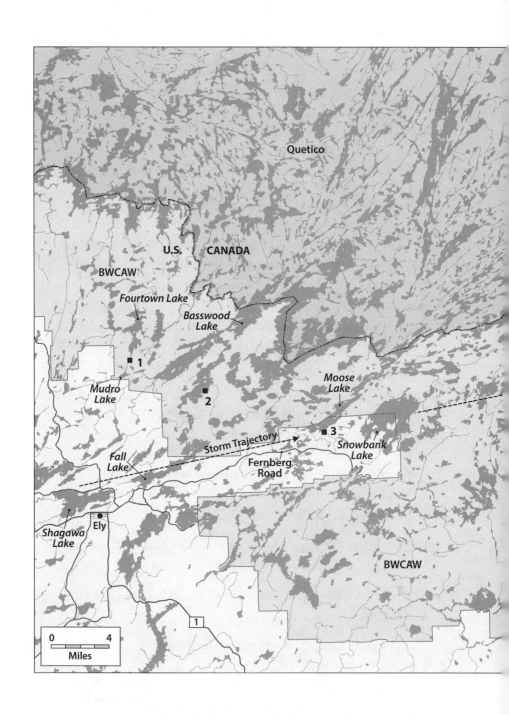

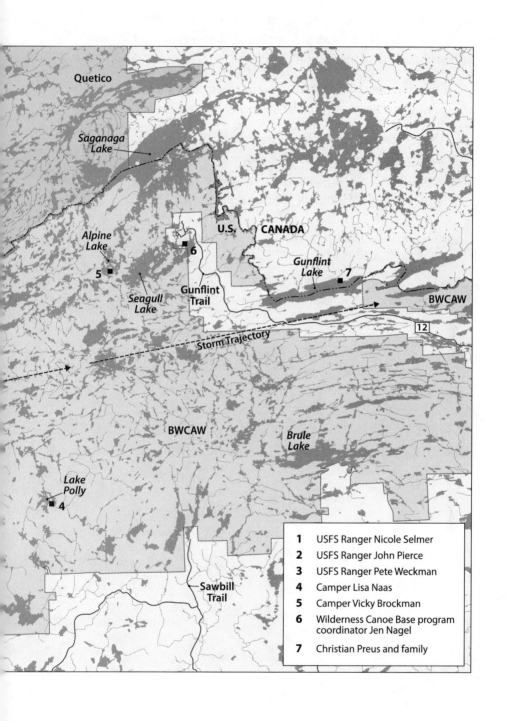

Quetico

Saganaga
Lake

Alpine
Lake

5 ■

U.S. CANADA

■ 6

Gunflint
Lake

7 ■

BWCAW

Seagull
Lake

Gunflint
Trail

12

Storm Trajectory

BWCAW

Brule
Lake

Lake
Polly

■ 4

Sawbill
Trail

1	USFS Ranger Nicole Selmer
2	USFS Ranger John Pierce
3	USFS Ranger Pete Weckman
4	Camper Lisa Naas
5	Camper Vicky Brockman
6	Wilderness Canoe Base program coordinator Jen Nagel
7	Christian Preus and family

Wilderness Canoe Base program coordinator Jen Nagel—one of the base's leaders spending the holiday weekend at the base, near the end of the Gunflint Trail

Christian Preus and family—visiting their recently completed summer cabin on the northeast corner of Gunflint Lake

Along with many other local, state, and federal officials as well as private citizens from every background, these individuals were significantly impacted by the blowdown. I am deeply indebted to all of them for sharing their stories.

PROLOGUE
SUNDAY, JULY 4, 1999

Wilderness Canoe Base
Fishhook Island, Seagull Lake, End of the Gunflint Trail

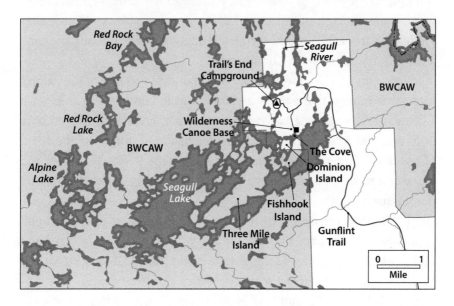

Since the still, hot start to the day, Jen Nagel had sensed foreboding. After the late-morning Sunday service, some of the attendees had lingered, sitting on the edge of the open-air chapel, seemingly overcome by the heat and humidity. Warm weather wasn't unusual for July in the Boundary Waters, but Jen couldn't recall this kind of heat, compounded by the air's moisture. And it was strangely calm, as though the entire area were enclosed in a bell jar.

Between the end of the service and one o'clock lunch, Jen decided to return to her cabin and change clothes.

/ / /

Jen Nagel had first been introduced to the Boundary Waters Canoe Area Wilderness (BWCAW) in the late 1980s. "I fell in love with the Boundary Waters on that trip," Jen remembered. So much so, she went to work at the Wilderness Canoe Base (WCB) over the summer of 1991, when she helped out in the trail shack and served as a guide and counselor. Before assuming her position as a program coordinator, Jen had worked throughout the 1990s in a variety of WCB jobs: wilderness guide, hospitality, trails director, pastor in residence, and more. At one point, after graduating from college and before attending graduate school, she took a year off to work at the WCB full-time.

Now, almost a decade after her first visit, she was one of the camp's leaders. She knew all the paths and buildings inhabiting the camp's two islands. She loved the area's old-growth trees, lakes, and rugged rock outcrops. Like many WCB employees, Jen had never forgotten the sense of awe and wonder she felt when first visiting the BWCAW. For her and many others, it was a place of startling beauty, a spiritual landscape that never ceased to amaze and inspire.

The Lutheran-based WCB resided at the northeast end of Seagull Lake, on the literal edge of the Boundary Waters. A turnoff near the end of the Gunflint Trail marked the ½-mile drive to the WCB parking lot and the Cove, where several camp cabins nestled along the shore.

At 4,300 acres, Seagull Lake is one of the BWCAW's larger bodies of water, stretching from northeast to southwest for approximately 4 miles. Its waters are dotted with more than one hundred islands. As one nearby outfitter has suggested, Seagull's shoreline is so jagged and the lake contains so many islands that a canoeist could explore it for days and never paddle the same route twice. The far northeast corner is home to several cabins and a few outfitters, including the Wilderness Canoe Base. The base and its cabins, outhouses, outfitting sheds, docks, boats, canoes, and kayaks were spread across the Cove and nearby Dominion and Fishhook Islands.

Fishhook Island gets its name from its shape: its southwest end forms a curved peninsula, giving the entire island the vague shape of a fishhook. Only the northeast end of the island, which contains the majority of the WCB's cabins and other buildings, lies outside the BWCAW. Much of the middle of the island, all the way down to its curved end, is technically in the Boundary Waters.

Fishhook and Dominion both had statuesque stands of old-growth white and red pine forest, some of the trees more than one hundred years old. Three Mile Island, a short canoe ride to the west, contained several stands of huge, beautiful old growth. It was often a destination for visitors who wanted to see God's natural cathedrals firsthand.

From inside Pinecliff Lodge, Jen and her colleagues at the base looked across the narrow strip of Seagull Lake to the older trees of Dominion. None of Dominion Island was inside the Boundary Waters, so its forest had been treated differently from the area within the BWCAW. Chainsaws could be used there, and much of the deadfall had been cleared out and cut up for firewood, making its forest more open, with wider, cleared spaces between the trees. A large mainland WCB dock supported the watercraft traffic visitors used to ferry to the nearby islands.

"You'd take a pontoon or a motorboat or a canoe or a kayak from the Cove to the islands," explained Jen. "Both islands have different landings and docking areas. Fishhook is the primary island. As you're coming across in whatever watercraft you're using, you would see, above and to your left, Pinecliff, which is the big, main kitchen, living room, and dining area. Pinecliff is the heart of a lot of things. Directly below Pinecliff sits the main dock. And a little beyond that you'd get to the canoe beach, where the canoes come in and out."

Jen Nagel had never thought of Pinecliff as being on a cliff. It was definitely on the highest western shoreline of Fishhook Island, but it was only a 50-foot trail from the dock up to the lodge. "From Pinecliff, you could stand and look across the lake toward the chapel on Dominion Island," Jen noted. "You looked west, and though you didn't have a long view of the lake, you definitely had a western view."

A 50-yard bridge had been built to connect Fishhook to Dominion, where there was a sauna and the open-air chapel. Jen and the others had traversed it earlier to worship at the beautiful sanctuary. "The chapel is stunning," she explained. "It has big, high peaks that rise into the nearby trees, but there are no walls, so you have a wonderful view of the lake."

/ / /

Contrary to WCB recommendations, Jen had worn sandals to the late-morning service. But on her return to her cabin, she felt more keenly the strange intensity in the air. The feeling caused her to slip into her hiking boots, careful to lace them tight.

By the time Jen climbed the hill to Pinecliff, what she saw to the west unnerved her. Having grown up in southern Minnesota, she was familiar with tornado season, and the wall of green clouds reminded her of the antecedent to twisters back home. As if responding to her thoughts, the day's vacuum-like stillness was broken by a light breeze.

Others were gathering for lunch. Typically, Sundays at the base were transition days. One set of weeklong campers would have left the previous day, and a new crop of visitors would be arriving throughout Sunday. But today was a holiday, and unusually, most of the people at the base were employees—guide counselors, base support staff, and a handful of leaders like Jen.

The WCB attracted a young, creative, and adventurous crowd. The community had a tradition of celebrating the Fourth of July with playful costumes, games of greased watermelon, and a cookout on the beach followed by a "paddle-in" movie. The group loved to have fun, and all the preparations were underway for another great Independence Day celebration.

Now everyone who had remained in camp gathered on the western side of Pinecliff to watch the weather come in. As the wall of green clouds approached, the breeze began pushing the trees. The rain came on, and there was another uptick in the wind.

WCB employees were familiar with being exposed to inclement weather. Many of them loved to experience meteorological histrionics firsthand. Now several of them stepped out on the western-facing deck and began dancing in the downpour.

Not long after the rain began, Jen thought she saw lightning approaching with the intensifying weather. The trees began to sway more wildly, and for fear someone was going to get hurt, she called out to the revelers to return to the safety of Pinecliff's interior.

Finally, the gathering storm forced everyone inside.

Amazingly, the wind intensified. As Jen and the others peered through the blurry rainfall, they could feel as much as see the mounting torrent. The forest was battered by the oncoming storm.

And then a phenomenon happened that shocked everyone who saw it. The massive trees of the surrounding forest began to lift and settle, as if some kind of seismic wave were sweeping toward them.

Jen had attended enough naturalists' lectures to know the forest of the Boundary Waters had shallow roots. The area was rocky, and the soil in many places was only inches deep. In consequence, the towering red and white pines' root systems spread out beneath them, some growing wider than their canopies. Under the soil, many of the trees' root systems were interconnected.

Now the tops of Dominion's old trees intensified their sway. Jen and the others watched in amazement as the carpet of huge, intertwined trees "were being lifted up out of the ground and set back down," as Jen recalled. "So as each of the trees were moving, it made the land look like it was breathing. But they were still standing. It was so strange."

Maybe if the wind had blown at 80 miles per hour instead of 100 or 120, the trees would have continued to rise and return to the ground, as though the earth were exhaling. "But instead, it loosened and pulled up big chunks. And as those trees went over, they knocked other trees over, because they're all interlaced."

The undulation was making the giant pines bend and weave and rise and drop like shocks of wheat succumbing to the sweep of a giant invisible hand. Then everyone felt an even stronger blast of wind. And the huge trees—on Fishhook and nearby Dominion and Three Mile Island and all over the heart of the Boundary Waters—began to fall.

PART I

BEFORE THE STORM

1

THE BEST-LAID PLANS

July 1–2, 1999
Journey to Lake Polly

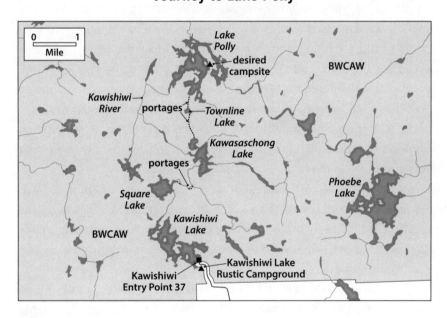

O ver the 1999 New Year's holiday, Ray Orieux (pronounced "Or-ee-you") had contemplated his next wilderness adventure. Ray had been all over the Boundary Waters, and he, his wife, Michelle, and their friends were thinking July 4 would be a good time for another trip. They were all relatively new in the workforce and had not yet banked a lot of vacation days, so they liked to leverage long holiday weekends.

And New Year's—the shortest, coldest time of year—was a good vantage point from which to contemplate a middle-of-the-summer Northwoods adventure. The idea of the warmth, verdure, and pristine waterways of the Boundary Waters Canoe Area Wilderness (BWCAW) was a welcome respite from winter's frozen fist.

The plan was for five of them to go into the woods: Ray and Michelle, Michelle's friends and fellow accountants Lisa Naas and Kristina Schwendinger, and Kristina's husband, Mark.

Michelle and Kristina worked for what was then a Big Five accounting firm. "At Arthur Andersen," Kristina recalled, "we spent a lot of hours working together, but then we spent a lot of time afterward at happy hour." They were often joined by Lisa, who had worked with Michelle at Cargill and subsequently became Michelle's roommate before Michelle and Ray were married.

"I would tag along, too," said Kristina's husband, Mark. "And Ray would tag along, and we all got to know each other really well."

As Ray considered his Boundary Waters maps, he began to conjure a plan that would take the five young adventurers into a less-traveled area of the wilderness. "I thought Lake Polly was a remote enough trip and wouldn't be too challenging for everybody to get out there with all their gear and some of the luxuries of home," Ray said.

Many BWCAW enthusiasts consider the best way to enter the wilderness to be from the east, traveling through Grand Marais and up the Gunflint Trail. Others prefer entering from the west, through Ely. While Ray had used both these BWCAW entry points, the way into Lake Polly was from the south.

Ray's plan would take them up Highway 61 to Tofte on Lake Superior's North Shore. From there they could go left, west, up the Sawbill Trail for approximately 17 miles to Cook County Road 33. Then there were a few more turns over roads that became narrower and more rugged over the next 12 miles before finally ending up at the Kawishiwi Lake campground and BWCAW entry point 37. The campground is located in the south-central part of the million-plus-acre wilderness.

"I'd been through that entry point multiple times," Ray said. "I consider it more of an easier quick day trip to get up to that area. That's kind of why I chose it."

Once through Kawishiwi Lake, paddlers can navigate the Kawishiwi River into Square Lake, to the north. The river continues north out of Square Lake, and though that paddle involves a couple of short portages, most of the way it can be traversed by canoe until visitors enter Kawasachong Lake. Because this is already three lakes into the Boundary Waters, many paddlers camp here. Others continue up the Kawishiwi River to the northwest. But for those interested in going farther north into Lake Polly, "There are two really long portages," Ray said. "You have a long portage through marshy low ground. It's a flat portage, and you don't have to go up any bluffs or anything like that. And it goes into another small lake . . . and then you have another portage into Polly." That long portage would be 189 rods, or more than ½ mile; the second would be 73 rods, or nearly ¼ mile.

At Ray's workplace, he had access to state-of-the-art printing capabilities. On top of a map, he superimposed his suggested route in red: through four lakes, over marshes, up rivers, and across six portages into Lake Polly. Also in red, he had printed ENTER POINT near the Kawishiwi campground. By the time his red line reached Kawasachong Lake, another note typed on the nearby shoreline joked POTENTIAL FIRST SITE. ARE WE TIRED YET? The red line continued through the next portage, into the small Townline Lake, and then another portage until it reached up a long northern peninsula on Lake Polly. Here a couple of lines ended on the shore with DESIRED CAMP SITES identifying the distant wilderness locations where Ray thought they should stay.

The group subsequently met over cocktails and dinner, during which Ray shared his plans and a copy of his detailed map. The buy-in was unanimous, and even though some members of the group had not spent much time in the woods, they were excited by the prospect of a Fourth of July holiday encamped in a remote section of the Boundary Waters with good friends.

Once everyone agreed, Ray obtained the necessary permits.

/ / /

After work on Thursday, July 1, Ray and Michelle Orieux climbed into their fully loaded black pickup and headed north. Ray had installed a rack atop the truck that would support a canoe over the rear cargo hold. "The canoe was up above and you still had access to the entire bed where all our gear and stuff was packed," Ray noted.

The couple had a lightweight 16½-foot Old Town river canoe. They had a good tent, bags, sleeping mats, a camp stove, large tarps for protection against the sun and rain, a solar shower, a portable table, and more.

Ray and Michelle were heading up two days before their friends and would spend their first night in the Kawishiwi campground. Ray had made enough trips to have acquired separate gear for car camping in the campground; their Boundary Waters gear was stowed in separate packs in the truck's cargo hold. In the morning, they would be able to just pack up and go.

Apart from the heat and humidity, the start of their trip proceeded as planned. They reached BWCAW campsite 1078 on Lake Polly around midday on Friday, July 2. Not only was the site open, but it was everything Ray had remembered about it. "There's a little island that's right across from the camp," he recalled. "I was very happy the site was open because it sits on a very large rock embankment that's probably 15 feet out of the water and gives you a good western view of the lake as the sun's going down."

There are approximately fifteen campsites on Lake Polly. On the Paddle Planner website, users have rated 1078 the highest of all of them, 4.5 stars out of a possible 5. Photographs show a small island 30–40 yards to the west-northwest of the site. The view west across the lake is expansive and clear. The rock and dirt escarpment that Ray recalled has a fire pit near its middle, with two log benches around the pit's southern and eastern sides. The opening is large enough for at least three tents. And there are enough nearby trees on which to string rope and hang tarps.

Kristina Schwendinger recalled one of the campsite's most interesting features: "The campsite wrapped around a little bit, and there was a small cove that faced north." Anyone viewing Lake Polly on Google Maps can see the rock escarpment that stretches due north approximately 30 feet away from the fire pit with benches. The lake wraps around that stretch of rock and does indeed form a small, protected cove, which is probably another reason Ray and so many other campers have appreciated the site.

/ / /

Ray and Michelle spent the rest of Friday afternoon establishing their camp, pitching their tent, getting their bedding in place, erecting their portable table, gathering firewood, hanging their solar shower, pulling out and tying off tarps, and more. They attached one of their largest tarps to nearby trees with one end tied off near the ground, so that it formed a kind of lean-to against the elements. Bad weather during the BWCAW's summer months almost always came from the west, and as the morning gave way to a warming day, the western-facing tarp would provide welcome shade.

On Ray's original map, he had noted two possible campsites on Lake Polly. The other, BWCAW campsite 1076, sits on the western side of the same peninsula, approximately one-quarter mile farther north. There are two very small islands in front of it. That site also faces west and would have had excellent sunset views.

Ray and Michelle finished setting up camp at site 1078 with plenty of time left in the day. They discovered a trail through the woods that headed north along the shoreline, and the afternoon was nice enough that they could hike along the water. Eventually, the trail ended at campsite 1076. At this point on Friday, it was still open. But once you enter Lake Polly, it is a longer paddle to 1076 than to 1078, so they were happy with their choice of site.

Once they returned to camp, they spent the evening around the fire, where the smoke helped ward off the bugs. They enjoyed their dinner and the views. Eventually, around dusk, the bugs drove them into their tent.

It had been a long, arduous day, and it felt good to climb into their soft down bags. The evening was unusually warm. They looked forward to the arrival of their friends the next day as they fell into contented sleep.

2

MAIDEN VOYAGE

July 2, 1999

Saganaga, Red Rock, Alpine, and Seagull Lakes Loop, BWCAW

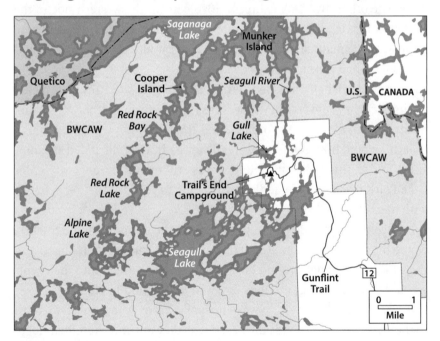

S ue Ann Martinson's first Boundary Waters trip had been, at least so
far, memorable. At fifty-five years of age, she had always heard about
the BWCAW, but until now she had never had a chance to visit. The
series of events that had induced her to make this trip with two friends
was, if she thought about it at all, fortuitous and serendipitous.

Sue Ann had recently met and been interviewed by thirty-eight-year-old Vicky Brockman as part of Vicky's PhD dissertation. Vicky had gotten to know the politically active Sue Ann and enjoyed her company. In fact, once Vicky finished her PhD, she invited Sue Ann to her celebration at her parents' Twin Cities home, which had more room than the apartment Vicky shared with her husband, Mike, in the Dinkytown neighborhood of Minneapolis. At that party, Sue Ann met a longtime friend and colleague of Vicky's, fifty-two-year-old Jan Fiola.

Over the previous fifteen years, Jan and Vicky had been on numerous BWCAW trips. Vicky loved going on wilderness trips with Jan, with whom she'd become good friends over the years. They shared academic interests as well as a love for the north woods. Jan enjoyed planning their wilderness excursions, and she loved preparing meals, even in the Boundary Waters, where she seldom spared expenses or cut corners with regard to what she was willing to carry into the woods. She was a careful packer and was familiar enough with wilderness rules and regulations to know what kind of equipment and packaging was optimal for paddling lakes and portaging trails. For instance, a well-known camping maxim is "leave no trace"—visitors must pack out everything they pack in. One of Jan's adaptations to this cardinal rule was boxed wine, as it was much easier to haul out boxes than bottles. When she was in charge of the wilderness cuisine, few people ate or drank as well as they did.

There was one Boundary Waters trip Vicky had taken with Jan that she had always wanted to revisit. The Fisher Company, known for its yellow and blue BWCAW maps, had a flyer that described the canoe route as "Trip No. 18: The Saganaga–Seagull Lakes Loop (17½ miles, 4 portages, 2 days)." In part, the flyer's description read, "This popular route begins and ends at the Trails End Campground on the Gunflint Trail, found 57 miles northwest of Grand Marais on Lake Superior. The canoe trail starts on Gull Lake and travels through Saganaga, Red Rock, Alpine, and Seagull Lakes before returning again to the Forest Service landing on Gull Lake."

When Vicky recalled this route, she remembered beautiful campsites, relatively easy paddles through gorgeous lake country, and a handful of manageable portages. It was considered a good beginner's foray into BWCAW travel, especially for canoeists who planned (as Vicky, Jan,

and Sue Ann did) to extend the duration of their paddle to four days instead of two.

Everything Sue Ann had heard about the trip—Vicky's memories of
the route, Jan's experience, their packing and wilderness cooking expertise, the boxed wine, and more—convinced her it would be perfect for
her maiden Boundary Waters voyage. When she considered how a serendipitous encounter with a PhD candidate had led to a wilderness adventure with new friends, she smiled at her good fortune.

/ / /

Vicky had tried to entice her husband, Mike, to join them. Mike was familiar with Jan and Vicky's wilderness trips—he knew that Jan left no
detail unattended and was prepared not only to eat well but also for
whatever unexpected incidents might befall them. But he was already
considering inviting some of his and Vicky's Dinkytown neighbors over
to celebrate on July 4. When he weighed lugging equipment and canoes
across portages against celebrating the Fourth in his own apartment,
where he would be able to sleep in his own bed, the choice was obvious.

Once the women knew it would be just the three of them, they
pooled their resources and bought a 9-by-7-foot nylon dome tent. It had
an ample rain fly, a large zippered screen door, and a top window. It was
not the kind of tent you could stand in, but it was spacious enough to
allow the three of them to lay out their bags and sleep comfortably.

Of the three women, Vicky had the largest car, a white Camry. The
plan was for Jan to pack the car Thursday morning, July 1. They would
drive to the end of the Gunflint Trail and camp their first night at End of
the Trail campground. On Friday, they would visit the nearby Way of the
Wilderness Canoe Outfitters and rent a canoe, paddles, and life vests.
They decided a single canoe would suffice for all their gear, with two
large packs and Sue Ann riding in the middle. Jan and Vicky had made
enough canoe trips together to be comfortable with the planned paddling duties: Vicky in the bow and Jan, the more seasoned paddler, steer-
ing in the stern.

They would enter the nearby Seagull River via the campground's public landing and paddle north. (On the north side of the Laurentian Divide,

the continental divide that separates the Hudson Bay watershed to the north and the Gulf of Mexico watershed to the south, the Seagull River flows north.) They would canoe most of the rest of July 2, heading due north through Gull Lake into the long, narrow southern arm of Saganaga Lake. Once out into the big open waters of Saganaga, they would steer west beside Clark Island and continue west along the numerous small islands and southern shore of the lake. They planned to stay well south of Munker Island, heading southwest into Red Rock Bay. Once in the bay, they would find a campsite, set up camp, and spend the night of July 2.

On July 3, they planned to paddle and portage into Red Rock Lake, canoe through that lake to the portage into Alpine Lake, and finally paddle to the southern end of Alpine—where, if their luck held, they hoped to find open a well-situated campsite Jan and Vicky had used before. There they would settle in, spending Saturday evening and all of Sunday, July 4, relaxing, reading, and taking in the ambience of the great Northwoods. They planned to paddle out on Monday, July 5.

/ / /

Their Thursday trip to the end of the Gunflint Trail had gone as planned, and on Friday, July 2, they awoke in End of the Trail campground. The morning dawned cool and hazy. Before they broke camp, Sue Ann snapped a picture of her two companions standing in front of their tent. Both were in good shape, definitely fit enough for the paddle and portages ahead. The pair wore khaki shorts and tennis shoes. The morning had enough chill to cause Jan to pull on a windbreaker and Vicky a light jacket. Sue Ann looked on from behind the camera's lens, her long silver hair tucked under her black lumberjack hat. Sue Ann's photograph shows two smiling women, obviously excited about the journey ahead.

On their first morning in the woods the travelers could already tell that it was going to be a warm and possibly sunny day and that by midmorning they very likely would be shedding their extra layers.

Jan and Vicky had also paddled enough to know that when you get onto the BWCAW's waters, if the sun was out, the light can be intense. In Sue Ann's photograph, Jan holds a blue baseball cap, while Vicky has already donned sunglasses—protection against what they suspected would be a sunny, hot day. They could already feel that, as this day progressed, the skies were going to clear and warm.

The three broke camp, went to Way of the Wilderness Canoe Outfitters, and were in the Seagull River, paddling north with the current, well before the day was fully underway. Sue Ann, comfortable riding in the canoe's middle, loved seeing the beautiful, endless expanse of water. Because her hands were free, she contented herself with snapping photographs with her disposable camera, a duty she would assume throughout the rest of their trip.

Sue Ann was glad she was traveling with experienced paddlers. Not only did they paddle well, but given the size of the lake and its numerous small and large islands, it was difficult to determine which direction they should take to get to their first campsite in Red Rock Bay. Fortunately, Jan had been on this route a few times, and Vicky had navigated it once before.

As the trio paddled north up Saganaga's long arm, clouds moved in. They were thick, puffy, gray and white, like huge cotton balls floating across the azure sky. At one point, with the sun trying to break through the clouds in the east and a cluster of small islands in the foreground, Sue Ann was struck by the beauty and snapped a photograph.

By midmorning, it was warm enough for Vicky, paddling in the front, to shed her hooded sweatshirt and wrap it around her shoulders. Sue Ann snapped a photograph of her in the bow. By now the clouds had largely dissipated, forcing Vicky to don her baseball cap. The photograph captures her hand, poised above her head, gripping the top of the paddle, ready to push with both arms in a downstroke.

Saganaga is a big lake. If it is windy, it can be treacherous. When whitecaps start breaking over Saganaga, only fools try to cross it in a canoe. Fortunately, this day continued calm, mostly sunny, and hot. As the trio approached Red Rock Bay, they grew close to the nearby forest. Sue Ann could see black spruce, cedar, alder, and other trees bunched close along the shoreline. Occasional white and red pines punctuated the land's edge, rising out of the shoreline like huge sentinels. From this vantage point, the forest appeared impenetrable.

The trio made the correct turns at the correct islands until they entered the north end of Red Rock Bay. At the mouth of the bay their map showed a small island called Cooper's Island. South of Cooper's Island was another island, larger and unnamed, with a campsite (BWCAW campsite 404) on its western side. It was a large site with plenty of space for several tents and at least three suitable trees for hanging hammocks. A gradual slope of granite angled down into the water, making it ideal for landing a canoe as well as wading out into the lake for a swim. On a rise over the granite beach there was an excellent flat spot for their tent. There were several nearby small islands off to the right and a small island bay to the left. The view was terrific, and the afternoon was warm enough for a leisurely swim.

The three women were readers, and all had brought along books. Vicky loved mysteries, especially those penned by Nevada Barr that featured Anna Pigeon, a National Parks ranger who visited parks all over the nation, where she stumbled on and then solved crimes. On this trip, Vicky had brought *Blind Descent*, a novel in which park ranger Pigeon finds herself descending into a cave system to rescue a woman who has been injured deep inside New Mexico's Carlsbad Cavern National Park.

After setting up camp and stringing their hammocks, the three settled in for some serious reading. Near the water, the light wind kept the bugs at bay. The view across the lake in front of them was the kind of scene that before now Sue Ann had only glimpsed in pictures. For their Friday-night dinner they enjoyed one of Jan's gourmet meals, accompanied by camp mugs of wine.

Their campsite faced west-southwest. July 2 was less than two weeks after the summer solstice, the longest day of the year, and on this evening the sun set around 9:00 p.m. Before it dropped below the opposite shoreline, Sue Ann faced her camera lens out across the water and snapped a photograph. The distant sunset had a flaxen hue, reflected in the lake's mirrored surface. Intermittent wisps of high clouds stretched across a dark blue sky.

Sailors have a favorite saying about sunsets: "Red sky at night, sailor's delight." This sunset was more gold than red, but nothing in the evening sky presaged anything other than another fine day ahead.

/ / /

In the middle of the night, they were awakened by the sound of movement outside their tent. When your walls are paper-thin nylon, unexpected nocturnal sounds can be alarming.

Anyone who has camped in wilderness and is awakened in darkness fears the worst. In that time and place, the imagination can run down shadowy alleys. Was a hungry bear attracted by the smell of food? Was a convict escaped from a Canadian prison trying to make his nefarious way across the border?

Fortunately, they quickly determined the distinct noise was a hooved animal who must have ventured out of the nearby woods. The island they were on was certainly large enough to host a deer or moose. The island was also near enough to the mainland for an animal to have easily swum to it.

They listened as whatever it was—something big, judging by the sounds—slowly wandered off.

A loon's tremolo broke the eerie stillness of the night.

Eventually, they all returned to sleep.

3

IN HARM'S WAY

June 30–July 3, 1999
Ely and the BWCAW

O n the final day of June 1999, wilderness ranger Nicole Selmer was
at the U.S. Forest Service's Ely Service Center, preparing for an
eight-day trip into the Boundary Waters. Nicole was leading a group
of eight, mostly volunteers, on a portage maintenance detail. Her crew
was going to rehab three portages from Mudro Lake into Fourtown Lake,
on the western side of the BWCAW.

"The Forest Service routinely supports work in the Boundary Waters
using volunteers," Nicole explained. A coordinator recruits volunteers
over the winter. "Volunteers typically stay for the entire season, but some
come for shorter time periods. In exchange they are given a place to live
and a small monthly stipend for food."

Given that the work is hot, strenuous, bug infested, and generally
thankless, why would people volunteer? "Many of our permanent workforce started as summer volunteers," said Nicole. Others are just looking
for a way to enjoy the wilderness with an experienced guide and use their
own labor to pay for it.

Six years earlier, Nicole Selmer had begun her career with the Forest Service in Utah. After four years working on trail maintenance out
west, she applied for and was hired as a ranger in the BWCAW. By experience and interest, she was familiar with wilderness, which is why she

was appointed to outfit and lead the group into the woods over the long Fourth of July weekend.

Nicole spent Wednesday at the Ely Service Center gathering her tents, food, and other supplies. She checked in her volunteers and let them know where they were going and what they would be doing. "Then we loaded up our canoes, tools, materials, and personal packs and waited for transport to our entry point."

Nicole was already familiar with some of her group members. Her second in command was Pam Kubichka, the only other paid employee on her team. "Pam was a student at Vermilion Community College and was working for the Forest Service over the summer months," explained Nicole. The group was rounded out with several other mostly young people, though not everyone was without experience. "One of our volunteers was a sixty-three-year-old woman named Lois Heskett, an RN," added Nicole. "So we were prepared for anything."

While venturing into wilderness with an experienced professional is one of the reasons some choose to volunteer, others are interested in learning about a wilderness ranger's job. On this trip, Nicole was leading a group using primitive tools to repair and improve portages. Other ranger duties include regulatory checks on visitors, identifying and monitoring invasive species, educating the public about wilderness issues, and performing a variety of other tasks as assigned. One of a ranger's most important jobs is something Nicole hoped she would not need to do on this trip: search for a lost visitor or help an injured traveler to safety. They were, after all, heading into the wilderness, where accidents can occur. If the unimaginable happened, she would be called on to help.

On Wednesday, June 30, the temperature rose to a moderate 72 degrees, typical for this time of year. At this point, the members of the team probably thought their work in the woods would be relatively temperate and expected no greater injuries than bug bites and branch scrapes. If any of the team had read the weather forecast, they might have seen predictions of unseasonable heat and possible precipitation. But everyone knows forecasts can be wrong, particularly two to three days in the future. And there was nothing in the current weather to suggest a future meteorological cataclysm.

By Wednesday afternoon, the crew was transported to BWCAW entry point 23 off Mudro Lake, approximately 10 miles east of Ely. They put in with all their gear and spent the rest of the day crossing three portages from Mudro into Fourtown Lake and setting up base camp.

Fourtown is a popular destination. Visitors were already on the lake, and Nicole knew, given the holiday weekend, that more would arrive. Presumably, everyone who entered the BWCAW had obtained and completed the necessary permits. Technically, as a wilderness ranger, Nicole could have checked. But given the tasks of organizing, equipping, transporting, and establishing her crew inside the million-acre wilderness, her hands and those of her teammates were plenty occupied.

/ / /

In 1999, the regulations governing BWCAW entry were relatively simple. While visitors needed a permit, the permits were easy to acquire and complete. Moreover, not every person visiting the wilderness needed to be listed on the permit. Ray Orieux completed the permit in advance of entering. He could have listed his name and destination and the number of visitors in his party, but a ranger or rescue worker looking through the permits would not know Lisa Naas, Michelle Orieux, or Kristina and Mark Schwendinger were part of Ray's group. With a bit of detective work, officials could have checked the license plates of the vehicles left in the Kawishiwi lot, run their registrations, and figured out Lisa, Kristina, and Mark had used the Kawishiwi entry point, like several other holiday visitors to the wilderness. But they would have no idea where in the wilderness they had paddled. And what if Lisa had driven up with Mark and Kristina? What if she had told her parents she was camping in the Boundary Waters and they suddenly needed to find her? It would, for all intents and purposes, be impossible. She would be lost.

Of course, over the Independence Day weekend of 1999, estimating the number of people camping in the BWCAW was a theoretical problem in search of a practical application. Essentially, going into the weekend, nobody cared. Depending on who you asked, you would get a variety of answers.

According to Bruce Slover, district ranger for the BWCAW's Kawishiwi District on the western side of the wilderness, the Fourth of July holiday typically saw a large influx of visitors each year. Bruce, who was in charge of all the wilderness rangers in his district, had instructed his lieutenants to send Nicole Selmer and many other rangers into the field to both perform trail and campsite maintenance and support the increase in visitors he was expecting.

Jo Barnier, district ranger for the Tofte and Gunflint Districts on the eastern half of the wilderness, believed just the opposite. She had given most of her rangers the holiday off. According to Steve Schug, Jo's wilderness program manager, "July 4 is not a big day in the wilderness. It tends to be more of a family-oriented time, not a high peak use day in the BWCAW."

Nicole estimated that there were six groups like hers in the field, each of which included several volunteers. In addition to these trail maintenance groups, there were also other wilderness rangers in the field.

Again, the issue of who went into the wilderness where and when doesn't really become a problem until someone is searching for them, or some cataclysmic event happens and officials are trying to determine the size of the problem. On this holiday weekend, how many people were taking advantage of the break and—like Sue Ann and her friends, and Ray and his friends—had decided to sojourn in wilderness? One hundred? Five hundred? Ten thousand?

When people are caught in a tsunami, earthquake, hurricane, tornado, wildfire, flood, or some other natural disaster, the immediate response is search and rescue. But first responders, like Nicole and many of her colleagues, need to know where to look and how many people might be affected. And those are just the people who have been directly affected. What about the loved ones of those in harm's way? Surely parents aware that their child was in an area that has been burned over by wildfire will want to know that their child is safe.

One million acres is approximately 1,600 square miles. On July 3, Sue Ann, Jan, and Vicky were comfortably encamped in the north-central BWCAW, while Ray, Michelle, Mark, Kristina, and Lisa were almost due south of them. Nicole was in the middle of her eight-day trip with her eight-person crew on the western edge of the wilderness. Of course, an area of 1,600 square miles can support many, many others.

"I remember our stats told us there were about ten thousand visitors in the wilderness," recalled Steve Schug. Those stats were estimated using the number of BWCAW permits that had been issued for that day. None of the ten thousand Boundary Waters visitors would have anticipated a cataclysm, especially one that reached into almost every corner of the wilderness.

/ / /

For obvious reasons, the preceding conjectures are about the number of *people* in the wilderness over the weekend. It's an understandable human conceit to only be concerned with the humans. But should some disaster befall an area, there is also the flora and fauna. On July 3, many of the trees across the region were more than one hundred years old, some older than two hundred years—older than any human. These trees had stood through centuries of weather, including severe cold, intense heat, windstorms, and rainstorms. Their green canopies continued to waver high above the ground, forming a vista above the surrounding trees, a favored site for eagle and osprey aeries. It is not difficult to give these trees, these majestic sentinels, characteristics worthy of our most beloved human heroes: noble, tall, straight, true. According to University of Minnesota forestry professor Lee Frelich, the oldest tree in Minnesota, which is more than two thousand years old, grew out of the shoreline of Seagull Lake's Three Mile Island.

And what of the area's abundant wildlife? One of the biggest reasons visitors come to the BWCAW is because it is filled with badgers and bald eagles; muskrat and moose; common loons, coyotes, and cougars; foxes and fishers; porcupines and painted turtles; lynx, wolves, bears, deer, and countless other animals that make the BWCAW their home.

/ / /

On Saturday, July 3, the 1,600-square-mile BWCAW was abundant with flora and fauna, including thousands of humans. As the day dawned, none of them had any reason to believe the holiday weekend would be any different from the stretch of relatively mild days that had preceded it.

4

A DESIRED CAMPSITE

July 3, 1999
Journey into Lake Polly

The Fourth of July holiday in 1998 had been Lisa Naas's first visit to the Boundary Waters. That year she had joined a group that included Ray, Michelle, Kristina, Mark, and several others—most of them young professionals who also worked at Arthur Andersen. While everyone enjoyed that trip, one of the equipment issues Lisa remembered was her canoe. She had taken that first trip into the BWCAW's waterways using an old aluminum canoe that weighed 85 pounds. It was a lot to carry.

"Lisa previously had one of the world's heaviest aluminum canoes," recalled Michelle. "For her to lift it, it was quite a sight." During that trip, Lisa had some help carrying the heavy craft. This time, however, she knew she would be doing her own portaging, and she was determined to manage her own canoe.

Lisa, Kristina, and Mark had all decided to enter the Boundary Waters on Saturday, July 3. In the accounting world, Lisa said, "month end is really critical for us. Of course, Fourth of July is pretty close after month end. So, I did all my work, and I worked really late to get everything done so I could be gone."

Mark and Kristina were able to knock off work early on Friday, July 2. Whenever they were able to get away early, they would follow Ray's lead and head up to the Kawishiwi Lake campground. "We would drive up," recalled Mark. "We would get there late, set up our tents, and then either have our entry permit or go get our entry permit and then enter the next day." They both planned to awaken in the campground Saturday morning and wait for Lisa's arrival, and then all three of them would make the demanding paddles and portages into Lake Polly, where they would meet up with Michelle and Ray.

/ / /

Saturday morning, July 3, Lisa awakened before dawn, climbed into her white Corolla, and began the four-and-a-half-hour drive north. Her first stop was at Sawbill Canoe Outfitters in Tofte. There, she had arranged to rent a state-of-the-art solo Kevlar canoe.

In 1999, Kevlar canoes were relatively new. One of their key benefits was being lightweight. For this trip, Lisa would be hoisting a 58-pound canoe rather than the aluminum beast she had carried last time.

The previous evening Mark and Kristina had driven up in a twelve-year-old utility hatchback. Because they already owned an aluminum canoe, they opted to bring it, rather than renting a lighter Kevlar one. "It weighed a ton," Kristina remembered.

"Probably 80 to 85 pounds," Mark said.

Still, Mark had used it enough to familiarize himself with hoisting and carrying the heavy craft. And besides, the price was right.

Well before noon Lisa arrived at Sawbill Outfitters. After she fastened her rented canoe to the top of her Corolla, she continued up the Sawbill Trail, making the necessary turns on her way to Kawishiwi Lake. Because Lisa wanted to make the most of her time in the woods, she had left early and made good time, arriving in the campground by midmorning. There, she met Mark and Kristina, who were loaded up and ready to embark.

The day was already unseasonably hot and muggy, but they were all happy to be heading into one of America's greatest wilderness areas by canoe. It did not take long for Lisa to park her Corolla, and with Mark and Kristina's assistance she got her lightweight canoe loaded with her gear and into the water. The trio spent the rest of the morning through midday following Ray's map along the trail Ray and Michelle had traveled before them.

There were approximately six portages between the campground and their destination on Lake Polly—"approximately" because from Square Lake into Kawasachong Lake, travelers paddle up the Kawishiwi River. During most years two sections of that river become too marshy and shallow to paddle. "When we went in, there were places that we had to portage because there were streams that were so small and so low that you weren't able to float through," Mark remembered. On these sections they needed to get out of their canoes and slog their way forward.

Mark also recalled the laborious process of hauling in their supplies. "On our way in we would double back on portages. One portage with canoe and one portage with gear."

"I think they said it took something like six hours to get through those six portages," Ray remembered. Regardless, by midafternoon, Ray and Michelle welcomed their colleagues and friends. The canoeists traveled up Lake Polly's peninsula shoreline and took advantage of the small natural cove, beaching their canoes with all their gear on a granite slab stretching down into the lake.

Michelle, who had not known what kind of canoe her good friend Lisa would be bringing, was happy to see her paddle up in the lightweight, modern Kevlar. "Seeing her in a one-person canoe was liberating," Michelle joked, remembering how unwieldy the much heavier aluminum canoe had been, particularly for Lisa.

Mark was pleased by Ray's choice of campsite. "One of the things we always wanted was a western-facing campsite," Mark said. This orientation would afford the best view of the sunset, and in the morning the sun would rise behind camp, rather than in front of it, minimizing the intensity of the morning light.

Everyone began unloading their gear, setting up their tents, and getting settled. Ray and Michelle had already pitched their blue tent near the open rock and soil top of the campsite. The orange lean-to tarp Ray had earlier strung up on a pair of large pines was nearby, with their portable table sitting in the shade. Mark and Kristina also chose a place near the main, open camp area. Lisa pitched her yellow two-person tent a little farther north, among a handful of trees.

While the others got settled, Ray and Michelle busied themselves with dinner preparations. Because they knew their friends would be tired and hungry from their long journeys, they wanted to cook a satisfying dinner. While the seasoned campers were familiar with the numerous freeze-dried options available from Backpacker's Pantry and similar meal packaging companies, "We probably would have had something that we had already cooked, that we would have packed in . . . pasta and spaghetti," Michelle recalled.

Kristina agreed regarding their shared meals: "We didn't actually do that much freeze dried. It was more like we would prepare spaghetti sauce we put in Ziploc bags along with noodles, or we'd bring a block of cheese and some refried beans and tortillas, and we'd make burritos."

Obviously, the wilderness visitors enjoyed their dinner. As Ray had already noted, he had in part chosen this Lake Polly campsite because—though it was a grueling, six-portage distance—it was at least near enough to bring "some of the luxuries of home." Besides, they planned on being in the Boundary Waters only the nights of July 3 and 4 and would paddle out on Monday, July 5. They could afford to tote in the good stuff.

Mark and Kristina brought a box of Merlot. "Oh, yeah," remembered Kristina. "We'd bring up a bladder of Franzia wine."

"I had a couple of smaller bottles of vodka," Lisa added. "Sometimes we would bring Crystal Light packets and mix that with water and vodka and make cocktails."

Many who have backpacked or canoed into wilderness areas can attest to the luxury (at least on the first night under the blazing stars) of having a few libations with a specially prepared meal while sitting on log seats around a campfire. The five close friends spent time sipping wine and talking. They each discussed the pros and cons, pluses and minuses, of their jobs. Lisa was mulling important news she had recently received from Cargill, her employer. "Lisa had a transfer," Michelle recalled. "She had a job offer from Cargill and was going to have to transfer to Nebraska. At that time she was really on the fence. She was considering not taking it, because she had just bought this cute little house in south Minneapolis. And she really liked Minneapolis." So at that point, concluded Michelle, "she was going to turn it down."

Presumably it was a beautiful sunset across Lake Polly, clearly visible over the western shoreline. Many writers have captured the sentiment of watching the sun set over the Boundary Waters: "The water was glassy and calm, still candy-colored in the afterglow of sunset," wrote Stephen King. And Gina de Gorna declared, "To watch a sunset is to connect with the Divine."

Eventually, the weary crew retired to their tents, burrowed into their comfortable sleeping bags, and welcomed the onset of sleep.

5

FIRST PORTAGE, LAST CAMP

July 3, 1999
Journey into Alpine Lake

Saturday, July 3, dawned unseasonably warm and mild, though still cool enough for Jan to pull on sweatpants and a sweatshirt, at least for now. When she, Sue Ann, and Vicky stepped out of their tent they discovered moose tracks. When they glanced into an adjacent wetland, they were excited to see the massive, horse-sized animal.

Later, after breakfast, they broke camp and prepared for their morning paddle and portage into Red Rock Lake.

From their campsite it was a short paddle to the southeast to get to their first portage (BWCAW portage 272). Still, they had to navigate several islands and a tricky long peninsula that jutted into the middle of Red Rock Bay. But again, since Jan and Vicky had navigated the route previously, it was relatively early in the day when they reached their crossing.

Ahead they could see the sand and gravel opening that marked the start of their exit from Red Rock Bay. The route was popular and well traveled, so the portage was easily identified. The three beached their canoe and stepped out into the clear water and up onto the rocky beach.

Their two large packs were heavy with food and equipment, and their aluminum canoe weighed at least 85 pounds. But Vicky knew Jan could single-handedly hoist and carry a canoe. She was not only an excellent cook; she was also strong. The three women got their supplies, canoe, paddles, and life vests across the 10-rod portage in short order.

The portage stretched almost due east–west. When Sue Ann looked back across it, she could see the morning sun over the trees on the distant side of Red Rock Bay. The trees on either side of the portage formed a nice tunnel through which the golden orb glowed. She snapped another memorable picture. The sun was high enough that it looked more yellow than any other color.

Sailors have another favorite saying, about sunrises: "Red sky in the morning, sailor's warning." But now the sun was well past sunrise, and it forecasted nothing more than another hot day. The three of them got into their canoe and began paddling into Red Rock Lake.

As they headed southeast away from the portage, they came to BWCAW campsite 408, on a rise of red rock off a small peninsula to their right. Jan and Vicky recalled the campsite, having stayed there in 1995. Vicky had circled it on her map and written nice next to it. But their paddle south through the rest of Red Rock Lake was different from their paddle through Saganaga.

"I remember going through Red Rock," Sue Ann recalled. "It didn't have a lot of trees on it, and the rock was very red."

It took them only a short while to paddle south through the lake to their next portage (BWCAW portage 290). The portage from Red Rock Lake into Alpine is approximately 60 rods, or around three football fields. It was also rocky and root strewn and had a slight rise. But it was largely straight and wide enough to accommodate Jan's overhead canoe carry.

While Red Rock Lake had approximately seven campsites, Alpine had twenty. Since it was the holiday weekend and Alpine Lake is near the edge of the Boundary Waters, most of the sites were occupied, but Vicky remembered camping on an island near Alpine's south end. The site (BWCAW campsite 347) was directly across from the main 105-rod portage from Alpine into Seagull Lake. The island was well forested, stretching about one-eighth mile from its west-southwest point to the clearing on its east-northeast point. It was a large campsite, and Vicky remembered it was well situated, with a gravel and sand beach sloping down to the clear lake water, perfect for beaching their canoe and taking a swim. There were also trees nearby for stringing their hammocks and for shade. The campsite was fairly open, with a nice fire grate surrounded by log seats. And since it was the nearest campsite to the start of the main portage into Seagull, approximately 50–100 yards across the water to the northeast, most travelers chose more secluded sites.

As expected, they found the site unoccupied and claimed it by pitching their dome tent on a flat space near a couple of mature jack pines. The nearest pine stood approximately 5 feet from the tent's northwest corner. Then they hauled their packs and gear up onto a ground tarp. Once the canoe was empty, they found a perfect spot to beach it, between two large boulders. On either side of the boulders stood more mature jack pines. After dragging the canoe between the boulders, they flipped it over, so that if it rained it would not fill with water. Then they continued getting settled.

Even though it was a warm, clear afternoon, Jan pulled on her sweats as protection against the bugs while she sorted out their camp.

A quarter mile nearly due north across the lake, another Alpine campsite sat at the end of a peninsula. In the afternoon they could hear some young campers, men and women, swimming. Sounds travel easily across water, though while they could hear voices and the occasional clang of a pot, the people weren't near enough to discern what was said. Still, there was comfort knowing the three women were not alone in the woods.

The afternoon and evening remained unseasonably warm and humid. Once their tent was pitched and their supplies stowed, the three spent the rest of the day much as they had the previous one: swimming, reading, feasting on another one of Jan's gourmet wilderness meals, and enjoying a mug or two of wine.

The plan was to spend Sunday, July 4, at the Alpine campsite. Then, on Monday morning, they would portage into Seagull.

They had a choice of two portages from Alpine into Seagull. The most well traveled is the 105-rod portage (BWCAW portage 307) directly across from their campsite. But canoeists can also travel due north up around a point and try their luck on a much shorter portage along the Alpine River (BWCAW portage 38). Most people recommend the 105-rod portage, even though it is much longer—it is clearly marked and easier to hike than the swampier, narrow waterway between the two lakes. Nevertheless, Jan was thinking they'd try the Alpine River on their way out, hoping they could spend most of the time paddling in the river.

Once they entered Seagull, they planned to paddle up to the northeast end of the lake. There was a landing on the far northeast side where they could beach their canoe and walk to Vicky's Camry.

/ / /

So far, Sue Ann's maiden odyssey into the Boundary Waters was everything she had hoped for. She'd seen stunning country. She'd heard one of the world's largest wild ungulates wander in the dark beside their tent, and then witnessed it feeding after first light. Magical loon calls had echoed against densely forested shorelines. She'd cleansed herself in pristine waters. And she'd bathed in a wilderness of unrivaled beauty. The three agreed that so far, their trip had been blessed by good luck in so many ways. The weather had been mild, the lake surfaces largely still and easily paddled, the portages obvious and open, and their desired campsites available.

As the sun set and they turned into their tent for the evening, they felt happy about the day and had no reason to think tomorrow would be any different from their first two days in the wilderness: a contented journey through woods and water.

PART II

JULY 4, 1999

6

DIRE FORECAST

West to East across Northern Minnesota

I n 1995 the Duluth office of the National Weather Service (NWS) moved into its new location at 5027 Miller Trunk Highway. From the street, the building is a relatively nondescript single-story brick edifice. Much more prominent is the nearby Doppler radar—the white sphere looks like a huge button mushroom sitting atop a multistory steelwork stem. This type of radar is still one of the most sophisticated, state-of-the-art weather tracking tools in use today, providing the NWS with detailed information about weather (especially storms). This one, installed in 1996, monitors Duluth's coverage area.

In essence, Doppler radar enables meteorologists to view a storm's breadth, depth, intensity, velocity, and precipitation (rain, snow, hail, and so on). Using these measurements, the NWS can forecast a storm's severity and path and forewarn people who may be threatened by oncoming weather.

Mike Stewart, meteorologist in charge at the Duluth NWS in 1999, didn't need Doppler radar to tell him the weather going into the Fourth of July weekend was problematic. Born and raised in southern Indiana, Mike was familiar with high humidity and temperatures in the 80s. But while weather like that was typical for Indiana, often presaging severe thunderstorms or tornadoes, it was atypical for Duluth, Minnesota.

"Our house," Mike recalled, "didn't have air conditioning. A lot of Duluth doesn't have air conditioning, especially in the older homes."

With an average July high temperature of 76.4 degrees Fahrenheit and a low of 55.4 degrees, the need for air conditioning is minimal. But going into the weekend, Mike remembered, "The heat was oppressive. Humidity was high, with dew points in the 70s. Temperatures were in the 80s. There was a stationary front just north of Duluth, running across the state from east to west. So, we knew we were going to have problems. We knew we were going to have some bad weather."

The Duluth NWS office is one of 122 offices spread over six U.S. regions. Each is responsible for issuing weather forecasts for a specific geographic area. The Duluth office tracks weather and provides forecasting for northeast Minnesota, northwest Wisconsin, and western Lake Superior.

Weather in the middle of the summer in the Upper Midwest generally moves from west to east. Despite the increasing sophistication of meteorological tools, however, severe weather events (tornados, derechos, thunderstorms) are not always easy to predict. Many climatological conditions must be present and interact in a specific way to spawn severe weather. For example, when a warm air mass meets a cold air mass, the warm air rises to cooler altitudes. If the warm air mass contains moisture, it condenses and forms clouds. If enough moisture is present, rising warm air masses can also produce precipitation. If the moisture is significant—from, say, a southern Gulf Stream and a saturated atmosphere from an abnormally wet spring and summer—something much more dramatic can occur. Hot air, cold air, and moisture are only three of the ingredients necessary to create deadly storms.

Because weather can be so difficult to predict, meteorologists seek input from a variety of sources. One of the most important is the NWS Storm Prediction Center in Norman, Oklahoma. This center considers the overall weather for a larger geography than the smaller 122 NWS regional offices. When a severe thunderstorm watch is issued, it generally comes out of Norman.

Since summer weather usually comes from the west, the Duluth NWS office also pays close attention to weather forecasts and reports from the NWS office in Grand Forks, North Dakota, due west of Duluth's coverage area. The Grand Forks office is responsible for eastern North Dakota and northwestern Minnesota. Ostensibly, weather coming from that direction (as well as farther west) heads toward northeastern Minnesota, including the BWCAW, and sometimes portends meteorological conditions literally downwind.

According to one historical account of the July 4, 1999, windstorm from the NWS, "During the evening of July 3, 1999, thunderstorms over southeastern Montana and western South Dakota merged into a mesoscale convective system (MCS)."[1] An MSC is more commonly understood as a collection of thunderstorms that act as a system, meaning they can spread and move over a large geographic area and become a significant storm event. The report goes on to describe this series of thunderstorms as driving "east-northeast across the Dakotas through the night . . . The system slowly weakened early in the morning of July 4th as it moved into eastern North Dakota. About 7:00 a.m. CDT, the storm *abruptly changed its character*, intensifying into an intense squall line about 30 to 40 miles west of Fargo, ND" (emphasis added). A squall line is a line of thunderstorms forming along or ahead of a cold front.

"Within 15 to 20 minutes," the report continues, "the storm struck Fargo. Trees and powerlines were brought down, many roofs in both residential and commercial areas were destroyed. At the Hector Airport, where a hangar was demolished, winds of 91 mph were recorded. Total damage costs exceeded 30 million dollars."

At the Duluth NWS office, the weather forecaster on the evening of Saturday, July 3, was Mike Stewart. Already concerned about high temperatures and humidity, as well as the stationary front settled over the region, he was keeping an eye on the developing weather out west. But it was still so far west its character would likely change as it crossed North Dakota and moved into Minnesota.

At 9:21 p.m., after reviewing the forecasts provided by the Storm Prediction Center in Norman, Mike posted a forecast for the northeastern Minnesota counties of Lake, Cook, and St. Louis (all of which contain significant BWCAW acreage), including the city of Ely. He predicted the rest of the evening would be partly cloudy, with a 20 percent chance of showers or thunderstorms. His forecast for this area the following day,

---

1. Norvan J. Larson and Peter S. Parke, *Boundary Waters Windstorm: The Blowdown of July 4th, 1999* (National Weather Service, 2009).

July 4, predicted a "warm and humid" holiday, with a 30 percent chance of thunderstorms. While storms were developing as far west as Montana and western South Dakota, there was nothing to indicate how, more than twenty-four hours later, those storms would abruptly change character.

/ / /

Sometime over the course of the evening, Stewart's shift ended, and he was replaced by meteorologist Dave Tomalak. Dave's first forecast was released at 4:15 a.m. on July 4 and was almost identical to Mike's from the previous evening. In particular, Ely and the surrounding area was expected to be "warm and humid. Partly sunny with a 30 percent chance of thunderstorms. High in the middle 80s. Southwest wind 10 to 20 MPH."

Before Dave made his next report at 7:39 a.m., he probably checked on the weather being reported by the Grand Forks NWS. The 7:05 a.m. forecast from Grand Forks predicted the July 4 weather in Fargo would be "partly sunny and continued humid. Scattered morning and late afternoon thunderstorms. High in the middle 80s. East to northeast wind 10 to 20 MPH and gusty." There was no indication of the weather that was just beginning to intensify 30–40 miles west of Fargo.

Checking his usual sources and finding nothing particularly untoward, Dave issued the report for his coverage areas at 7:39 a.m. For the Ely area, he repeated the exact verbiage from his 4:15 a.m. forecast: warm, humid, and partly sunny with a 30 percent chance of thunderstorms.

By 8:00 a.m. or soon thereafter, Dave must have been hearing news from his colleagues in Grand Forks. By that time, according to the NWS report, the storm had already "abruptly changed," blowing through Fargo at about the same time he released his 7:39 report and causing significant damage.

As the storm moved east-northeast, blowing into western and central northern Minnesota, it intensified. Reporting and forecasting weather in this region was the responsibility of the Grand Forks NWS, and at 8:45 a.m., that office finally issued a severe thunderstorm watch for the Bemidji area and surrounding communities that would remain in effect until 1:00 p.m. The 8:45 report predicted "scattered thunderstorms . . . some severe with large hail and damaging winds."

In fact, as Mike Stewart had feared, as the storm moved into Minnesota, it was building into something much more significant than the squall line that had moved across North Dakota five hours earlier. According to the historical report, "The bow echo seemed to divide its energy just after 8:00 a.m. CDT in extreme western Minnesota, near Detroit Lakes." A bow echo, as the National Oceanic and Atmospheric Administration (NOAA) explains on its website, "is a radar signature of a squall line that 'bows out' as winds fall behind the line and circulations develop on either end. . . . Brief tornadoes may occur on the leading edge of a bow echo."

The NWS report recounts:

> The southern portion [of the bow echo] produced one or two small tornadoes and resulted in numerous reports of winds over 60 MPH, hail up to an inch in diameter, and widespread, minor damage. This part of the storm reached the north shore of Lake Superior, just north of Duluth, about noon CDT . . . The stronger northern portion reached Bemidji about 9:30 a.m., resulting in a report of 75 mph winds and one-inch hail nearby. Winds of 81 mph were reported at the Chisolm–Hibbing Airport as the storm passed through about 11:30 a.m. CDT.

By late morning, the Duluth NWS was both tracking the reports issued by Grand Forks and using its own Doppler radar and other tools to glimpse some alarming atmospheric developments. By 10:55 a.m., the Duluth office issued a severe thunderstorm watch that would be in effect until 3:00 p.m. for Ely and the surrounding area. It also predicted scattered thunderstorms and warned that "A few storms could produce hail and damaging winds."

"Issuing a severe thunderstorm warning is a good news, bad news situation," explained Mike. The good news: people in front of the storm are getting as much time as possible to prepare. "The bad news is that if you can issue a warning that far in advance, the weather is usually very bad."

/ / /

According to Carol Christenson, another Duluth NWS meteorologist at the time of the blowdown, there would normally be three people working. But on July 4, 1999, "We had five or six."

By noon on July 4, Mike Stewart, who had the day off, had been called back in. Dave Tomalak's shift ended late in the day, but he remained at his post. The developing weather was troublesome, and the Duluth NWS was staffing up to make sure the office could cope with the expected fallout.

"We have some people who are there to answer phones and take spotter reports and issue local storm reports," explained Christenson. "Some people are warning forecasters. They are the ones who issue the warnings. Others are communicating with our emergency managers and 911 dispatch centers. And then there's our public service desk. People are still working and making sure that all our normal public services are still being met. It was a very, very busy day."

By late morning on July 4, someone responsible for determining the safety of the Ely holiday parade, scheduled to begin at 1:00 p.m., must have seen or heard one of the reports coming out of Duluth and decided to postpone the event until the storm blew through. By the time the Duluth NWS issued its 1:20 forecast for Ely and the surrounding area, no one needed to be told about a "severe thunderstorm watch in effect until 3:00 p.m. today." Or that there were "scattered thunderstorms." Or that "A few storms could produce large hail and damaging winds." Ely, of course, was still within the boundaries of civilization. Everyone had access to radio or TV, and if the weather turned particularly bad, the city could sound its warning sirens.

But only a few miles to the east lay wilderness. There are no radio or TV transmission towers in the BWCAW, let alone devices or the electricity required to use them. There were no strategically positioned sirens that could blare to forewarn people in the wilderness. Once visitors passed through a Boundary Waters entry point, they were on their own. More explicitly, in determining what kind of weather was headed their way and what they should do about it, wilderness visitors could only rely on the same senses and instincts that have guided people in the region for thousands of years.

As the storm blew across the North Dakota–Minnesota border, it became serious, causing intermittent damage. But so far, the weather damage had been erratic, downing trees and power lines in one area while skipping over acres of country as it blew east. In some places it caused temporary flooding, but otherwise the oncoming storm wasn't demonstrating the sustained severity that might be considered a once-in-a-lifetime, let alone once-in-five-hundred-years, weather event. The bad weather continued its erratic behavior as it headed into Ely. If it retained that character moving farther east, into the Boundary Waters, then wilderness damage would be minimal.

Unfortunately, the Duluth Doppler radar was showing the emergence of a meteorological event rarely seen at this latitude, and even more rarely with the intensity the NWS meteorologists were seeing.

"That was before cell phones and cell phone towers were all over the place," remembered Mike, "so you really couldn't contact anyone up there. When we saw it going into the Boundary Waters, we knew we could be having a lot of problems. We estimated there were 3,500 to 4,000 people camping in the wilderness, and we knew none of them would be able to hear a severe thunderstorm warning. So we made phone calls to the Forest Service and the Park Service to let them know what was coming. But I just had this feeling that this was not going to be good."

By now the trajectory of the stormy weather was clear. There was the southern branch of a bow echo that spawned a couple of tornadoes and blew across the center of Minnesota, continuing into the open water of Lake Superior a few miles north of Duluth. And there was a much more serious east-northeastern bow echo that was moving in an approximately straight line from Fargo toward Ely, taking aim on the tip of the state's Arrowhead Region. If the evolving trajectory maintained its new direction, a large swath of the BWCAW would be directly in its path.

/ / /

What no one could foretell was how truly bad the weather would become. While a storm of the intensity that blew through the BWCAW the afternoon of July 4 may have happened before, it had never happened as far north as the Boundary Waters and southern Canada. The intensity of the derecho was not only monumental—it was unparalleled in the annals of known meteorological history. Perhaps most astounding was its length, breadth, and duration. As a singular weather event, it would continue heading northeast like a juggernaut. Parts of the country as far away as Maine would be blown apart. Trees would fall. Power lines would be snapped like overstretched rubber bands. Roofs would fly heavenward, and people would die.

When it finally reached the Atlantic, it would start heading south, causing more destruction before it returned to land along the Mid-Atlantic Seaboard. It would then travel west and eventually blow itself out in Missouri.

While the damage farther east would be bad, nothing else in the derecho's 6,000-mile path would rival the most intense and comprehensive destruction that was, at midday on July 4, bearing down on the remote BWCAW. Perhaps most consequential of all, no one who had chosen this holiday weekend to enjoy one of Minnesota's most wild, natural areas had any idea a weather catastrophe of truly historic proportions was about to befall them.

7

AN UNEXPECTED MORNING

Eveleth, Tower, Cook, and Ely

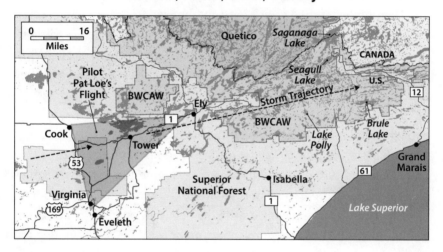

The Ely day dawned hot, humid, and still. It would be perfect flying weather, providing the elements held. Since weather was a crucial consideration when flying planes, especially small ones, Forest Service pilot Pat Loe had checked the day's forecast. There was a prediction of winds coming out of the west, but nothing inclement enough to prevent him from finishing his quick flight from Ely to Eveleth, Minnesota, and back again.

Pat had the day off. He was following a fellow pilot and his aircraft to Sky Harbor Seaplane Base. It was supposed to be a quick trip down to the base, 42 miles from Ely as the crow (or pilot) flies, where the friend needed to leave his plane for maintenance. After Pat picked him up in his Cessna 180, they planned to circle back to Ely well ahead of the town's one o'clock holiday parade.

As soon as both pilots were in the air, they began seeing storm clouds build in the west. They were headed at a 45-degree angle to the oncoming clouds. From this vantage point they could see the weather growing more serious than the forecasts had predicted. Pat still hoped they were far enough in front of it to be able to return to Ely on schedule. He radioed his friend and suggested they make a rapid turnaround.

"As soon as we drop off your plane," he said, "we turn and burn."

His buddy agreed.

They landed at the Eveleth base and hurried to check in and secure his friend's plane, but the weather came on faster than anyone expected. The base was hit by strong winds and a downpour. Even though they were on the edge of it, the clouds drenched the short airstrip, and they had no choice but to ride it out on the ground.

They kept their eyes skyward, and by eleven o'clock there was a big enough cloud break to again get airborne. West of Ely they could see it was still blowy, as though the region's air had not yet finished expelling its unexpected tumult. But it appeared as though the heaviest weather had moved east. There were more clouds to the west, but Pat had enough confidence in his flying abilities that he believed, once he gained more altitude and obtained a better vantage point, he'd be able to dodge the worst of it, find an open seam, and make it back to Ely in time for the afternoon's festivities.

Pat nosed the plane down the runway, lifting into what he hoped would be calmer skies.

/ / /

Though he was only in his midthirties, Pat Loe was already a seasoned pilot, having logged more than a decade of serious flight time. After obtaining his bachelor of science degree in aviation at St. Cloud State University, he became one of the school's flight instructors. Following a brief stint teaching, he signed on to fly for United Airlines' regional carrier.

Three years of commercial flying taught Pat a valuable lesson. The work was routine, but boring. Pat knew he craved more flying variety. Since he had served in the army and been stationed in Alaska, he suspected a good place to find the antidote for piloting boredom might be north of the 48th parallel. So, at the age of twenty-five, he headed up to the place where wilderness knows no bounds.

Growing up in Ely gave Pat a special appreciation for wild places. In Alaska he became a bush pilot, flying Beavers and Super Cubs. The Beavers taught him the intricacies, difficulties, and thrills involved in landing on water. And the Super Cubs, with their oversize wheels, taught him how to land on remote, rough airstrips and gravel bars, at high altitudes, and in every kind of weather.

He worked for a hunting and fishing operation. Almost every flight was a run into remote wilderness, either dropping fishers on distant lakes and rivers or hunters on tundra. He became particularly adept at tracking and spotting game from the air. Ten years spent flying into Alaska's back country provided Pat with the kind of practical education few bush pilots ever get a chance to experience. "It was definitely extreme flying," Pat recalled. "I had some pretty intense moments up there. You cut your teeth flying in Alaska and most other places in the world seem tame."

After Pat turned thirty-five, he decided to return home to Ely, and by April 1998 he was flying for the Forest Service out of the Ely airbase. Moored to the airbase's large extended dock sat three de Havilland Canada DHC-2 Beavers, more simply known as Beaver planes. Beavers have floats that enable them to land on water, crucial for a region with so many lakes and rivers.

Pat had spent much of his Ely youth guiding, fishing, and exploring the region's waters. During that time, he became familiar with the wilderness there, especially the part that stretched from Lac La Croix—40 miles to the northwest, up on the Canadian border—to well east and south of town. He knew most of the region's lakes, rivers, and portages because he had traveled them by foot and canoe. He knew almost all the best watercourses for landing. And if he was flying into an unfamiliar region, he knew how to find the safest places to land.

/ / /

For a pilot with as much airtime over wilderness as Pat Loe, the idea of being grounded in Eveleth by what appeared to be a mild blip in the weather seemed ludicrous. He felt certain he could find an opening in the clouds that would enable him to dodge it, and so by a little after eleven o'clock, he and his pilot friend were up in the air, peering through the clouds for that opening. But what they saw was alarming.

It took only a moment for them to understand that the weather forecast (an oxymoron most pilots read with suspicion) had seriously underestimated the severity of what was building on their horizon. In the clouds, the weather grew darker and more ominous. Pat's small plane began to be buffeted like a kite in gale-force winds, forcing him to deviate.

From his present altitude he could look east and see his hometown getting hammered by the storm. Pat's first thought was to try to put down in Tower, less than 20 miles west-southwest of Ely. But as he began nearing the Tower airport, he was still getting tossed around; the intense winds were far too dangerous to attempt a landing. The air had grown still more problematic, and after zigzagging through the clouds, waiting for an opening, he was forced to tack another 20 miles west. Finally, he put the Cessna's wheels down on the airport tarmac in Cook, Minnesota, happy to be on the ground.

Cook and its airport had been hit by the same intense weather that was now moving east. Some of the planes that had been tied down were twisted in their ropes. The door to the airport's operation building had been blown open, and water was pooling across its entryway.

The damage at Cook prompted Pat to call the Ely airport to check on current conditions. It was a little after noon. The Ely attendant told him the town had been hit, and a few trees were down, but otherwise it wasn't too severe. He told Pat the air seemed to be easing a little, with the worst weather moving east of town, entering the Boundary Waters. The storm had forced them to postpone the parade, but the attendant thought it had eased enough that by the time Pat and his friend covered the 40 miles from Cook to Ely, he should be able to land.

Airborne for the third time that morning, Pat made a beeline toward town. The trip east was less tumultuous than their earlier flights, but he could see bad weather far out ahead, fanning out into the Boundary Waters in a dark, amoeboid mass. That far out, the sky appeared dangerous, which prompted the seasoned bush pilot to start thinking about the rest of his day.

Around one o'clock, Pat nosed his Cessna down into Ely. Like Cook and Tower, the area had been buffeted by strong winds. There was spotty damage, but it was manageable. Still, he remembered how the sky had appeared farther east of town, and since the parade had been delayed, he had enough time to head home and check in with work. He suspected his services might be needed sooner, rather than later—for search and rescue or medevac. As soon as he walked through his door, he called his supervisor, stationed at the Minnesota Interagency Fire Center in Grand Rapids.

Pat related the effects of the storm as it had passed west to east over Cook, Tower, and Ely. He knew there had been some damage and assumed, given the trajectory, that it continued into the wilderness. That would likely mean downed trees. Some of those trees could have fallen on campers huddled in their tents. A nylon flap was adequate protection against a downpour, but not a falling hundred-year-old white pine. And if people were caught out on the water, they could have blown off course or, worse, capsized in the middle of a large lake.

When storms blow up in wilderness, terrible accidents sometimes happen.

Pat's supervisor confirmed that the radars were still showing severe weather, particularly over the BWCAW. But so far dispatch had received no requests for assistance. The supervisor also confirmed that Wayne Erickson, Pat's fellow U.S. Forest Service Beaver pilot, had taken the afternoon off. It had been a wet spring and summer, the area receiving much more precipitation than normal. As a result, the trees and plants (and air, for that matter) were full of moisture, and the fire risk was extremely low. Consequently, Wayne had decided to check out of the air base and attend Ely's parade. That meant no pilots were on duty.

For now, Pat's supervisor told him, there was no reason to head in to the air base. Still, he suggested it would be prudent if Pat stuck close to a phone and maybe checked in later.

That sounded fine to Pat, who was looking forward to the celebration. But in the back of his mind he recalled the menacing look of the eastern sky as he had dropped down into Ely. He knew intense storms took pity on no one. That would mean he was going to get a call: medevac, search and rescue, or both. Pat felt certain it was only a matter of time.

8

RANGER IN THE WILDERNESS

Ely and the BWCAW

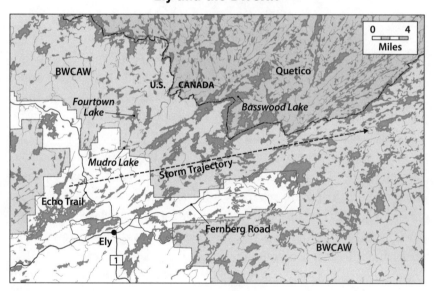

For wilderness ranger Nicole Selmer, the morning of July 4 was not much different from the previous three mornings in the woods. She was on the fourth day of her eight-day trip, leading a group of volunteers in the backbreaking task of portage maintenance. It was challenging work because the weather in the Boundary Waters had been hot and sticky, the bugs merciless, and the labor physically demanding.

Nicole's team was camped on the south end of Fourtown Lake. As was their custom, they used their handheld radio to check in with their home base, the Kawishiwi Ranger District. They let the district know they were okay and that they planned to spend their day rehabbing one of three portages between Mudro Lake, to the south, and Fourtown. The district told them there was the potential, later in the day, for thunderstorms in the area, some possibly severe. But otherwise their work on the portages should continue.

On this day, Nicole's boss, wilderness ranger Nancy Pius, was paddling into the BWCAW via entry point 23 off Mudro Lake. She and a companion were going to cross Mudro and head toward Fourtown to have a look at the portage work. Because it was a holiday, Nancy carried with her enough Snickers candy bars to provide Nicole and her team with some welcome Fourth of July treats.

The first portage from Mudro into nearby Fourtown involved traipsing along a boulder-strewn 30-rod trail. The portage was short and flat. But while it lacked steepness, the rocks meant a sprained ankle waiting to happen. Nicole's team had spent the first three days of July smoothing out the portage. Because the area was designated wilderness, they were forced to use primitive rather than power tools.

This region of the Boundary Waters is on the north side of the Laurentian Divide. The three portages between Mudro and Fourtown lie almost due north and are separated by brief waterways. When paddlers enter the waterways, they paddle north with a current that flows north.

The 141-rod middle portage between Mudro and Fourtown is so rocky and hilly that it is colloquially called the Billy Goat Portage. After traveling the Billy Goat, canoeists paddle through another small section of water before hauling their craft and gear across a 30-rod portage, after which they enter the south side of Fourtown Lake.

Every morning, Nicole's team left their camp on Fourtown and traveled south to get to the location where they would begin their day's work. This morning, they turned their attention to the Billy Goat Portage. If the first portage was designed for ankle sprains, this one was designed for broken legs, particularly when carrying a canoe. "It's called the Billy Goat Portage because it has a kind of peak in the middle," explained Nicole. "You go uphill both ways. And it's a longer portage, really rough and rocky."

During the morning of July 4, the team was sweating through the heat and swatting bugs. By Nicole's seasoned reckoning, finishing work on the Billy Goat Portage would take more than the four remaining days of their eight-day tour of duty.

/ / /

Nicole Selmer was no stranger to wilderness trail maintenance. Her career with the Forest Service began in Utah in 1993, when she was hired to do the same kind of work she was now doing in the Boundary Waters. But trail maintenance in the BWCAW was different from out west. The previous year, she had come to work in the Superior National Forest's Kawishiwi District, and while her experience in Utah had been excellent training, repairing portages in the Boundary Waters involved different considerations. In Utah, the ground isn't nearly as rocky as in northern Minnesota. Out west, when she needed to use soil to augment or repair a trail section, she could easily find what she needed nearby. But in the rocky Boundary Waters, soil needed to be mined using a borrow pit.

A borrow pit is a construction term that describes a location where soil has been dug for use in another location. To find and dig a suitable borrow pit in the Boundary Waters, Nicole and her team often had to move away from the actual portage trail. Once they found a location with suitable soil for digging and hauling, they had to excavate the borrow pit using primitive tools such as soil augers and shovels. Then, they needed to carry it in 5-gallon plastic buckets to wherever it was needed on the portage.

Nicole had spent the previous day scouting the Billy Goat Portage, determining what trail work was needed and finding suitable locations for borrow pits. Since this was her second season leading a team in the BWCAW, she had a good idea of the scope of their work. Not only was this middle portage long, rocky, and in parts steep, but on the morning of July 4, it was busy.

Whenever wilderness travelers crossed a portage, Nicole and her team had to step aside and let them pass. "We would be on our hands and knees," Nicole recalled, "digging and repairing stuff. And every time someone comes through, you have to stop. And the people portaging don't make just one trip. First they haul their canoes, and then they return for their gear. And on that morning, some of the groups were big, carrying four canoes. So, throughout the morning, our work was frequently interrupted."

Nicole continued, "Fourtown is one of those destination lakes. When travelers get through those three portages out of Mudro, they tend to find somewhere on Fourtown to camp and remain there for the rest of their stay."

During the long, hot, bug-infested Fourth of July morning, Nicole and her crew—when they weren't stepping aside to let canoeists pass—were working on different sections of the Billy Goat. "We were working in the middle of that portage. We were putting in some check dams, which are kind of like steps, with some rock." Check dams minimize soil erosion, particularly during heavy rainfall.

"We would hang a radio in the borrow pit for the people working there," Nicole said. "One person would dig and fill the buckets while others shuttled them back and forth to wherever the soil was needed. You're sitting back in the woods. There's lots of mosquitoes. You're digging and hauling dirt all day. It's not a very great job. So, to boost morale we'd listen to WELY, because that's the only radio station you can receive where we were on the edge of wilderness." WELY was the local Ely radio station. "Because of our morning call with the Kawishiwi office, we knew there was a potential for storms. And because we had the radio at the borrow pit tuned to WELY, we were getting weather updates."

Sometime during the late morning, Nancy Pius appeared with her welcome supply of Snickers. Near noon, she, Nicole, and others were taking a lunch break, listening to the radio, when they heard the weather reports about the storm as it blew through Ely. The town is about 10 miles south-southwest of the Billy Goat Portage. Nicole knew weather hitting Ely at this time of year would be heading into the Boundary Waters next. What she and her team didn't know was that the storm had moved out of Ely on an east-northeast path, building intensity as it plowed into the BWCAW. The worst part of the storm would strike south of their location. But the storm was building so much strength and breadth that as Nicole looked to the western skies, she was shocked to see them turn an ugly green.

The obvious onset of a pending thunderstorm caused the group to leave the borrow pit with her boss and take cover.

Preparing for an oncoming thunderstorm was a common occurrence, and Nicole and her team were familiar with the protocol. First, they stowed their gear and made sure everything was secure. Since they were in the middle, higher portion of the Billy Goat portage, they needed to find lower ground so that, if lightning struck, they would be out of harm's way. And since radio antennas and electronic devices could attract electricity, they made sure their radios were turned off and set aside somewhere safe out of the rain. Lightning could strike trees and be conducted into the nearby ground, so they also knew they should sit on life vests or some similar kind of insulation.

The team had been split up all morning, half working on one side of the Billy Goat peak while the second group repaired the other side. As the storm threatened, Nicole sent one group back to their canoes, both to make sure they were turned over and secured and because the location was a safe, lower spot on the portage. She and the rest of her colleagues found a similar low spot where they could ride out the storm.

"We didn't think it was any different than any other thunderstorm we had to sit through," Nicole said. "We were off the portage, but right next to it. It was a nice low spot. There weren't any large trees around us because they were all above us on top of the hill. And that seemed like the safest place to be out of the lightning and wind. We didn't have time to put up a tarp. So, like any other storm, we hunkered down and waited.

"But when that weather hit, it was clear this was not your normal thunderstorm."

While the winds were less intense than in the wilderness to the south, "the trees around us began moving in circles," Nicole said. "I remember looking up and seeing the trees spinning. The aspen had a lot of heavy branches on all sides. They were being pushed in one direction, then they'd snap back and be pushed in the other direction, so they'd spin back around. It looked like they were literally going in circles while the rain poured down on top of us. All of us were thinking, 'Oh my god, we have never been in a storm like this.' The skies were green and intense. We were just caught in the moment, experiencing the power of nature."

9

NEVER SEEN ANYTHING LIKE IT

Moose Lake and Basswood Lake, BWCAW
Twenty-four Miles East-Northeast of Ely

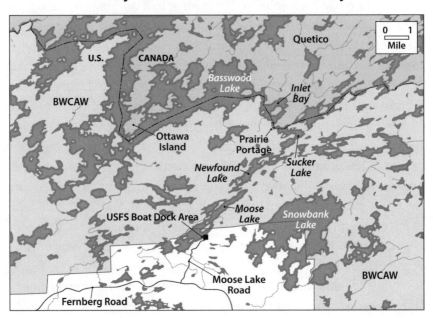

The Kawishiwi Ranger District in Ely, Minnesota, has a district office and a service center. On July 4, 1999, the district office was located adjacent to the John F. Kennedy Elementary School and housed the administrative offices of west zone timber manager Ralph Bonde, Kawishiwi District ranger Bruce Slover, fire management officer Jim Hinds, law enforcement officer Chip Elkins, and other members of district leadership. Whenever a serious event befell the Boundary Waters forest to the east, the district office and its leaders would be involved with addressing whatever needed to be done.

The service center was located on the outskirts of the town and housed the trucks, boats, motors, and other equipment needed to run and support the Kawishiwi District. It was also staffed by many U.S. Forest Service employees, like Nicole Selmer, who spent more time in the BWCAW than behind a desk.

Early on the morning of July 4, wilderness ranger Pete Weckman was in the service center checking on weather forecasts issued out of the Duluth offices of the National Weather Service. Pete had a work crew up on Basswood Lake's U.S. Point near the Canadian border. One of his first morning duties was to check in with his crew and share any relevant news. Today, given the hot, still start to the morning, that news was about the weather.

Pete radioed his team and let them know that according to the NWS report, there was a 30 percent chance of thunderstorms in their area that afternoon. He was familiar with the antecedents of potential storms, and he was feeling them today.

"I'm from southern Minnesota," Pete said. "In Ely, it was like 85, 90 degrees and humid as hell. I remember cornfield country Mankato, and when you had days like this, it either spawned a tornado or something [else] bad happened. It was just in the back of my mind. I knew something was gonna happen that day." He shared his prognostication with his work crew and readied himself to go out on patrol.

On this day, Pete was the lone ranger in his section of the center. He was scheduled to drive out on the Fernberg Trail and up Moose Lake Road to the southeast end of the lake. There, the Forest Service maintained a dock with a few different boats, boat lifts, a work shed, a fuel tank, and a few other necessities.

Before leaving, he heard someone in the separate area of the work center known as the fire cache. Investigating, he found Duane Whalen, one of the employees who worked in the timber shop. Duane told Pete he was supposed to go out in the woods today, but he wasn't looking forward to it. The hot, still air meant the bugs would be pestilential.

Pete patrolled Moose Lake all the way up to Prairie Portage and into Basswood Lake on the U.S. side of the border and used the Moose Lake Forest Service station as his disembarkation point. "We're basically out there meeting people and doing various kinds of checks," he explained. "Fishing licenses, day-use motor permits, overnight permits, checking for bottles and cans, and giving people directions."

He invited his colleague to accompany him up to Moose Lake, where they could at least be out on the water, avoid the bugs, and enjoy the breeze as they headed up to Prairie Portage and then into the northeastern stretch of Basswood Lake.

"I could use a bowman," Pete told him.

Duane liked the idea. Since bad weather appeared likely, he returned to his locker to get his boots and raingear.

/ / /

Moose Lake is long and narrow, stretching northeast all the way to Prairie Portage on the Canadian border. Getting to the portage involves boating up to the end of Moose and zigzagging through a narrow gap into Newfound Lake. Newfound, like Moose, is long and narrow and continues northeast up into Sucker Lake. Prairie Portage is located at the northwest end of Sucker Lake. A river runs along the portage from Sucker Lake, flowing north into Basswood Lake's Inlet Bay; the Sucker Lake side of the river is dammed.

At this point, the U.S.–Canadian border largely runs north–south. The western side of the river is the U.S. side of Prairie Portage, and the eastern side of the river is in Canada. On the U.S. side, a mechanized portage facilitates the transfer of boats from Sucker Lake into the U.S. side of Basswood Lake's Inlet Bay. A Canadian ranger station sits on the Inlet Bay side of the portage, where visitors can pass through border customs and into Canada. One key consideration made Prairie Portage a great place for Pete Weckman to journey into the upper reaches of Basswood Lake: the Moose Lake chain all the way up into Basswood was one of the few regions in the BWCAW that permitted the use of 25-horsepower motors rather than solely canoes. An informal agreement between the Forest Service and the Canadian ranger station allowed the Forest Service to maintain a boat on the Canadian station's docks. Forest Service rangers like Pete parked their boat on the Canadian side of the Sucker Lake dam and walked across the portage to the Canadian ranger station, where they could board a Forest Service boat and motor into the U.S. side of Inlet Bay, and farther down Basswood's long stretch of water to the southwest.

/ / /

Around 10:30, Pete and Duane pushed off the Forest Service dock on Moose Lake and headed northeast toward Newfound. The air was still and hot.

"Wow," Pete said. "It's gonna feel nice to get out in the boat and get going."

While the pair were anxious to get underway, they could also see the skies, to the west, growing darker.

With their 25-horsepower motor, it didn't take long for them to reach Prairie Portage. From there, Pete knew, they could cross into Canada, where they would use a similar boat and motor on the Canadian side. Once in that boat, they'd be able to speed out into Inlet Bay and eventually, after a short ride, reach a far northern point where they'd have a clear view a few miles out over Basswood's waters to the southwest. Since that was the direction from which the weather was coming, they would be able to gauge the intensity of the storm.

"And that's what we did," Pete said. "First we checked in with the Canadian rangers to see if they needed help with anything. Then Duane and I jumped in our boat to head down Inlet Bay. Then it opens up into Bailey Bay."

From that location, Pete and Duane could "see quite a ways down to the Washington Island area. It was just that dark blackish color."

That color in the clouds on the distant horizon to the southwest, which were approaching, was ominous enough to cause the pair to abort their planned entry into Basswood. If they had continued, they would have been two men in an open boat in the middle of a huge body of water. If the weather turned the way it was looking, they would be at the mercy of the wind and rain.

"We ain't in a good spot," Pete finally said, recognizing their vulnerability. "We need to get back to the dock on Moose Lake."

They quickly turned their boat around and backtracked to Prairie Portage, where they mentioned the approaching ominous weather from the west-southwest. The Canadian rangers told them their own weather service out of nearby Atikokan, Ontario, also reported bad weather headed toward them.

Pete and Duane hustled back to their boat on Sucker Lake and began speeding across the water, hoping to reach the dock at the southwest end of Moose Lake before the skies opened up.

"We headed down the lake and went through Sucker and Newfound," Pete recalled.

Racing through Newfound Lake, they encountered a group of paddlers and were forced to stop. Pete told the canoeists about the approaching weather and implored them to get to shore and find cover. Then they sped through the zigzag cut from Newfound Lake into Moose and continued into what now looked like the black maw of the approaching storm.

"It's starting to get really dark now," Pete recalled. "It's like, I don't know if we're gonna make it or not. In the distance you could hear rumbling."

As they raced toward their dock, they encountered another group of paddlers out in the middle of the lake.

"People were just lollygagging," Pete said, incredulous. The Moose Lake public landing was not far off, and the paddlers were hoping they could reach the landing before the skies opened up. But Pete knew it was too distant for them to reach it in time.

"I told them, 'You need to get over to that small island right there.'" He pointed to an island much closer than the landing. It was large enough to have a good coverage of trees. "I told them they needed to flip over their canoes and take cover."

As they raced toward the Forest Service dock, the rising wind began churning the water into whitecaps. Moose Lake is narrow; given the slim stretch of water it was unusual for the wind to be strong enough to create whitecaps. Still ¼ mile from the dock, Pete and Duane looked ahead and could see a black wall coming toward them.

And then it started to rain. At first, it was a stronger burst of wind with light rain. They were still a couple hundred yards from the dock, speeding forward, when the weather started going from bad to worse. The wind increased while the water fell out of the sky like a curtain.

The 25-horsepower Johnson motor enabled Pete to speed at 25–30 miles per hour. Finally, in the middle of the tumult, they reached the dock. "We have a boat lift there. It was all I could do to get out of the boat and hold it and feed it into the lift."

Pete told Duane to grab their day packs and get into his Forest Service truck. Fortunately, he had parked the truck in a clearing, which meant that if trees began falling, they should be out of harm's way. It was also facing due west, so they would have a clear view of the approaching storm.

Pete used the manual crank to get the boat up in the lift and chain it down. The wind and rain were coming down in blasting sheets. He fought his way to the truck and yanked open the driver's-side door, climbing in and slamming it shut behind him.

"And I kid you not, the truck started swaying from side to side," Pete said. He started the truck and got the windshield wipers going. Incongruously, there was a brief lull in the storm. But when they looked into the southwestern sky and saw the near horizon turn blacker, then green and purple, they realized the lull was only the storm gathering strength.

When the full force of the weather finally hit them, "It was like a tidal wave of low-level clouds coming right at us," Pete remembered. "I've never seen anything like it." The wind and rain rocked the F-150 truck like an earthquake. There were trees off to their left; Moose Lake Bay sat in front of them. From their vantage point in the small clearing, they witnessed the storm roll in.

As the rain, wind, and clouds bore down, pummeling the truck, Pete glanced up to see a blue heron trying to find some kind of flight pattern. But it was being blown sideways by the hurricane-force winds. "It had no control whatsoever," Pete said. Then some mallard ducks suffered the same fate, hurled back by the wind, slapped away like badminton birdies.

There was a picnic table to the side of them, set near a pair of 50-foot balsam firs. As the wind increased, the tops of the balsams snapped off and blew away. The power lines behind them suffered the same fate as the balsams. Once the poles snapped, the lines fell to the ground, whipped back and forth by the mayhem. It was the most intense weather Pete and Duane had ever seen.

After a while, the wind and rain ratcheted down—but only a little. They watched and waited, struck silent by what they'd just endured. After a few more minutes, Duane finally opened the door to what both men knew would be a changed world.

Pete's first thought was that people had died in this storm. There had to be people in the woods or on lakes who had perished.

"The first thing I did was walk down the driveway to see if we could get out of there," Pete said. But it only took a moment to determine they were trapped by a fallen forest blocking everything. There would be no return to civilization anytime soon. He looked back to where the power line poles had been snapped and saw live wires sparking across the ground.

"And then, all of a sudden, there was this young gentleman walking down the road from the opposite direction, from Canadian Border Outfitters. He was checking to see if they could drive down the Forest Service driveway to get out of their resort." The newcomer, too, quickly understood they were all stuck in the blowdown from the storm's aftermath.

"Eyes opened in the Big Blow," Pete said. "It was right there in front of me. And I won't forget it. That darkness in the sky. The blacks and purples and even greens. It was that rolling tidal wave at tree level. What an experience."

/ / /

At that point, Pete used the truck radio to call Forest Service dispatch: "Dispatch, this is Officer Weckman. I'm up on Moose Lake. We just had a severe windstorm. We've got power lines down. I can't get out of here. We need to get some crews with power saws up here." He also suggested they get the Forest Service Beaver planes in the air to survey the damage farther east, where the storm was heading. And it would probably make sense, given what he'd experienced, to get an incident management team called up, to begin to address what he was certain would be some serious search-and-rescue efforts. He recommended they contact the Lake County Sheriff's Office, which would take the lead in search and rescue. Pete suspected they would be busy for the foreseeable future. But at this point, he had no idea the "foreseeable future" would stretch into days, weeks, months, and eventually years.

10

FIRST RESPONDERS

Western and Eastern Zones, Superior National Forest

Ralph Bonde was looking forward to Ely's Fourth of July parade. He was one of the members of the Ely Area Honor Guard who would be leading the event, and as the skies west of town began to stir, he and his fellow guards were assembling by a nearby school. Around noon, the parade planners announced a fast-moving storm was forming, and the parade would be postponed until at least 2:00 p.m. Since he was only a few blocks from home, he decided to wait out the storm from the comfort of his kitchen table.

As Ralph drove across town, the wind came up sudden and intense. It grew stronger the closer he got to home, slamming into his car. The rain began to fall.

Ely, which was incorporated as a city on March 3, 1891, was old enough to have plenty of mature trees, some of which lined the streets near Ralph's house. "I thought the big maple tree and the big basswood were going to blow over," Ralph said. "I couldn't see anything."

Then a falling branch suddenly tumbled on top of him. Thankfully, it wasn't large enough to cause any damage, but like the uptick in wind, it was unsettling.

Now the rain started to fall in earnest, forcing him to slow to a crawl. There was another blast accompanied by a cracking sound. Ralph squinted through his windshield; a larger branch fell in front of him, large enough to have certainly damaged his car. He skirted the fallen branch and crept along the rain-drenched street, nearing a side street.

"And then out of the alley comes this big thing, this big ball rolling," recalled Ralph. The large object startled him. Squinting through the rain and wind he recognized a four-person tent, obviously empty, pulled up by the blow, tumbling into the street. It was like an image out of a bad dream. The tent rolled straight into him, disappearing beneath his car. "I went over the top of it and kept going," Ralph said.

He finally reached home and the comparative safety of his garage, which is when he examined the undercarriage of his car. The tent was caught up in his chassis. It took him nearly an hour to tease the twisted nylon free. By the time he entered his house and cleaned up, it was nearly two o'clock. The storm had finally blown through. There were downed trees and some property damage, but for the small, hardy town of Ely, there was nothing substantial enough to cancel a holiday parade. Ready to reassume his position in the Honor Guard, Ralph returned to the starting point.

/ / /

Being a guardsman was just one of Ralph Bonde's occupations. In 1964, he had begun working for the U.S. Forest Service as an assistant in timber management. By education, he was a silviculturist; by training and experience, he added forest fire management to his growing list of duties. Over the ensuing thirty-five years, Ralph Bonde had found ample opportunities to work his way up the fire management ladder. He was a firefighter, then a crew boss, then a division group supervisor, then an operations section chief. His work experience was augmented by training and the necessary classroom time, enabling him to earn a series of red cards (interagency certifications) that qualified him for progressively higher positions of responsibility. By 1999, Ralph had worked his way up to the position of Type II incident commander.

According to the National Wildfire Coordinating Group, "The Incident Commander Type 2 (ICT2) is responsible for all aspects of emergency response, including developing incident objectives, managing incident operations, setting priorities, defining the organization of the incident management team, and the overall Incident Action Plan (IAP).

The ICT2 also has responsibility for ensuring incident safety and establishing and maintaining liaison with other agencies and stakeholders participating in the incident. The ICT2 supervises all Command and General Staff positions and reports to the Agency Administrator."

While forest fires were the most common type of emergency, especially in the Ely area, they weren't the only disasters on which Ralph had worked. "I have been on floods. I've been on wind events. And I've been on fire," he said.

As an ICT2, Ralph led one of Minnesota's three incident management teams. During fire season, from around May 1 through September, one incident management team was always on call. Coincidentally—and fortuitously, given Ely was about to become the headquarters for a major incident—the week of July 4, it was Ralph's team's turn to be on call.

But given what Ralph had seen of the blow that came through Ely—a sudden dust-up that had caused damage, but not the kind of devastation that would have required a Type II incident response—he had no idea that before the end of the day he would get a call that would change the trajectory of how he was going to spend his next two weeks.

/ / /

U.S. Forest Service law enforcement officer Chip Elkins was standing on an Ely street when the weather suddenly changed. "I was in the area with my brother and his two boys, and we were gonna watch the parade when it struck town," Elkins remembers. "And that's when I told my brother we need to get back to the house. The wind was swirling around Ely."

Chip Elkins was a longtime resident of the town who had begun working for the Forest Service during summer 1977. His first job with the agency was as a forestry technician, responsible for maintaining campsites and trails in the Superior National Forest. After graduating with a two-year degree in conservation technology, Chip became a full-time seasonal forestry technician, and during the next two years, 1978–79, he led groups of teenagers who came up to the area to work, building and maintaining trails and campsites. Then by 1980, Chip and his wife, Cindy, who were both fluent in sign language, created the first USFS program in which Deaf and hard-of-hearing youth could work in the BWCAW on trail and campsite maintenance.

By the mid-1980s, Chip had augmented his forestry technician training with eighty hours of law enforcement training, enabling him to add Forest Service law enforcement to his duties. When the opportunity arose for more training, Chip attended the Federal Law Enforcement Training Center program in Brunswick, Georgia. Not long after he graduated, the Forest Service decided, for the first time, the BWCAW needed a full-time law enforcement officer in the field, and Chip took the job. In his new position he was authorized to carry a weapon, use a marked vehicle, and, when necessary, make arrests.

The day of the storm, Chip suspected there was enough wind damage in Ely to require some sort of law enforcement presence in the area. He turned on his radio and immediately heard emergency transmissions over Forest Service and county frequencies. The chatter caused Chip to tell his brother and two young nephews that he had to go to work. Unfortunately, he wasn't sure when he might return.

/ / /

As head ranger of the Kawishiwi District, Bruce Slover had oversight of an area that stretched several miles east–west from just west of Ely into the heart of the Boundary Waters and approximately 20 miles north–south from the Canadian border to the Laurentian District.

The trajectory of the intense winds that blew through Ely unsettled Bruce. "I remember that storm rolling in, and it was a fierce-looking cloud," he said. "I think you call it a shelf cloud? It went all the way across the sky. It was bright on one side and extremely dark on the other. And it was scary looking." The darkening clouds presaged worse weather as they entered the eastern section of the Kawishiwi District.

Bruce was familiar with the kind of weather that preceded midwestern thunderstorms, and what he saw in the skies over Ely reminded him of it. In response, he did what most midwesterners familiar with tornado weather do: he took refuge in his basement. In Bruce's experience, the Fourth of July holiday in his district typically saw a surplus of campers and visitors. In consequence, he had made sure many of his wilderness rangers were active and in the field. In the immediate aftermath of the storm blowing through town, he worried about those employees in the wilderness. "When I came out, I thought, 'Man, I'd better check on our folks in the field.' So, I went to the service center just to listen to the radio a bit and see what was happening."

/ / /

Jim Hinds was the fire management officer for the Superior National Forest's west zone, which encompasses the Laurentian, Kawishiwi, and LaCroix Districts. On July 4, he and his wife, Jeanne, were on their back screen porch, watching the storm as it approached from the west. The wind was stronger than the average storm, but at their home, 3 miles west of Ely, it bore little resemblance to the intense and prolonged derecho it would eventually become. "I often watch storms from this vantage point," Jim recalled. "On July 4, 1999, however, as the storm's intensity increased and debris started to blow about the yard, I decided it was wiser to go inside. The storm was strong, blowing branches and lawn chairs around, but no trees came down."

After the winds died down, Jim and Jeanne headed into Ely to watch the parade. When they arrived in town, they could see some wind damage. "There were scattered trees down in town, on a scale not often seen, but not devastating." The Hindses found a place from which to watch the parade, and settled in.

"During the parade, I spent time visiting with a friend and fellow Forest Service employee, Wayne Erickson, a Forest Service pilot. I remember talking with him about 'the storm,'" Jim recalled. At that time, neither he nor Wayne had any idea how "the storm" would dramatically affect the rest of their day—or the remaining years of their Forest Service careers.

/ / /

Tim Norman was the Superior National Forest's fire management officer for the east zone, which covers the Isabella, Gunflint, and Tofte Districts.

Tim was not on duty on Sunday, July 4—he was getting ready to enjoy one of the year's most popular events, the Tofte Holiday Parade.

As the crow flies, Tofte is approximately 50 miles southeast of Ely, on the eastern side of the wilderness. By car, it's nearly two hours away. The small town perched on Lake Superior's shore is also 30 miles southwest of Grand Marais.

"Tofte has one of the biggest Fourth of July celebrations on the North Shore," Tim explained. "We'll typically get 1,200 to 1,500 people." Cars line up on Highway 61, which goes through Tofte, all the way to the North Shore Market on the northeast end of town. "We have that little town park road, and a fire hall right on the lake. It's a popular place. We open the fire hall and get one of the trucks out and have vendors who come in. Then we have a parade."

On this day, Tim and his wife, Diane, were getting ready to line up and enjoy the parade. Their fifteen-year-old daughter and one of her friends owned horses and wanted to ride them in the parade. Earlier, Tim had trailered the horses down from the acreage where they were boarded. "We had them unload in the staging area," Tim remembered.

Tim was a firefighter for the Tofte Volunteer Fire Department, which had a truck in the parade along with the volunteer departments for Schroeder and Lutsen. There were always a few kegs of beer at the fire hall, and Tim was getting ready to serve it. "When the storm hit," he re-called, "we were all getting ready for the parade, thinking we were going to get rained on." But when Tim looked up, he saw ominous, rolling purple clouds heading straight toward them. "We had a couple hundred people crammed into the fire hall, trying to get away from that storm."

Kids from Tofte's Birch Grove elementary school had used reams of crepe paper to build a parade float. When the storm hit, all the paper on the float was stripped away, like leaves blown off a tree. "I remember those kids getting worried and saying, 'Oh my god, we're gonna die.'" Tim laughed. "One minute there was a float, and the next it was gone."

While the storm was bad, this was its initial, early southern front. Most of the full-force derecho would happen much farther north, tearing through the Boundary Waters and the northwest end of the Gunflint Trail. Tofte would be hit by part of that second storm later, when it would dump 8 inches of rain on the town and the surrounding region. But for now, as in Ely, the weather did little more than delay the parade.

"When the parade was all over, the part I remember was how freaked out those horses were," Tim said. "We could not get them to go back into their trailer. They were so spooked from that event. We were thinking, 'What's the deal? Just another thunderstorm going through?' It took us a couple hours to get those spooked horses trailered. The horses knew something big was going on."

Eventually, when Tim Norman's pager started to go off, so would he.

/ / /

Steve Schug began his Forest Service career in Ely in 1979, when he was a wilderness ranger for the BWCAW. In 1988, he had an opportunity to become a wilderness program manager in the Boundary Waters' Tofte District, and he still held that position in 1999. But on July 4, he wasn't working. "I was just about ready to start my second beer at the Tofte Fourth of July celebration," Steve remembered. He seldom drank beer, but like Tim Norman, Steve was a volunteer firefighter, in this case for nearby Schroeder. "The fire department has a beer stand, and it was a fundraiser, and so I had to help."

While he was working the fundraiser, a temporary Forest Service employee approached him.

"Steve, you should go over to the office, because all hell is breaking loose," she said.

"Why?" Steve wanted to know.

"The storm."

Like everyone else in Tofte, Steve had experienced the storm that had come through town earlier. While he recalled the cloud cover being unique and having an interesting hue to it, and while there had been some winds and heavy rain, it had passed. However, recognizing the urgency in the woman's voice and eyes, he immediately put down his beer and went over to the ranger station to find out what was happening.

Most of the Forest Service employees were in vacation mode, it being a holiday. The local office was being staffed by this temporary employee, who was primarily on-site to issue wilderness permits and answer phones. But when she started getting radio calls and listening to the initial chatter about what had happened in the wilderness, 25 miles to the north, she decided she had better find a more senior official to respond. She could not find the district ranger or any assistant rangers, so she had come down to the celebration, where she knew many of the office's employees would be.

The Tofte Ranger District only had one or two groups of wilderness rangers out at that time. As previously discussed, based on the number of issued BWCAW permits, Steve Schug estimated that there were ten thousand visitors in the wilderness.

/ / /

"On July 4, the storm had already passed where I live, in Littlefork up by International Falls," remembered Jody Leidholm, Forest Service air attack supervisor. "We didn't have severe winds like they did south and east of us. But we had lots of rain, and it was ungodly humid and hot." Sometime in the early afternoon, after the rains passed through Littlefork, Jody got a call from the Minnesota Interagency Fire Center (MIFC) dispatch. "They told me there had been some kind of blowdown event and I should report to Ely. But they didn't know any details."

As an air attack supervisor being called up for a blowdown event (rather than a wildfire), he suspected he would be coordinating search-and-rescue work over the wilderness. "My main job at the time was to make sure a search was carried off in safe fashion and it's coordinated, with all aircraft adequately separated in the airspace," he explained. In that role, Jody would plan the search-and-rescue process with whatever aircraft were available. That meant ensuring all aircraft and pilots were identified and there were clear procedures for keeping in touch with radios. It also meant Jody would take to the skies with the other pilots doing the actual search-and-rescue work. "Somebody's got to take the lead and make sure it's a coordinated search and it's been covered the best it can be done."

But in the early afternoon, details were few and sketchy. "I didn't know if the assignment was a day, a week, or longer," Jody recalled. "So I had to take a little while to pack and get my gear."

By late afternoon, he was in his vehicle, headed toward Ely, a two-hour drive from Littlefork. Once he arrived, he would need to find a room and maybe grab a quick bite to eat. But he expected to arrive in the Ely Forest Service offices no later than early evening, when he would learn more details about what had happened, and how he could help.

/ / /

Steve Jakala was the area fire management officer for Voyageurs National Park, headquartered in International Falls. He was also the operations section chief (OSC2) on Jim Tarbells's Minnesota Incident Command Center Type II incident management team, another of the three Type II teams in Minnesota on call throughout the fire season. In addition, Steve was an OSC2 on a National Park Service Fire Use Management Team, which managed fires in the western United States, mostly in wilderness areas. "We were just getting ready to leave on a camping trip to Rainy Lake," Steve remembered, when he got the call from MIFC. While there had been no official declaration for a Type II team, MIFC wanted to be ready. Ralph Bonde's team was on call, but the normal operations chief was unavailable. Consequently, they asked Steve to report to Ely to stand in as the OSC2, at least for a while.

"Another family trip interrupted by a fire/all risk assignment," Steve said. "My wife and kids were disappointed but had become used to it." That said, he told MIFC he was only able to commit to four days. For now, that would suffice.

Steve was a former smokejumper—a skydiving firefighter who is often dropped into extremely dangerous situations that can only be accessed by air. Because the work can be so harrowing, it takes a special person to become a smokejumper. According to Steve, every effort that requires smokejumpers begins with the same message: "This is no shit." Steve, figuring the storm had been significant, guessed it was an appropriate sentiment for what he was headed into.

Like Jody Leidholm, Steve was called up by midafternoon. It was a two-hour drive from International Falls to Ely, so Steve had time to secure a room, grab a bite to eat, and arrive at Forest Service HQ by early evening, if not before. "It's always hard to mentally game out what I was up against," Steve recalled. "But knowing the BWCAW, it was definitely going to be an air show."

/ / /

Presumably Jo Barnier, head ranger of the Tofte and Gunflint Districts, was, like many of her employees, taking the holiday off. Since she lived in the area, she had doubtless experienced the same early stormy weather as Tim Norman and Steve Schug. Even if she was up in Grand Marais, she may have experienced some wind and rain, but nothing on the scale of what was about to happen in the northern reaches of the BWCAW. Regardless, at some point, probably later in the day, when MIFC would have had at least some sense of what had happened in the wilderness, she would have been notified. Jo Barnier's Tofte and Gunflint District leadership duties, at least for the foreseeable future, were about to change.

/ / /

The Minnesota Interagency Fire Center is located in Grand Rapids, Minnesota, approximately 80 miles west-northwest of Duluth and 100 miles west-southwest of Ely. According to its website, "MIFC serves as a hub for mobilization of wildfire and emergency resources." Because there was little to no cell coverage in the BWCAW, and the most intense areas of the storm had taken out electricity and land lines in and around the wilderness (especially at the end of the Gunflint Trail), on the afternoon of July 4, MIFC had no clear idea of the extent of the damage. But because its personnel began hearing radio transmissions and reports from others impacted by the storm, including calls for help, they began calling up people and directing them to Ely. Though Ralph Bonde's IC Type II team was on call, no official callup had yet been made.

11

WE THOUGHT SHE WAS DEAD

Lake Polly
South-Central Boundary Waters

That day was very unusual," Michelle Orieux said about Sunday, July 4. "The humidity was so high—we knew a storm was coming."

"Calm, hot, humid and muggy," agreed Kristina Schwendinger.

After waking, the five campers kindled a fire, in part because the day was so quiet the smoke would help keep the bugs, who buzzed through the still air, manageable. Because their campsite was a small, thumb-shaped peninsula largely covered in rock, previous visitors had already culled the nearby forest for firewood. Fortunately, the previous day, Ray had figured out there was abundant firewood on the small island across from their campsite. Yesterday, he had gathered enough for their campfires the previous night and this morning. But he knew that later in the morning, he would need to replenish their supply with another trip to the island.

After coffee and breakfast and awakening around their campsite, the five spent the rest of the morning in various pursuits. Most of them decided to go swimming—everyone except Michelle, who described herself as "a pool girl."

"In the morning it was very hot," Ray said. "We swam out to the point on that island."

After cooling off with a quick swim, Ray returned to the campsite while Lisa and Kristina decided to take their life vests from the canoe and continue cooling off in the water.

"We had our life jackets as floats," Kristina recalled. "We had our arms on the jackets, just kind of hanging out. It was hot. It was really hot. So we were just chilling and having a relaxing morning. We were all thinking, 'Wow, how hot is it going to be?'"

Michelle remembered that Ray hooked up their solar shower, a large black bladder with a hose extension and a shower nozzle. The bladder holds a few gallons and can be hung in a tree, in the sun. The black surface absorbs the sun's heat and warms its contents.

"Usually that water's got to heat for a while before you want to stand under it," Michelle said. "But we were so hot out there, I think I took two showers that morning just to cool off."

Lisa and Mark eventually decided to try their luck fishing. They had both brought fishing poles, and in the holiday morning they paddled away from their campsite in Mark's canoe. Everyone was dressed lightly, either in cutoff shorts or swimsuits. After getting out of the water later in the morning, Lisa kept on her bikini top and pulled on a pair of cutoffs over her swimsuit bottom.

Late morning, Ray decided it was time to replenish their firewood supply. Because Lisa's Kevlar canoe was lightweight and small, and he was curious about how it handled on the water, he commandeered it and again paddled across the brief stretch of water to the island. It took him the rest of the morning to forage and fill Lisa's canoe with firewood.

Lisa and Mark, fishing, had paddled offshore no more than 100 yards. "It's hard to fish in a canoe when you don't know the lake," Mark said. Still, they spent perhaps an hour trying their luck in the oppressive heat. "The fish weren't biting at all," he added. The heat and absence of fishing activity eventually drove them back to their camp.

An hour or so before noon, Ray noticed the western sky beginning to cloud and decided it was a good time to return to camp. "I knew a storm was coming," he said. He paddled around the point to the inside of the cove and beached Lisa's canoe. While the sky to the west continued to cloud, there was still enough time for Ray to unload the wood, bring it up to their campsite, and begin cutting it.

"Mark and Lisa had come back from fishing," Ray noted. "They knew the storm was coming, too. We all just started getting our stuff out of the canoes and bringing it up to the campsite."

Although the five campers sensed the impending arrival of bad weather, they believed it was still distant enough that they had time to fix something for lunch. "Something quick, like peanut butter and bagels," Michelle said.

Their portable table was under the large tarp Ray had earlier affixed to a couple of nearby trees. Now he made sure the bottom of the tarp was facing west and securely fastened near the ground against the approaching weather.

As the group had a quick bite to eat, the western sky took on an ugly hue. "The sky got really eerie," Lisa recalled. "If a storm cloud rolls in, it gets dark. This one turned a different color. Like green. The sky had this kind of greenish tint to it."

Suddenly, the wind increased, beginning to flap Ray's carefully positioned tarp. All of them wondered whether they should retreat farther to the east, into the trees, for protection. But after a quick debate they decided to stay on the rock ledge, in the open. Even though it was 15 feet above the shoreline and exposed, it had fewer surrounding trees than the adjacent forest. When the inevitable rains came, the tarp should provide some protection. And because they were in the open, they might suffer wind gusts and some pelting precipitation, but—if the wind grew strong enough—they would avoid broken-off branches and falling trees.

"Ray had tarps over stuff," Lisa remembered. "He had everything in its place. But [the storm] came up really fast. When the wind started kicking in, it was all-out chaos."

"The thing that was remarkable to me was how quickly the wind came up," commented Kristina. "At first, we thought it was normal rain—so when the wind started, there was some stuff blowing around the campground. People began to chase down and secure stuff so it wouldn't blow away. And then the wind just started going up and up and up and up."

In the growing hurly-burly, Ray's tarp began flapping wildly. The edge that had been anchored near the ground was pulled out of its mooring. Now it whipped and flailed, and Mark, fearing the intensifying gusts could tear it or, worse, blow it away, grabbed hold of one side and held on tight.

From her vantage point atop the granite slab, Lisa watched her canoe, which Ray had pulled halfway up the granite shoreline. Now it began to blow sideways. "The wind caught it and started pulling it out into water again," Lisa recalled. "So, I ran out and grabbed it and started dragging it back onto shore."

Mark and the others were still atop the campsite's main granite slab, trying to hold on to whatever they'd managed to save from the straight-line winds. Given the chaos, the intensifying wind, and the trees that began to sway wildly, Michelle realized remaining in the open, on top of the granite rise, had been the right call. Now everyone on the campsite believed it was only a matter of time before the trees began losing limbs, torn off in the wind—or, worse, began falling. Better to be in the open, exposed to the torrential downpour, than in the woods and vulnerable to falling spruce.

Mark still gripped the tarp, which was whipping in the wind. "As I'm watching the tarp and wondering 'Is this gonna hold? What's gonna happen?' I was glancing up at the trees," Mark recalled. "I saw how violently they were shaking. I was watching it, but I was not really comprehending what was happening. I would see the tree swaying back and forth violently. And then all of a sudden, just like that, it swung away, but it didn't do the bounce back.

"I was thinking, 'Okay, when is it going to start coming back?' It took me a few seconds to realize the tree had snapped off and was falling down. And that's when I kind of followed it all the way as it was coming down and I realized it was coming right in line with Lisa, because she had gone down to the water's edge to pull up her canoe."

The downpour was turning everything opaque. The wind was pushing the torrent sideways, driving the massive onslaught of water onto everyone and everything. The hurricane-force winds were howling across the site, making it difficult to hear or see anything.

Down by the water, Lisa had hold of her canoe. "I was looking at the inside of my canoe," she said. "I heard a big crack that I thought was thunder. . . . I thought that was maybe the tree breaking. It was super loud and made me flinch. But I had my arm out and grabbed one of the crossbars of the canoe and I'm dragging it out and looking inside the canoe . . . the last thing I remember . . ."

"As I'm watching the tree—I think I was watching it because it was one of the trees the rainfly was tied to—it just came down and went right along her line and it just brushed the left side of her head," Mark remembered. "She was reaching down and kind of holding the canoe. Not even looking up. She had no warning, no nothing that something was going on up above.

"I saw the tree fall and hit her on the side of the head. And I say alongside the head, but it brushed her head, and she was knocked out. It would have been a very, very different outcome if it had landed on her."

Mark was the only person atop the main campsite area to glimpse Lisa getting struck by the tree. The moment was so chaotic and confusing that those who were exposed to the full blast of the storm, trying to hold on to themselves and whatever else they had grabbed on to, to keep their equipment and supplies and food from blowing away, glimpsed different parts of the calamity around the campsite.

"It was pouring torrential rain," Ray recalled. "But I don't think Lisa made it to the canoe, because the canoe was still down there, and the tree had fallen over the canoe and broke that front part. . . . I don't remember her making it all the way down to the canoe."

The pummeling storm was like the fog of war. Everyone was trying to hold on. But above the helter-skelter of the wind they all heard Mark's scream.

"She's down. She's down!"

"Food was flying everywhere," Michelle recalled. "Trees were flying. It was chaos."

"Everything was straight-line winds," Ray added. "The whole campsite was falling apart."

The tarp Mark was holding continued flapping like a flag in a typhoon. Their table blew over. The food they had earlier set out was picked up by the wind and flung east.

As soon as everyone heard Mark say Lisa was down, Michelle said, "We all ran down, honestly expecting that she was dead. That was my and Mark's first thought, we later admitted."

12

WHEN THE SKY FALLS DOWN

Alpine and Seagull Lakes
Near the End of the Gunflint Trail

July 4 dawned quiet, unseasonably hot and humid. Vicky Brockman knew it was uncharacteristic weather for the Boundary Waters. But she, Jan, and Sue Ann enjoyed the dead calm, the placid lake stretching in front of their campsite flat as a mirror.

It was going to be a great last day in the woods. The three women planned on spending the entire day at their campsite; maybe they'd take a paddle in the afternoon. Their hammocks were strung and waiting for a lounging read later in the day. And they looked forward to their last supper in the Boundary Waters—Jan was planning something special.

By late morning it was already warm enough that they decided to go for a refreshing swim. They stepped down the beach into the water. The lake would cool them off and help them keep the bugs at bay.

While they were swimming, they noticed clouds to the west beginning to gather. The day had broken hazy, but the sky had presaged nothing untoward. They spent some time enjoying the lake water.

Eventually, they climbed back onto shore and began milling around camp, talking. As the morning tilted toward midday, the western sky grew darker. Vicky had grown up on a farm in southwestern Minnesota, so she was familiar with the onset of storms. She was pretty sure she could feel one approaching, but the dense forest west of their campsite obscured their view of the horizon.

Sensing a storm, they decided it was a good time for a quick lunch. If it began to rain, they could take cover in their tent and ride out the squall.

While they ate, a freshet rippled across the lake's surface. They could see the near western sky continuing to turn an ominous shade, but the light breeze breaking the hot, still air was refreshing. Then in another few minutes they felt the first raindrops begin to fall, intermittently at first—big, fat drops being pushed by a quickening wind. Vicky could see from the clouds the rain would likely soon intensify.

The three campers made the obvious move, into the dry environs of their tent. As the weather came on, Sue Ann lay down on the southern side of the tent, her head facing east. Vicky lay in the middle, facing the opposite direction from Sue Ann. Vicky had enough time to find her book, open it, and begin reading. To her right, on the other side of the tent from Sue Ann, lay Jan, also reading. Jan lay on her stomach, in the same direction as Sue Ann, with her legs angled toward Vicky's head.

They were expecting to wait out the storm in relatively dry quarters, though it was hard not to notice the intensifying elements. Contrary to a typical squall, the winds kept increasing. And increasing. The blow began buffeting their nylon walls like a jib in a gale, enveloping them on all sides. There was a moment, with the winds blowing harder, when it felt as though the tent might be picked up and carried away. In response, Jan stretched across the floor, placing her hands against one wall and her feet against the other, hoping to keep it from collapsing. The gale out of the west-southwest began shaking the treetops.

Vicky sat up.

The peak of their tent had a screen window. Vicky, concerned about the sudden onslaught, peered into the forest behind them. Most of the trees were pine; their stiff-needled arms were flailing in the squall. And then the rains grew worse. Water spilled out of the sky, drenching their nylon walls. The outburst intensified the shaking trees.

Through the downpour, Vicky watched a distant treetop snap off. Then another. She screamed to her companions, dropped to the floor, turned onto her side, and leaned into the nylon side to help Jan anchor their tent. Fearful of a falling tree, she shielded her head with her arm.

To the northwest of their tent stood a 60-foot jack pine, its trunk at least a foot in diameter. While they struggled to keep the tent anchored, they heard the sickening sound of the tree being pulled up by its roots, starting to topple. There was an interminable moment while the maelstrom howled and the tree, as though in slow motion, continued to fall. And then it pounded down on top of them, slantwise, flattening the paper-thin walls and the three women who lay inside.

The tree pinned Sue Ann to the ground. The trunk lay across her side and chest, and she struggled to breathe. When she opened her mouth to gulp air, the heavy rain prevented her from catching her breath.

Vicky took a direct blow from the jack pine's trunk. Fortunately, her arm protected her head. But because she was on her side, her hip absorbed the full force of the impact. When it landed, Sue Ann said, "We could all hear something crack." Vicky remained conscious. But excruciating pain was accompanied by the sickening certainty that something in her lower extremities had been seriously injured.

"And that's when I started screaming," Vicky said.

Because Jan's feet had been angled toward Vicky's head, several of the tree's branches had fallen on top of her. She, too, was being pinned to the ground.

"Jan got the end of the tree," Sue Ann said.

The storm was still howling around them, the skies filled with lightning and thunder and a deluge. There was nothing they could do but ride out the bad weather and wait for the uproar to subside.

Vicky was the most grievously hurt. Her first thought was that she'd broken a leg, but the side of her hip had been higher than her tapering thigh. Now she was held tight between the ground and the fallen jack pine, as though fastened in the jaws of a vise.

Sue Ann wasn't much better. The tree trunk and branches lay across her chest and side. She was now managing to catch her breath, but she couldn't crawl out from under the tree.

Jan was pinned only by her feet and lower legs. Branches were holding her down like the scraggly fingers of a wicked hand.

Under the onslaught of rain, they struggled to keep breathing, tensing their bodies against the storm.

"So there we were," concluded Sue Ann.

13

IT'S A HURRICANE

Northeast Canadian Side of Gunflint Lake
Ten Miles East-Southeast of the Wilderness Canoe Base

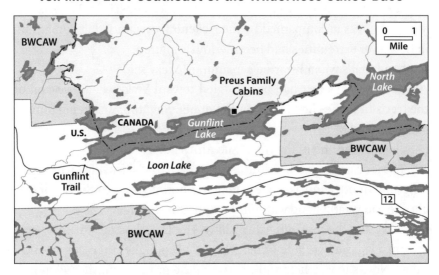

S ometime during the morning of July 4, Christian Preus turned to his wife, Cindy, and said, "Enough. We're done. I'm going to take the boys fishing." For their sons, Caleb (ten) and Luke (twelve), it would be welcome news. Given that the morning was hot, still, and humid, the family recalled that the kids—who also included Kristiana (seven) and Erika (fifteen)—were sleeping in. Eventually they and their Shih Tzu dog, Tobie, would all rise and gather around the kitchen table for breakfast, unaware of their father's pronouncement. But Christian's early-morning observation to his wife was significant because it involved much more than fishing: he was putting a verbal exclamation on a process that had begun three years earlier, and that had—in one way or another—involved all of them.

/ / /

In 1996 Christian Preus's mother, Donna Mae Preus, established a family trust. The trust gave her children and grandchildren the right to use and enjoy her interest in more than 200 acres of wilderness property that included 3,000 feet of forested shoreline on the northeast Canadian side of Gunflint Lake. To seven of her ten children, she gave the right to build on one of the lots included in the trust property.

Christian's family lot stood in a spectacular stand of old-growth forest. Because it was remote, and because Christian's grandmother Idella Preus (married to Christian's grandfather, Jacob A. O. Preus, who was the governor of Minnesota from 1921 to 1925) had owned the property since 1929, the substantial parcel had never been logged. And while fire had at times crisscrossed every corner of the region, the Preus property had, at least for the past two centuries, escaped the blazes.

After the trust was established, Christian, Cindy, and the kids didn't wait long to begin working on their dream northern retreat. They chose a spot approximately 80 feet from the lake, up through the old-growth wood, careful to remove only the trees that grew over their cabin site. "We started building in 1997," Christian recalled. "We worked really hard for two years." The Canadian side of Gunflint Lake has no roads; the only access to the area is by water. "We hauled everything across by boat."

Christian, an attorney, recalled the grueling two-year schedule required to construct and finish their place. "During the week I would work until 6:00 on Thursday night and then drive up." Travel time from his home in Plymouth, Minnesota, to Heston's Lodge on the south side of Gunflint Lake, where they stored their boat, was approximately six hours. Christian, Cindy, and the kids, when they were along, made the crossing to their North Shore retreat in the dark, arriving at the cabin late. "I'd get up early Friday morning and put in ten to twelve hours on Friday, Saturday, and Sunday, leaving around 5:00 p.m. to return home."

During the two-year effort, they did most of the work themselves, at times assisted by friends and relatives. "I had a cousin who was a concrete guy," Christian explained. "He helped with the foundation. And I had some friends help with the subfloor, floor, and framing. And I had another friend help with the electric."

The north side of Gunflint Lake is so remote public utilities have never run electrical lines to the area. Christian and Cindy acquired a generator and had another friend wire the cabin for electricity. "And then *we* did everything after that," Christian continued. "Everything inside. All of the pine paneling and the tiling and all of the outdoor siding. Everything."

The cabin layout was classic Northwoods. It faced south, toward the lake. The front door opened onto a deck that extended across two-thirds of the front of the cabin, with stairs leading down to the forest. Christian and Cindy's bedroom stretched along the cabin's southeast corner, with another smaller bedroom next to it. A third bedroom was tucked into the rear northeast corner. An open living room, dining room, and kitchen with a vaulted ceiling anchored the west side of the cabin. Large picture windows covered its front. Because the trees had been so carefully preserved, if you were looking from the cabin toward the lake, most of the water was obscured. Similarly, if you were standing at water's edge it was easy to miss the cabin concealed in the woods. At the bottom of the front deck's stairs, a meandering path wound through the trees to the lake.

On the morning of July 4, 1999, when Christian turned to Cindy and said "We're done," it marked a turning point in the three-year journey that left them and their four kids with a cabin in one of the most beautiful wilderness areas on the planet. To be sure, some cleanup remained. There was a table saw still standing on their deck, waiting to be covered by a tarp and moved to storage. And as Christian well knew, "You never really finish work on a cabin." But it felt good to be finally finished, for all intents and purposes, with the fire-in-the-belly effort. Christian had labored over every inch of the cabin, from the concrete footings and the foundation to the top of their peaked metal roof; he could honestly say he was familiar with every crevice of the place by muscle ache and brow sweat.

/ / /

After their return from fishing, the two boys joined their sisters in swimming off the end of their remote cabin's dock. The cool Gunflint Lake waters provided a pleasing respite from the heat.

Christian was down on the dock with his kids. As the day progressed, he glanced westward over the lake to where the skies were starting to darken. As the clouds grew more ominous, headed their way, he felt certain they would usher in a serious thunderstorm. He had often experienced storms on the north side of Gunflint Lake—he was one of those people who, if caught on the water in a good old-fashioned Minnesota thunderstorm, would not typically return to shore. To Cindy's dismay, he loved the feel of a good downpour.

The clouds continued their darkening approach. As they thickened and continued to swell, their color began to morph into an eerie green. Faced with the possibility of bad weather, Christian and the four Preus kids decided it was time to head back to the cabin. Besides, they were all hungry from their morning's efforts. Time to go up into their kitchen and eat lunch.

Back in the cabin, Cindy had prepared the midday meal. Inside, surrounded by the trees, they no longer had a clear view of the oncoming storm. While they finished lunch, the only change in weather was an increasing blow out of the west.

Then, around one o'clock, it started to rain. No one thought much about the cloudburst; it was July, and thunderstorms often blew through the area. But the pelting quickly turned into something more substantial, as though all of that summer's excessive precipitation had been sucked up into the clouds and a pair of hands was wringing them out like an overfilled sponge.

Christian suddenly remembered the uncovered table saw on his deck. By the time he stepped outside, the rain was a downpour. He retrieved the tarp and quickly fitted it over the saw, the torrent drenching him. He also noticed a serious uptick in the wind.

Christian knew that if the breeze became too strong it could damage the boat or the dock or both—maybe even yank the boat from its mooring and send it crashing ashore. Since he was already drenched, he decided to hike down their path to the lake and haul the boat onto their beach rocks. Besides, an admirer of foul weather, he knew the best place to see the full breadth and depth of this storm's intensity was at lake's edge.

The overhead canopy muted the full intensity of the rainfall. But even under the trees, the weather forced Christian to keep his eyes down, focused on the blurring path in front of him. He hurried along the trail, in less than a minute reaching the water.

While he loved watching thunderstorms—the stronger the better— what he saw now was something else entirely. The wind had worsened. Gunflint's surface raged. Whitecaps churned out of the water like foaming boulders. Breakers were ravaging the rugged shoreline. The squall and rain were so intense he could not tell where the lake ended and the sky began. The world had suddenly transformed into a howling hurricane. His Alumacraft boat was being flung around like a toy boat in a typhoon, impossible to haul in.

Christian had grown up on this property. He had spent every childhood summer at his parents' cabin, had traversed the entire north shore of Gunflint Lake and paddled most of Gunflint's waters as well as the lakes and rivers surrounding the Gunflint Trail. He had seen plenty of bad weather, but nothing rivaled this storm's cyclonic fury. For the first time in his life, the weather made him fearful.

He turned back into the trees, knowing he needed to get to the safety of his cabin. Suddenly, behind him, there was a thunderous crack. Turning, he watched a huge spruce topple, its canopy shuddering the ground. Impossibly, the wind worsened.

Christian began to run.

The wind out of the west was a blitzkrieg. As he approached the cabin he swung around its right side, using its structure to blunt the storm's ferocity. He hurried to the back door. As he came around the corner, the forest to the west was filled with bending trunks, splintering canopies, and debris. The air was rife with pelting rain.

/ / /

Inside, Cindy and the kids had been listening to the weather unfold. The rain was coming down so heavily the cabin's windows were opaque, as though everyone inside peered from beneath a waterfall. The metal roof overhead was fastened directly to the rafters, and the absence of an intervening plywood sheath amplified the pounding rain, filling the cabin with a deafening clamor.

The kids were at a rear bedroom window, watching the raging weather sway the trees. For the moment, from inside the cabin, despite the rain noise that made it difficult to hear each other speak, they thought the July thunderstorm was bad, but not dangerous.

There was an old poplar to the side of the cabin's back door, its trunk at least 20 inches in diameter. As Christian finally reached and opened the door, the poplar's crown snapped off, its canopy slamming onto their cabin's roof.

After the huge poplar's topple and boom, Christian watched a second tree fall. Incredibly, the weather was gathering more strength.

As he stepped inside, Cindy turned and said, "I think we were just struck by lightning."

"That wasn't lightning. That was a tree, and they're falling all over. It's a hurricane out there!"

By this time Erika, the Preuses' eldest, had come out of the bedroom. The expression on her father's face shocked her. In her fifteen years, she had never seen him afraid.

Another explosive roof boom rattled the entire family like a face slap. In an instant Christian realized that if more trees fell, their roof might cave in. The storm was attacking from the west. The safest place would be on the furthest eastern side of their cabin.

"Everyone into our bedroom!"

They all bolted to the cabin's southeast side. The wind howled. They heard another tree snap and fall. The overhead metal boomed.

There was a closet in Cindy and Christian's bedroom. Christian knew that the closet was probably the most protected place on the main floor and structurally the strongest. He considered having the family cram into the tight space.

Another break and boom were followed by a crash and the unmistakable splintering of their cabin rafters. From inside the bedroom they could not see the ceiling breach, but they could feel the storm rush in.

The wind's howl made Christian wonder whether they were living through a tornado. If the entire roof caved or was blown away, they'd be exposed to the storm's ferocity. The fury was wailing out of the west. Several old-growth trees towered over the western side of their cabin. If the blow continued, it was only a matter of time before a behemoth toppled and crushed them.

For a moment Christian thought about pulling the mattress off the bed and having everyone scramble beneath it. But there was no way they could all fit, and a mattress would be mashed beneath the massive weight of a giant white pine.

Amid the chaos and terrifying tumult, Christian struggled to think of any crevice, nook, or cranny the six of them might squeeze into, something large enough and strong enough to offer respite from the storm. Having labored over every inch of their cabin, he knew the place by heart. He recalled the lay of the ground on which their cabin had been built, and the structure's solid floor beams anchored into concrete footings.

The crawlspace! It was like a hollowed-out cave, big enough to hold them all. The subfloor's plywood covering rested on expansive beams. The space beneath them was where the ground made a low impression. The subfloor was strong enough to support the cabin's walls, rooms, and roof. If anyplace was strong enough to withstand the felling of an old-growth pine, it was the careful latticework of rafters and boarding beneath them. And they could reach it in moments—out the front door, a straight shot across the deck, down the stairs, and then just steps around the foundation's corner. They would be exposed for three, maybe five seconds. The crawlspace was at least 4 feet high and protected by a makeshift door. In the manmade cave, Christian felt sure they could ride out an EF5 tornado.

"Under the cabin!"

He and Cindy grabbed the kids and dog and ran to the front door. They crossed the deck, leaped down the stairs, turned the corner, flung open the door, and scrambled into the crawlspace. Suddenly they were in a hollow, out of the wind.

They could still hear the fury blowing out of the west. Their door opened to the east. They watched the torrential rain and the wind tear through the trees, several of them bent over by the blow. They watched in awe as some of the trees snapped, falling away from them, while others toppled over, their root balls torn out of the waterlogged earth.

Christian hoped his instincts had been sound. All they could do now was wait and watch as one of the region's most cataclysmic storms continued to unfold, praying their sturdy cabin in the woods would hold.

14

TOUGH CHOICES

Lake Polly
South-Central Boundary Waters

The first thing Michelle noticed was a seizure. Lisa, clearly unconscious, was beginning to seize. Michelle estimated they were all by her side within thirty to forty seconds. With the storm still howling around them it was difficult to determine the exact length of Lisa's convulsions, but Michelle guessed she lay on the ground, trembling, for fifteen to twenty seconds.

"She was shaking, and we knew she'd hurt her head," Kristina recalled.

"It was very obvious that she was not well," Mark noted. "We were concerned she was going into shock."

"When we got to her you could tell her pupils were dilated," Ray remembered. "Her whole body was convulsing on the ground. I mean, it was significant, like getting hit with a baseball bat."

Ray rushed back to the top of the campsite, grabbed the flapping tarp, cut off all the strings that still held it, and pulled it back down to where Lisa lay on the ground, still being pummeled by the torrent.

"We started to cover her up," Mark said. "She was wearing a bikini top and shorts. And she was getting wet, and it was obvious she was cold. There was no consciousness at all."

"The side of her head was smashed," Ray added. "I don't think she could open that eye. Her whole face was terribly swollen. She looked terrible."

"Where she'd been struck," Michelle noted, "the side of her face was blue and purple."

The wind blew and the rain fell onto the hapless five. Lisa, prone and still, was being inundated. The temperature, which had been dreadfully hot a half hour earlier, was suddenly chill.

"We knew she wasn't safe where she was," Kristina said. But now the group had a dilemma. Everyone knew you never moved a person with a neck injury. The result could be something as catastrophic as permanent paralysis—paraplegia or quadriplegia. The thought was enough to sober anyone, though at this point the calamity that had just happened to their good friend focused everyone.

"We made a choice," Kristina said. "She couldn't stay where she was at. She was getting more wet and going into shock. So we had to choose between getting her warm and dry or not moving her because of neck injuries. We decided we'd do the best job we could, with everyone doing it all at once in a synchronized manner."

It had been only a few minutes since the tree had fallen onto Lisa, who still lay on the ground unconscious. Fortunately, the weather was beginning to abate.

"It wasn't coming down in the torrential line that it had been," remembered Mark. "But it was still raining."

"And at that point we weren't even paying attention to the rain," said Kristina. "It could have been coming off the trees. At that point we were very focused on her."

Miraculously, Lisa Naas began to awaken. "When I came to, I was on my back on the rocks," Lisa recalled. "Rain was pelting me in the face. And the four of them—Mark and Kristina and Ray and Michelle—were huddled. They were going through their plan of what they needed to do. And trying to decide that, yup, they were going to move Lisa. And they were just very . . . I can remember I was laying there and I'm thinking, 'They're very systematically going through what they need to do.'"

While Lisa recognized her friends, she was disoriented and coming in and out of consciousness. "At that time, really what was going on in my head is 'What the hell just happened?'" she recalled. "Because I didn't know, right? I had no idea. Pain was, you know—I was being pelted. I had pain. I knew something huge happened. I felt horribly nauseous and dizzy. I couldn't focus on anything. I was wearing glasses at the time, and those obviously came off somewhere. So I didn't have glasses either."

While Lisa tried to make sense of where she was and what had occurred, her four friends carefully, painstakingly, moved her onto the tarp. Trees and branches lay pell-mell across the site. Lisa's tent was thankfully unscathed, and the others decided it was the best place to get her dry and out of the elements. They carried her on the tarp from where she lay to where her yellow two-person nylon tent was pitched among the trees, climbing the escarpment and carefully picking their way through the debris. Fortunately, Lisa was small enough that Ray could grip one side of the tarp with both hands, while Kristina and Michelle lined up across from him, gripping the other side. "I remember I had the job of holding her head while we were carrying her up the hill toward her tent," Mark said. They all worried she had broken her neck.

Over the next several minutes they began to realize the severity of their situation. "It was crazy," Michelle remembered.

While they struggled to get her up the rock embankment and into her tent, Lisa still felt disoriented, continuing to come in and out of consciousness. Once in the tent, her disorientation turned into severe nausea. "I think at some point they had to stop because I was sick," she recalled. "I remember being on my hands and knees and I was vomiting."

After Lisa's sickness, Michelle and Kristina got her into dry clothes and then into her dry sleeping bag. They knew they needed to raise her body temperature.

Mark and Kristina remembered they had packed a first aid kit. Obviously, Lisa's condition was too extreme to be treated by the contents of a wilderness first aid kit, but it held an information pamphlet. While Michelle and Ray got into the tent with Lisa, trying to keep her conscious, talking to her, Mark and Kristina began poring over the pamphlet's contents. "We started to literally read through it for the first time," Mark said. "'Okay, what are we supposed to do in this case?'"

"It said if they have a blow to the head and they start vomiting you need to get them out," Ray recalled.

Reading through the booklet they quickly determined Lisa was in shock, severely compromised, and should not be moved again without help. And as they talked, they realized there was no way they could get her out of the wilderness in a canoe. Given her condition, it would likely kill her.

"As they were having that conversation," Lisa recalled, "I think one of the things I heard was 'Well, it's the Boundary Waters. Can we have them come in with a motorized vehicle, with a plane or whatever, to get her?' And I do remember laying there and thinking to myself, 'If I'm not taken out in a plane, I'm going out in a body bag.' I was very matter-of-factly thinking that. I knew it was serious. Whatever it was, I knew it was really serious."

She added, "The four of them were intense and in problem-solving mode. We were there having fun. So, if they're intense and they're in problem-solving mode, it's big. And I will tell you that there are not four other people that I would want there solving that problem for me at that time than those four."

At this point everyone recognized, given the terrain and portages and paddles they had taken to get here, the only way Lisa would get to safety and the care she needed was by plane.

"We had no idea what the options were," Kristina said. "But we knew we couldn't move her in her current state."

"That was the pivotal moment that we decided two of us needed to head back and call for help," Ray said.

"The four of us talked and decided that Ray and Michelle would stay with Lisa," Kristina added.

They knew Lisa's survival clock was ticking. They knew they needed to get to a phone and call for assistance as fast as humanly possible. Hurriedly, they tossed granola bars and water bottles into a day pack. They managed to retrieve some warm, dry clothes. Kristina and Mark found and pulled on their rain gear.

As they hustled through their preparations, they also took note of the condition of their campsite. "When it was all said and done, we stopped counting," Kristina said. "We stopped at about eighteen or twenty mature large trees that were down at our campsite."

"Where our tent was," Mark added, "one of the stakes was hanging in the air because the root ball had gone up with the tree that was right there.

And this was on the complete other end of the campsite [from where Lisa had pitched her tent]. The trees went down in a spray of angles."

Then Mark and Kristina rushed to their canoe, grabbed their paddles, and shoved off into the narrow cove. They dug in, pulling their Alumacraft toward their first portage, the air still soaked with rain.

15

IF I SCREAM

Alpine Lake, BWCAW

To Vicky Brockman, Sue Ann Martinson, and Jan Fiola, it seemed like a very, very long time before the rain, wind, lightning, and ear-piercing thunder began to subside. The storm still howled over and around them. The downpour continued pelting their flattened tent. But the atmosphere seemed less intense. The gasping rattle and the falling rain eased enough that the women could finally breathe.

Gradually, it diminished enough for Jan to try to work her way out from under the tree.

"Fortunately," recalled Sue Ann, "because Jan was on her stomach and not her back, the branches scratched her legs, but nothing else happened to her, and she was able to wiggle free."

The rain was still falling, and the wind remained intense. The jack pine had flattened them and their tent. The nylon was draped across the three of them like a wet sheet. After Jan crawled out from under the soaked tent she stood and considered the scene.

The world had changed. Downed trees and other forest damage lay on all sides of their camp, and across and around the lake. But Jan didn't spend time considering the extent of the damage. She looked at the tree that was pinning her friends to the ground and wondered whether she might be able to move it. Part of it was tangled and intertwined with another fallen tree. Jan was a strong woman, but as she gripped the tree and tried to shift it off her friends, she quickly realized it was too much weight and too enmeshed for her to manage alone. She felt frustrated, powerless, and alarmed.

The storm continued to slacken. Vicky remembered that Jan packed for their wilderness trips with an eye toward preparing for anything that might befall them. Now she yelled to her friend, "Do you have a saw? We've got to get this tree off us."

Of course, Jan had packed a camp saw. She searched through their scattered supplies and found the small plastic handle with a short, serrated blade. While it wasn't designed to cut through a 12-inch-diameter tree, she figured with patience and brow sweat she might be able to free her friends.

"I remember the saw was just large enough to be able to cut through that trunk," Vicky said. "So, Jan started sawing through the tree."

While Jan labored, the storm continued to ease. Sue Ann also continued to try to free herself.

"I struggled and struggled and I could not get out from under that tree," she said. "It was so frustrating, and Jan was doing her best. But it was a small saw."

Every time Vicky moved, she felt pain—any effort to fight against the tree trunk only increased her discomfort. Finally, she willed herself to grow as calm as possible in conditions more conducive to panic and fear. She was able to lift her head enough to consider their predicament. Glancing down the length of the jack pine trunk, she noticed something about the tree and its weight. Given the place where Jan was sawing, when the trunk was finally severed, the bulk of the remaining section would drop on her, increasing the weight now resting on her hip.

Vicky quickly shared her observation with her companions, and when they all saw the veracity of her perspective, they realized the only way they could get out from under the tree was to lift it. Jan had already tried mightily to move it, but it was too heavy and cumbersome for her to manage alone.

At that point, Sue Ann suggested they yell for help. "Because across the lake we had heard voices over there the night before. Sound carries over the water. I thought, 'Well, if I scream, I'll get somebody.'"

They all began yelling and screaming. The racket was eventually enough to get their neighbors' attention, and they were relieved to see two men start out in their canoe, paddling across the water toward them.

By now Jan had also located her first aid kit and managed to dig out some aspirin, trying to assuage their aches and pains. Especially Vicky, who was, like Sue Ann, still pinned under the tree and was suffering from a much more serious injury than either of her companions.

The men beached their canoe and began to survey the damage. By all accounts the storm in this vicinity had been devastating. The men had been across the water, camping with two women. Like the rest of the area, their camp had been demolished by fallen trees and branches. In fact, one of the women had been struck by a falling branch, and they thought she might have a slight concussion. But she was at least conscious and, for the moment, doing well enough that when Vicky, Jan, and Sue Ann began screaming, the men were able to come over and help.

"They were fit, young guys," Sue Ann recalled. "Probably in their late twenties or early thirties. And they were strong."

They immediately turned their attention toward the tree pinning Vicky and Sue Ann to the ground. The three of them together were finally able to lift and move the tree off to the side, freeing the two women.

"Some of Sue Ann's ribs were bruised and battered," Vicky said. "And she had some back pain, but she was still able to get up and walk around. I wasn't able to move."

The ground was soaked, and so was Vicky. There was general recognition that they needed to at least move her to try to get her as dry as possible, and comfortable. The two men were certainly strong enough to move her. But given her pain and injury, it had to be done carefully.

The uber-prepared Jan remembered she had packed a Mylar blanket, which could be folded to the size of a large wallet. While Mylar is thin and shiny, like aluminum foil, it is tough, designed to be weatherproof and waterproof and to retain and reflect body heat.

As delicately as they could, Jan and the two young men managed to lift Vicky enough that Sue Ann could place the blanket over the wet ground beneath her and wrap the rest of it on top of her. Vicky gritted her teeth and endured the pain.

Clearly, given the agony of being moved, Vicky would try to remain still and on the ground until a more refined method of transport, like a gurney, became available.

Jan and Sue Ann thanked the men, who needed to get back to their own wounded. Then they did whatever else they could to make Vicky comfortable.

Before leaving on their trip, Jan had reminded both her companions they should line their clothes bags with large garbage bags or something similar to ensure they remained dry in case of rain, never imagining the intensity of the storm they had just experienced. Fortunately, they'd heeded her advice. Now Jan and Sue Ann reached into their sealed bags and found dry clothes to change into.

In the aftermath of the storm, the day had cooled. What caught Jan's attention in her bag was a pair of bright red sweatpants with a matching red jacket, red as a stop sign. She knew, given their predicament, they were the right color to wear. She pulled on the sweatpants and a long-sleeved button shirt, then pulled on the red jacket over it.

As much as Jan and Sue Ann could, they helped Vicky into warm, dry clothes, or at least tried to make her as dry and comfortable as possible. Then they covered her with a blanket and a tarp.

When Vicky had packed for her trip, she had remembered how her head could get cold on some Boundary Waters nights, sleeping on the ground in a tent. As a precaution she'd brought along a purple stocking cap. Now her friends made sure her head was covered and elevated.

Obviously, Vicky could not be moved without significant help. The most popular portage from Alpine Lake into Seagull was almost six football fields, open and wide. Given the destruction around their campsite, they guessed that main portage might now be impassable, and the river channel Jan had earlier considered as a different way to portage into Seagull Lake was now probably the best way to exit Alpine. But Jan knew Vicky's condition precluded her from paddling and portaging around a swollen Alpine River.

"Get a plane," Vicky said, as she continued to consider her condition. It was a mantra she would repeat more than a few times.

The best solution, they all knew, was obviously to be medevacked out by seaplane. But they had no idea how bad the storm had been, and whether any planes were flying. It was, after all, July 4. The only logical next step was to stop whoever they saw heading into Seagull and ask them to send help.

While they waited, Sue Ann and Jan helped Vicky take more aspirin. Then they examined the destruction in their camp.

In every direction, trees lay flattened, most of them snapped at the bottom of their trunks. Those that were still standing looked haggard from the blow, their deciduous leaves or pine needles frazzled and mostly stripped. The trees had fallen from west to east. There were several still precariously aloft, their topmost branches hanging on a stronger or more fortunate neighbor or on a tree that had fallen before it.

Down on the shore, where they had stowed their canoe between two boulders, the mature jack pines on either side had fallen across the canoe and each other. Fortunately, the boulders were large enough to have caught the trees' fall. Now the mature jack pines hung over their canoe like two toppled wooden pillars. The boulders and the fallen trees had kept their canoe from being damaged or crushed.

Looking farther around, they could see the destruction all around them. The forest had been hit hard. Across the lake the shoreline looked as though it had been put through a buzz saw. Many of the trees were down, and those still standing were partially denuded.

Everyone encamped on Alpine Lake had suffered through the intense blowdown. Most were now understandably anxious to exit the shattered forest and return to civilization—that is, providing they still had functional canoes.

Within an hour of the storm the first canoeists paddled by, searching for the 105-rod portage in the hopes it might still be open. When they came near enough, Jan and Sue Ann called out to them, explaining their predicament.

"Please send help," they said. "We need a plane."

The canoeists assured them they would.

Jan and Sue Ann watched them search for and finally find the start of the main portage out of Alpine. The area was so damaged it was difficult to locate. Once the canoeists paddled near enough to see the extent of the damage, they determined it would be impossible to carry a canoe over the 10-foot-high latticework of fallen trees and branches.

Jan yelled across the water, telling them about the Alpine River crossing, just a short paddle north. It was advice she would continue giving paddlers throughout the afternoon. The canoeists took her advice and turned north, continuing up the shoreline, deciding to try their luck on the river.

Jan and Sue Ann watched each canoe disappear around a distant point, hoping the paddlers would be able to navigate the river, and that they would remember to send help.

Sue Ann wore a wristwatch, but she had been too busy to even think about checking the time. While she milled around their camp, occasionally checking on Vicky, picking up debris, and sorting through their scattered equipment, she finally glanced at it. Its crystal was scratched and broken. Its hands had stopped at exactly 12:30.

16

UP THE GUNFLINT TRAIL

The Gunflint Trail

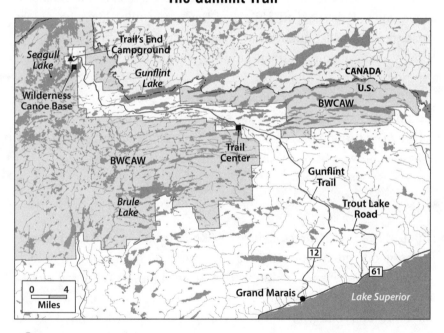

After the midmorning chapel service, Wilderness Canoe Base director Jim Wiinanen and his wife, Rebecca, decided it was time to hunt for some new blueberry patches, preferably nearer to their Grand Marais home than the base at the end of the Gunflint Trail. The morning at the camp on Seagull Lake had dawned hot, still, and sultry. It was uncharacteristic weather this far north. Jim had heard something about strong winds out west, in North Dakota, but the camp was nearly 300 miles from the border. Here, the day was preternaturally muggy and calm, at least for now.

The Gunflint Trail is a two-lane blacktop road that reaches 57 miles north-northwest out of Grand Marais into the heart of the Boundary Waters. Jim and Rebecca, who was the Cook County Soil and Water Conservation District manager, had lived and worked in the region most of their adult lives, so they knew the deepest lake in the world had a moderating effect on the weather. The temperatures in Grand Marais were often markedly different from the temperatures elsewhere, especially farther inland.

They had decided to drive nearly 50 miles down the Gunflint Trail to the Trout Lake Road turnoff. There they hoped to encounter the lake effect and possibly cool off while they drove a few miles down the remote road to an area that might contain a productive blueberry patch. Given the wet summer and optimal growing season, they were planning on picking some fresh, plump berries.

Trout Lake Road runs for approximately 15 miles before the T intersection at Cook County Road 14. At that intersection Jim and Rebecca planned on turning toward the Lake Superior shoreline and taking Highway 61 southwest into town and their home.

/ / /

Jim had been WCB director since 1992, but he had worked for the organization off and on since 1965, the summer after his junior year in high school, when he was hired to work as a swamper. In WCB parlance, a swamper is someone who helps out in a variety of ways and does a little bit of everything. But an early change in personnel resulted in Jim becoming an assistant quartermaster, working in the Trail Shack, the center responsible for outfitting campers heading into the wilderness.

After two summers working at the WCB, Jim attended college at the University of Minnesota Duluth. During his college years and after graduating, he worked a number of jobs, some of which involved wilderness, until November 1975, when he finally returned to the camp as assistant director. Over the next seventeen years he would be assistant director under three different directors before finally being appointed director himself in 1992.

The WCB is literally on the edge of the BWCAW. In fact, most of Seagull Lake is in the Boundary Waters. The south half of Fishhook Island, on which the main WCB buildings reside, is technically BWCAW. If you paddled south-southeast down the shoreline of Fishhook Island or circled around to visit the barb end of the hook that gave it its name, you would be in the designated wilderness. Over his more than three decades in and around the woods, Jim had traveled all the main routes in the million-acre wilderness and in Canada's Quetico Provincial Park, just across the border, as well as many other explorations off the beaten paths.

Having spent so many Independence Day holidays at the WCB, Jim knew it was the midpoint of their busy season. "Saturday, we had welcomed fourteen canoe trip groups coming out of the woods," he recalled. "They had a noon meal with us and then we sent them home Saturday afternoon. We had one group left in the woods down somewhere around Little Sag and Tuscarora. But they were expected to exit the woods that Sunday." Otherwise, July 4 marked a lull in the WCB's hectic summer. Jim knew it was a good time for him and Rebecca to drive closer to home, search for blueberry patches, and spend some time in Grand Marais.

They left the WCB before noon and began their drive down the trail. Covering the distance to the Trout Lake Road turnoff takes a little more than an hour. During that time, they did not notice the skies in their rearview mirrors beginning to change. "By the time we turned, that's when it started getting windy," Jim recalled. "I remember the clouds were kind of greenish. That would have been west of us, so the storm back at camp could have very well been active at that point."

Over the years they had experienced plenty of storms in the area. For now, he and Rebecca figured this one, like the others, would be a passing squall.

They made the turn and kept driving.

"We had driven just 3 miles or so, and the wind was blowing hard. The trees were really swaying." They came upon two trees that had blown down over the road. But they were small enough to be easily removed. "We felt we could continue down to Highway 61. But then we came upon a downed tree that was too big for us to move."

They were forced to turn around and try to make their way back to the Gunflint Trail. "We met some friends of ours that weren't far behind us,"

Jim recalled. "They turned around, too. And then there were more trees down. But we were able to move them enough to get our cars around the downfall and back to the trail. At that point, we still thought we just had a windstorm. I didn't think anything of it. Rebecca and I continued toward town and got to our house, and that's when things started to happen."

/ / /

Back at the WCB, the derecho had blown through, leaving a felled forest and the base and its employees in turmoil. After the wind and rain subsided enough for Jen Nagel and her colleagues to take stock of their situation, they wanted to make sure no one was missing or in need of medical attention. Or worse.

"We had this food board that we used to track everyone who was supposed to be showing up for meals," Jen said. "At the canoe base, people are going in and out constantly, so your numbers are fluctuating by meal." Fortunately, when they compared their food board list with everyone present in Pinecliff—the kitchen, dining hall, and main lodge—the numbers matched up. That's when they decided to use the same list to get organized, sending out search-and-rescue parties and others to perform various tasks.

By the time Jen and her colleagues finally ventured out of Pinecliff, what they encountered was startling. "Everything felt alien, otherworldly," Jen said. "As we went out of Pinecliff the trees were stacked far higher than us."

The first thing they tried to do was assess the damage. But the trails that crisscrossed Fishhook Island—down to the nearby dock, the canoe beach, and the other numerous cabins and outbuildings—were choked with fallen trees. Moving around involved climbing over the debris left by the storm, much of which was the remnants of the large trees that once towered over Fishhook. Fortunately, from what they could determine from their initial, partial foray into the devastation, "Most of the buildings were intact," Jen remembered. Some trees had fallen on buildings and caved in roofs, but it wasn't nearly as bad as it could have been. And no one was hurt.

"Obviously, our power and phones were out," Jen said. "I had one of our base radios." But the base radios were only good for communications with other nearby base employees. Jen decided her first task was to get to the mainland and get word down to Grand Marais about what they had just endured, and that miraculously, everyone at camp was okay and accounted for.

After making her way to the dock, Jen managed to find one of the base's boats and use it to get to the Cove, the mainland part of the WCB. When she got there, she encountered a ½-mile drive with fallen trees stacked as high as they'd been on Pinecliff. Eventually, she managed to pick her way out to the nearby Gunflint Trail Volunteer Fire Department station, where she was able to use the emergency radio to get word to Cook County dispatch in Grand Marais. She tried to put into words the extent of the devastation. She also conveyed the more important messages that everyone was okay and that the power and phones were out.

Once she got this basic information out, she headed back to help with the cleanup.

/ / /

Farther up the Gunflint Trail, at nearby Voyageur Canoe Outfitters, owners Mike and Sue Prom were having a staff meeting when the storm struck. Voyageur was located near the terminus of the 57-mile Gunflint Trail. After a quick turn up Sag Lake Trail, visitors followed the Voyageur signs and were soon in the outfitter's parking lot. Mike and Sue had started the business out of college and grown it into one of the larger canoe outfitters in the area. In fact, for the July 4 holiday they had outfitted several trips into the Boundary Waters, and farther north into Southern Ontario's Quetico. Unfortunately, as Voyageur's employees were equipping people for their wilderness trips, Mike had noticed a lull in their usual high level of customer service.

"Typically, we have an end-of-July or first-of-August all-hands staff meeting," Mike said. "By that time everyone's a little tired of the season, and so we remind them they need to provide the same levels of customer service that we began with when the season first opened."

While Mike was familiar with this kind of meeting, he was disappointed they needed to have it at the midpoint of the season rather than later in the summer.

Voyageur sits on the banks of the Seagull River. The docks, boats, canoes, and boathouse and a handful of cabins are nestled along the river's banks. A main building sits back from the water and houses the Prom family living quarters, the store, and a main lodge where visitors can enjoy a meal or two before or after their wilderness trip. For this Fourth of July staff meeting, they were gathered in the main building's second-story lodge.

Among his many other duties, Mike Prom had recently joined the Gunflint Trail Volunteer Fire Department. As part of his volunteer firefighting duties, he was issued a pager. Normally, catastrophic events like a forest fire or a major, destructive storm would result in some kind of notification going out on the department pagers. "But I don't remember anything coming out saying that this storm was coming," Mike recalled. "We were pretty surprised by it."

When the skies darkened and the wind came up, everyone sensed the onset of bad weather. Since Voyageur sits on the narrow river and is surrounded by mature trees, they didn't have a clear view of the skies to the west. Also, they didn't yet know it, but they were on the northern edge of the storm. Voyageur is approximately 1 mile almost due north of the WCB and a half mile north of the terminus of the Gunflint Trail. The derecho's primary wind front was, at times, approximately 12 miles wide, moving in an east-northeast direction and flattening everything in front of it. Voyageur was on the northern edge of the swath. Still, there was clearly enough wind and rain to wreak havoc where they were. Once the skies grew particularly menacing, Mike paused their meeting.

Down near the banks of the Seagull River stood a pyramid of Kevlar canoes. As they felt the storm come on, some of the staff members went down to secure the canoes.

Bonnie Schudy was working in the lower level of the lodge at the time the storm began to come on. "I remember looking out the office window and seeing this really dark green sky coming our direction," she recalled. Unlike the second story of the lodge, whose windows all faced north, the office provided a western view of the oncoming sky. "The next moment,"

Bonnie continued, "the wind and rain started coming down. A few of us went outside to try and tie the canoes down because they were getting blown all around."

"They were going down to throw a rope over the canoes when the full force of the storm hit," Mike recalled. "I remember looking out the window. We don't think about tornadoes up here. But the canoes started rifling off the pyramid like they were being blown by a tornado."

Mike yelled to his staff members to get inside.

"The wind was so strong we decided to get back in the lodge," Bonnie said. "I remember pushing on the lodge doors to get them to close tight because the rain was coming through the door cracks. We just sat inside the lodge building looking out the windows and watching the trees bend—boats, canoes, and equipment getting blown all around."

From the safety of the lodge, everyone at Voyageur watched the catastrophic weather pass in front of them.

"I remember looking out the window and seeing canoes rolling around the yard," Mike recalled. There was nothing to do except wait for the severe weather to blow itself out." Because they were on the northern edge of the derecho, they didn't yet have a full sense of the tempest's destruction. "We had a few trees down in the driveway. We had some trees fall on a van, and some of our aluminum canoes."

After the skies finally calmed enough to venture out, Mike and his staff began clearing fallen debris. While Mike supervised the cleanup at Voyageur, he sent a couple staff members down the Sag Lake Trail to make an accounting of any damage south of them, and to clear whatever debris needed clearing. When they returned, they told him the destruction farther south was much more extensive than at Voyageur, and that the Gunflint Trail was impassable.

"Our power and phones were out," Mike said. "So we didn't have any sense of who had been hit or how hard." And nor could they tell anyone how hard they had been hit, or how bad it was farther south.

All they could do now was feel fortunate no one had been injured and continue cleaning up and digging out.

/ / /

Twelve miles from Voyageur, down the Gunflint Trail toward Grand Marais, is the iconic Gunflint Lodge and Outfitters on Gunflint Lake. Because of the way the Gunflint Trail cuts into the heart of the BWCAW, the last 7 or 8 miles of the trail travels almost due north–south. If Voyageur sat on the northern edge of the 12-mile swath of the worst blowdown cutting through the area, Gunflint Lodge and Gunflint Lake sat in the middle of it.

The lodge was established in 1925, and not long thereafter, in 1934, it was taken over and managed by recently married couple Bill and Justine Kerfoot. Justine's family, the Spunners, had owned the lodge for a few years before Justine met and married Bill. Eventually they became Gunflint's sole proprietors. The Kerfoots had three children, one of whom, Bruce, ultimately took over running, managing, and eventually owning the lodge with his wife, Sue.

Gunflint Lodge is positioned on the far southeastern shoreline of Gunflint Lake. While the lake is surrounded by some of the most beautiful cliffs and rugged shoreline in the north country, the lodge has beautiful sand beaches. The view from the patio looking due north across the lake is spectacular. And at least on the start of July 4, the country around the lodge and the lake boasted a mature forest of aspen, cedar, white and red pines, and more—some of the trees more than two hundred years old.

Bruce Kerfoot doesn't recall the approach of ominous clouds building in the west. He remembered it was hot, muggy, and sunny. Until it wasn't. "We were just going along, and then all of a sudden the wind started to come up," Bruce said. "And then the clouds came on."

A 100-foot floating dock extended into the lake in front of the lodge. Since Gunflint Lake is on the edge of the BWCAW, the lodge had both canoes and approximately twenty-five aluminum fishing boats and motors as well as a pontoon boat. A boathouse stood to one side, with watercraft resting along the shoreline.

Gunflint Lodge and Outfitters is one of the largest resorts in the area. Like Voyageur, it outfits wilderness trips into and around the BWCAW and the Quetico. Its staff can send out parties on solo expeditions or supply a wilderness guide to lead the group. They also keep a stable of horses for horseback riding and maintain nearly 50 miles of wilderness trails. The trails are used for cross-country skiing in winter and horseback riding in the summer.

With the onset of clouds, the wind increased. "Then," Bruce recalled, "holy smokes—the wind kept coming up. At that point we didn't realize the severity of the storm. Our first concern was the safety of the boats tied up to our dock." The winds came up strong enough to begin blowing the boats back and forth. Some of them began to break loose. Others began to take on water. Some capsized.

When the skies opened up and sheets of rain began falling, Bruce and his lead wilderness guide, Kevin Walsh, ran down to the dock and began tending to several of the boats in trouble. "We were bailing like hell and losing ground quickly as boats started to sink and motors went under," Bruce said. Somehow, the 100-foot floating dock kept its mooring. But their pontoon boat broke loose and in the intense wind started blowing down the lake.

"I thought, 'Well, hell, we'll just run down the shore and wade out and get the pontoon boat before it smashes up too bad,'" Bruce recalled. "We started down along the path by the cabins toward the boat, and all of a sudden the wind notched up a little more and I looked up and . . . we had a lot of mature aspen trees on our property . . . and all of a sudden I looked up and they were breaking off halfway up and the tops were just flying, you know, in among the buildings and dropping to the ground. I looked at Kevin, and I said, 'Turn around. Let's get the hell out of here.'"

At that point Bruce Kerfoot no longer cared about his pontoon boat. Or rather, he cared about his boat, but not enough to risk his life or that of his guide to try to retrieve it. "Now we were worried about our safety," Bruce said. "I've never seen multiple trees just breaking off 10 and 20 feet up and the tops just going all over the place."

After they returned to the safety of the lodge with the rest of Gunflint's employees, everyone waited and watched as the cyclonic fury of the storm blew past and through them. What they could see of Gunflint Lake's waters roiled with massive waves and whitecaps. Trees continued to fall. Branches and other debris flew across the near shoreline, dock, and boiling waters.

"I don't even know how long it lasted," Bruce said. Eventually, of course, the winds began to subside and the rain settled down. "At that point, we looked at each other and thought, 'Oh my god.' Because you start to look around."

Above the lodge stood Justine Kerfoot's cabin and Bruce Kerfoot's boyhood home, a log cabin that had been built in the 1930s. "She had so many big poplars on her cabin that we couldn't even get into the building. They were just jackstraws of poplar trees all over the place," Bruce said. "When we started to get our marbles organized, we decided to do a safety check."

Gunflint Lodge is a large operation with many cabins, employee quarters, and more. After checking to ensure everyone was okay—there were, amazingly, no injuries—Bruce Kerfoot and Kevin Walsh decided to each take a motorboat and head out on the lake. Bruce knew in the middle of the day, particularly one that had dawned as hot, still, sunny, and muggy as this one, there would have been people recreating on and around the lake. Canoeists could have been exploring the nearby Granite River or could have boated across the lake to the forested Canadian shore of Gunflint, searching for blueberries or places to hike. Before the storm the opposite shore had been forested by beautiful stands of old-growth forest. After the storm it looked as though someone had taken a wrecking ball to the trees. A wrecking ball that swung west to east.

"We wanted to get out there and see if there were any people stranded or really desperate," Bruce recalled.

His personal motorboat was tethered near the end of his 100-foot floating dock, in 8 feet of water. His lead guide went for one boat, and Bruce walked down to his boat at the end. It had weathered the storm well but needed to be bailed and set aright. While getting the boat shipshape, Bruce felt something out of place. But it wasn't until he finally started his motor that he realized he was only in 4 feet of water.

Gunflint Lake is more or less a 7-mile rectangle stretching almost due east–west. At 1 mile across, it holds a lot of water. The winds that came out of the west, blowing almost due east, blew long enough and hard enough to move the millions of gallons of water from the west side of Gunflint Lake toward its east side, an unbelievable phenomenon.

"The storm lowered our end of the lake by 4 feet," exclaimed Bruce. "It reversed the rapids, and our waters began flowing in the opposite direction. We had never imagined there could be that kind of force that could move that many millions of gallons of lake water and create an 8-foot differential between our end of the lake and the other."

Eventually Bruce and Kevin were able to get their boats onto the water and motor out in opposite directions, hoping they would find cabin owners and vacationers safe and alive. If so, Bruce thought, it would be a miracle.

/ / /

When Jim and Rebecca Wiinanen finally made it to their Grand Marais home, there was a message on their answering machine from the Cook County Sheriff's Office dispatch. "It was sort of cryptic," Jim recalled. "It said everyone's okay, but the power and the phones were out up at camp." Not only was the message cryptic, but Jim was perplexed by the call. Power outages at the WCB were familiar events. Why, and how, would Cook County dispatch have any reason to know the power was out at camp, or to be concerned enough to report it?

"So, I called them, and they said the staff had used the public safety radio in the fire truck." Jen Nagel, one of Jim's lead staffers who had been left in charge, had used the radio to call down and convey what had happened. Cook County told Jim that it was quite a storm and that the Gunflint Trail was blocked, but the county highway department was going up with a grader, clearing fallen trees off the road. "The Forest Service was working their way down from the upper end of the trail, cutting away trees. They also said an ambulance was caught in that traffic, trying to make it down."

At that point, Jim and Rebecca recognized they needed to return to camp.

Jim's years of going back and forth along the entire length of the Gunflint Trail had left him with an intimate knowledge of the road and the woods through which it traveled. The road was the main artery, accessing the heart of the BWCAW, and the only road they could take to get back to the canoe base. But it was two-lane blacktop, much of it with narrow shoulders and heavy forest that grew nearly to the blacktop's edge. If the trail was blocked and graders were trying to move trees, Jim knew it might be difficult returning to the base.

"I was trying to figure out how to be useful. I thought maybe if I had a chainsaw, that would be a ticket to getting up in front and helping," he said. But Jim's chainsaw was back at the WCB, so he called a friend and borrowed his. "I said, 'We'll probably not have to use it, but I'd like to have it along.'" (In the days to come, when chainsaw use was ubiquitous and constant, he would recall the comment with a wry smile.)

The first 30 miles of the Gunflint Trail travels west-northwest away from Grand Marais. At that point visitors are approximately halfway up the trail, which is also the location of the store/restaurant on Poplar Lake called Trail Center. Because the path of the main derecho had passed several miles north, encompassing the last 30 miles of the Gunflint Trail, Jim and Rebecca made it all the way to Trail Center before encountering a roadblock. They fell in behind a line of twenty to thirty cars.

"I could see a Cook County deputy's squad car up ahead, parked in the Trail Center parking lot, and thought I should check it out," Jim recalled. He approached the deputy, who had been forced to close the road and wouldn't let anyone through until a grader up ahead finished its work.

"I chatted with the deputy," Jim said. "Understandably, he was occupied with radio traffic to and from dispatch and trying to answer questions from the folks backed up in the line." When Jim told the deputy he had a chainsaw and could assist, the deputy let him and Rebecca through.

"We pulled out and around all these other cars and finally got up the road about 4 miles to where the grader was pushing trees and debris out of the way at the Laurentian Divide overlook. There's a little turnoff there. We could also see, just up ahead, the Forest Service truck lights flashing, coming from the opposite direction."

It was afternoon, and there was still a lot of road to cover to get to the canoe base. "At that point we were aware it was only going to be a one-way road. The Forest Service staff let the downbound traffic with the ambulance come through first. There were probably twenty-five to thirty-five cars of people just wanting to get out of there. As soon as they passed, we started up with all the other traffic from Trail Center."

What Jim and Rebecca saw, weaving through the one-lane road, driving slowly up the Trail, was "jaw-dropping. It was a holy cow moment, there were so many trees down."

17

IN THE WAKE OF STORM

Mudro and Fourtown Lakes and up the Moose Chain, BWCAW

There are no rain gauges in the wilderness. Forest Service ranger Nicole Selmer guessed that over the first ten minutes of the storm more than 4 inches of rain fell. Despite being far enough north that they dodged the storm's full intensity, it was torrential. "In retrospect," Nicole opined, "if we had been in the center of that storm, there's no doubt in my mind we wouldn't have survived. There was no place to go. If the trees had all come down similar to what they had done elsewhere, we couldn't have gone anywhere."

Once the rain and wind abated, Nicole and the volunteers who had hunkered down with her were able to get back onto the portage and reconnect with the rest of their crew. There were many downed trees. As they hiked the trail, Nicole counted at least twenty before realizing they were far too numerous to get an accurate count. Most were small and easily navigated. And unlike farther south, much of the forest was still standing. But walking along the portage, Nicole remembered, "was like walking through a streambed." So much rain had fallen so quickly they waded through the portage as though walking in the center of a creek.

Thankfully, they found the rest of their group safe and their canoes intact.

"At that point, we turned on our radios and began hearing all the calls from the other wilderness rangers in the field. And that's when we realized how bad it had been south of us."

She learned fellow ranger Pete Weckman had been caught in the storm on Moose Lake, approximately 10 miles east-southeast of her location. Moose Lake and the surrounding area had been in the direct path of the storm.

"I remember hearing Pete Weckman call in," Nicole said. "Pete was asking for someone to bring a chainsaw. 'Because I can't leave here. I'm stuck. Someone needs to come and cut me out.' We were hearing a lot of stories like Pete's."

While Nicole's boss, Nancy Pius, headed back toward Mudro Lake, Nicole's crew headed back into Fourtown to check on their campsite as well as the campers on that lake. Nancy, on her way back to Ely, would check on the lone Mudro campsite.

Most of the travelers who had portaged that morning into Fourtown were just getting to their campsites when the storm hit, so they hadn't unpacked. Fortunately, no one needed assistance.

The team's home base on Fourtown had been hit hard: drenched in the downpour, tents uprooted, their sleeping bags soaked. Because their tents were all the same make and model, they managed to salvage enough intact tent poles to reestablish some cover for the night.

"And we just settled in," Nicole said. "We were all going to be fine. A little wet, since our sleeping bags were soaked. But we were just basically living off the high and the adrenaline of that crazy storm. And then listening with fascination to our handheld radios. It was like listening to an audiobook. All the reports and the Beaver planes taking off and landing. It was one of those weird things. We were all totally fine. We had food. We had shelter. We were just a little bit wet and listening to how bad it was in other places."

/ / /

Pete Weckman and fellow Forest Service employee Duane Whalen spent at least a half hour considering their predicament. The Moose Lake Forest Service dock parking lot was open, but everything around them— trees, telephone poles and lines, branches, and more—lay scattered across the ground. They were trapped, unable to get out to Moose Lake

Road and return to Ely. And they had to mind the live wires sparking over the rain-soaked ground.

After Pete used his truck radio to contact dispatch, explaining what had happened and requesting help getting the road cleared, both he and Duane knew it would be some time before they could expect assistance. They also had no idea how Moose Lake Road or, beyond it, Fernberg Road and the city of Ely, had been affected. Those areas might have also been impacted, and if so, it would be a long while before they could return home.

Fortunately, Pete had parked his boat in the boat lift, raised it, and chained it to the lift, so it had come through the storm largely unscathed. They would need to spend some time bailing water, but once it was bailed, it would be fully operational. They also figured, with so many trees down, they might eventually have need for an axe and a crosscut saw. Pete retrieved both from the Forest Service boathouse and stowed them in the boat.

After touring the dock, prepping his boat, and getting it back into the water, Pete made another call to dispatch. "I still have a watercraft available," he told his colleagues. "I know there's potential damage up the Moose chain—Moose, Newfound, Sucker, and potentially all of Basswood Lake." Pete also mentioned Prairie Portage. "If that's completely blown over, people aren't going to get out of the lake." And there were cabins across the bay on Moose. They were only accessible by boat, and Pete and Duane could see, looking across the southern stretch of Moose Lake, that the forest around those cabins had been severely damaged.

Pete let dispatch know he and Duane were heading back out onto the lake, and then north up the chain, to help anyone needing assistance.

"At this point," Pete said, "we were getting back in the boat to start our search and rescue."

As they headed out onto Moose Lake, the first thing they noticed was the water. "It was like an ocean," Pete recalled. Moose is a narrow lake, so the wind doesn't usually have an opportunity to build across the water and create large waves or whitecaps. When waves happen, they have shallow troughs and narrow bands. "But these were like huge surfing waves," Pete said. It was as though the weather had been so intense it affected the entire lake system.

As they pushed out into the bay, tree limbs and floating debris were cresting with the waves. "I can't see certain things," Pete told Duane. "You've got to be my point man and keep an eye out from the bow."

Duane moved into position and scanned the lake's surface as the boat made headway across the water. While the winds had largely abated, a light rain continued to fall.

First, Pete boated to the handful of cabins on the other side of the lake. Because there were no roads to those cabins, Pete knew they'd be the last visited by county law enforcement. As they grew close, they saw several cabins with trees toppled onto their roofs. "When we approached, someone would come down to their dock," Pete said. "I hollered at them: 'Everybody all right?' And when they gave me the thumbs-up and said they were fine, we went down to the next cabin." Fortunately, there were no injuries.

They continued working their way up Moose Lake. The weather continued to moderate, though the lake still surged with huge ocean-like rollers. While the water would have been too rough for canoes, Pete's boat was large enough to navigate it. But progress was slow.

Halfway up Moose Lake there was a bay on the northwest shore that marked the start of a 175-rod portage into Wind Lake. From Wind Lake, Pete knew, you could portage into Basswood Lake.

When Pete and Duane boated across the bay, they saw a 14-foot boat at the start of the portage. Two fishermen stood nearby, puzzling over a medium-sized black spruce that had fallen across the boat's bow. When they saw Pete and Duane, they waved them over.

As Pete and Duane approached, they looked down and saw the portage choked with trees. For Pete, who was the wilderness ranger for this area, it was an "oh my god" moment. "This is bad," he thought. "There could be people in there portaging and no one even knows they're there. There could be day fishermen on Wind Lake and now they're stuck." He also worried that the portage from Wind Lake into Basswood might be compromised as well, causing possible harm to anyone who might have been portaging during the storm, or trapping those who might have been on Basswood when the storm came up.

There was nothing to do now but search for survivors and help those who needed it.

Pete and Duane manned the crosscut saw and cut the tree off the fishermen's boat. While they worked, the fishermen told them about the intensity of the storm and the way the forest had fallen down around them. They had managed to escape the fallen trees, but like excited players in the aftermath of a big game, they wanted to share the drama of their experience.

Pete, gregarious and normally willing to share stories of his own, commiserated with the two fishermen. "But I knew I couldn't spend too much time chewing the fat with people, because I had a long day ahead of me." Once the fishermen's boat was freed, they could motor back to their Moose Lake resort.

Pete and Duane continued working their way up the lake, keeping their eyes open for anyone else in need of assistance. In moments, they were abreast of the island where Pete had sent the paddlers earlier in the day, when the storm was nearly upon them. The canoeists had thought they'd be able to make the distant public landing, but he told them it would be safer to take cover on the island. The island had been covered with a beautiful stand of seventy-year-old Norway pines. Now those pines were almost completely horizontal, several having fallen on the paddlers' overturned canoes.

Pete and Duane stopped to assist. One of the canoeists had some puncture wounds from fallen branches, which Pete doctored with his first aid kit. Taking stock of the group, he could tell they were frightened. "They were so scared," Pete recalled. "They had never seen anything like it. They were just happy we were there."

Pete and Duane helped them cut the trees and branches off their canoes, which were dented, but still serviceable. They had lost one of their canoes but could see it had blown across the lake in the storm and was now resting against the distant shore.

"You feel comfortable paddling over there and getting your other canoe?" Pete said. So far, he and Duane had only traversed the southwest half of Moose Lake. They had a lot more territory to cover if they were going to reach the border. And given the damage, they had no idea what they might encounter.

The paddlers assured them they were fine to retrieve their other canoe, so Pete and Duane shoved off and continued boating up the lake.

They managed to make it to the zigzag narrows separating Moose Lake from Newfound Lake. "All of a sudden I caught myself," Pete recalled. "There was just something." He had worked this area of the Boundary Waters for approximately two decades, and during that time he'd grown intimately familiar with Moose, Newfound, and the other lakes up this chain. Something in the narrows didn't look right. And then Pete realized: "Trees weren't in the spots where they had been before. Huge, towering white pines were gone. I looked down the lake and islands and everything was completely leveled. In places, all you could see were stumps and root systems flipped up in the air. Everything was running southwest to northeast . . . the trees just flattened all in one direction."

They continued down Newfound Lake and encountered several other parties. In every instance they stopped and made sure the people were okay. And in every instance the survivors conveyed a stunned amazement. After living through the storm, and for the most part having survived it with nothing more than scrapes and dents, they had decided not to push their luck. They were all leaving, heading back to their cars or resorts and presumably homes—providing they were able to find a way out.

There is another zigzag narrows separating Newfound Lake from Sucker Lake. When Pete and Duane boated through it, they were again stunned by what they saw. "There were these giant, big white pines on the right-hand side, and they always had an eagle's nest," Pete recalled. Eagle's nests are among the largest nests in the bird kingdom, especially in the Boundary Waters. Sometimes they are used year after year, and some have been estimated to weigh at least a ton.

"Now the trees, the eagle's nest, everything was gone," Pete said. The only remaining remnant was the stump of a three-hundred-year-old white pine, sticking up out of the pile of a fallen forest.

After getting through the narrows, they ran into a party paddling down from Birch Lake. Normally, canoeists would portage between Birch and Sucker Lakes, but these travelers had taken a long paddling detour because the portage was impassable. When Pete motored over to examine it, "All I saw were big root wads with trees going across it. There was no way anyone could cross that portage." He hoped no one had been trapped in the middle of the portage when the storm blew through. He also knew there was no way he and Duane could begin to clear a path through all those fallen trees. That would take a large work crew several days—providing they were allowed to use chainsaws, which were normally forbidden in the wilderness.

When they looked at the forest all around, they were dumbfounded by the destruction. Pete was partially responsible for tending 130 campsites up on Basswood Lake, which they ultimately hoped to reach. There were numerous portages along the way, like this one from Sucker into Birch Lake. It was hard for Pete to fathom the amount of work it would take to clear them all if they were all as bad as what he was seeing on Sucker.

Knowing there was nothing to be done, Pete and Duane continued up Sucker Lake toward Prairie Portage. "I went over to the truck portage because there's a lot of day-use motorboat fishermen that go from the resorts on Moose Lake up across this motorized portage into Basswood," Pete recalled. "They go up in the morning and usually come back between three and six o'clock."

By now it was nearly four, but Pete didn't see or hear any movement on the truck portage. If it was blocked and day fishers were backed up on Basswood, hoping to get out, it could be problematic. They might have to spend the night on the water, and if another storm like the one they just endured came up, it could be deadly. He also worried, having already dispensed some first aid, that someone on the other side of the portage could be hurt and in need of assistance.

Pete knew the truck portage's operator, whose name was Jeep. Pete pulled up near enough to see the portage covered with fallen trees. He docked their boat, walked up the portage halfway, and found Jeep driving a tractor with a bucket loader, trying to clear away the debris.

"Well," Pete told him, "I'll go across to the Canadian side and see if they got a power saw that I can borrow." If he could get a power saw, he and Duane could help cut away the trees from the portage faster than Jeep working alone.

They returned to their boat and motored across to the Canadian side. At the Canadian ranger station he spoke with Kathy, an employee with whom he was acquainted: "Mind if I grab your power saw and go over and give Jeep a hand opening up the portage?"

From this vantage point they could all look out into the bay on Basswood Lake and see a buildup of boats, waiting for the portage to open. A few of them were tied up, the boaters going onto the portage to assist Jeep with the cleanup. But without a chainsaw it would be a long, painful, and arduous process.

Fortunately, Kathy loaned Pete their chainsaw.

"I grabbed the power saw with Duane, and we motored back over to where Jeep was working," Pete said. "He had the tractor and I had the power saw, and along with all these people that were helping us as I'm cutting . . . they're throwing logs and Jeep's got the tractor going. I was the sawyer and they were my swampers." In Forest Service parlance, sawyers are people with chainsaws and swampers are those who clear away the cut debris.

Gradually, fallen tree by fallen tree, the portage began to clear.

/ / /

As Kawishiwi District ranger Bruce Slover sat by the service center radio, he heard plenty. He heard Pete Weckman's call from Moose Lake, describing the destruction of the place, and how he was trapped. He heard several other employees calling out, conveying their own stories of destruction and asking whether others they knew in the field were okay.

When Bruce heard his district's radio chatter, he decided he needed to have a firsthand look. Since he had heard Ranger Weckman describe the destruction at Moose Lake, he figured a good place to begin his reconnaissance would be by driving out Moose Lake Road.

Bruce wasn't the only one at the service center. A conservation officer (CO) had also come in to the center, suspecting it was an all-hands-on-deck moment. When the CO let Bruce know he was heading out Moose Lake Road to survey the damage, Bruce decided he would ride along.

/ / /

Law enforcement officer Chip Elkins drove out the Fernberg Trail and headed east-northeast out of Ely. Approximately 20 miles up the Fernberg was the Moose Lake Road turnoff, heading north into wilderness. The Northern Tier scout base was near the end of Moose Lake Road. Chip knew that if he drove up Moose Lake Road and turned north, heading to the scout base, he'd get a good sense of what damage, if any, had struck the BWCAW.

By midafternoon, shortly after the storm passed through Ely, Chip was on the road, driving a route that followed the same path the winds had taken as they passed through town. As he traversed the Fernberg, what he saw unnerved him. The woods on either side of the road were filled with downed trees. There were sections in which the forest was still standing, but there were increasing sections in which the trees had toppled into a surreal latticework of fallen trunks. By the time he reached Moose Lake Road, the turn north to the scout camp was impassable— driving to the base was out of the question. There was simply no way to get through, or around, so many downed trees.

Moose Lake Road and the Northern Tier scout base are on the edge of the BWCAW. In fact, most of Moose Lake is in the Boundary Waters. If the road leading to the base was blocked with falling trees, it was a good bet the forest farther east and north had also been struck.

As Chip approached the blocked road, he saw Bruce Slover with the CO, also surveying the damage. The CO needed to remain in the area, but Bruce knew the best way to get a better sense of the extent of the damage would be from the air.

"Let's head back to Ely," Bruce suggested to Chip, "and see if we can get a plane up over the area to get a better look." Chip, who had also seen enough of the damage, was happy to oblige.

Not long after they headed back down the Fernberg Trail, Chip's cell phone began ringing. Inexplicably, he and Bruce began fielding emergency calls from deep inside the BWCAW. As the two men drove in Chip's official vehicle, they took notes on a yellow legal pad, identifying and—as more emergency calls came in—prioritizing which calls should be answered first.

Unbeknown to either of them, the local Minnesota State Patrol (MSP) had temporarily routed all 911 calls coming in to the MSP office from cell phones in the wilderness to Chip's official phone. When the decision was made, the skies must have been sunny. No one at MSP or anywhere else outside northeastern Minnesota could have foreseen how the weather would change and what impact it would have on those in its path.

"My phone lit up, and we're driving down the road taking calls," Chip recalled. "As we continued to the seaplane base we began to prioritize medevac flights." Some victims of the storm had minor cuts and bruises. Others broken bones. And still others were more serious.

/ / /

By midafternoon, Jim Hinds, Forest Service fire management officer for the Kawishiwi District, had returned home from viewing the Ely parade. Jim was no stranger to the BWCAW or to the numerous significant events—fire, floods, wind, and more—that could trigger an incident command team call-up. He had begun his Forest Service career in June 1970, working summers as a wilderness ranger for the district. When he graduated from college in 1974, he began working for the agency full-time. During his more than two decades of service, he'd worked in a variety of capacities. In 1999, he was working as the west zone fire management officer for the Superior National Forest, but like many of his colleagues, he had also worked his way up the incident command chain and now held a red card qualifying him as an incident commander for a Type III event as well as an operations or division chief for a Type II event.

Some time after the blowdown swept through the Boundary Waters, Jim Hinds received a call from Bruce Slover. Given what Bruce already knew about the storm, he was concerned. He knew Jim should be included in any early discussions about next steps, so he asked Jim to meet him in the Forest Service administrative offices in Ely.

Jim was happy to oblige.

18

THE FOREST SUPERVISOR

Duluth, Minnesota

July 4 marked the end of a two-week vacation for Jim Sanders, his wife, Pat, and their two kids. They had driven east to spend time in and around the state of Virginia, attended a wedding, and on their return to Duluth picked up Pat's mother in Wisconsin, who was coming for a visit. By the afternoon the family was home. Jim was unloading the car when he got a call from Jim Thomas, fire management officer for the Superior and Chippewa National Forests. Thomas was calling from the Minnesota Interagency Fire Center up in Grand Rapids, Minnesota. He apologized for bothering Sanders on his vacation, and over the July 4 holiday, but said, "Has anybody talked to you about what's going on?"

For the past fourteen days Jim Sanders, forest supervisor, the head of the Superior National Forest, had literally been in vacation mode. Driving through Wisconsin, where the weather had been typical for the Fourth of July, he'd heard nothing about the dramatic climatic conditions up north or their impact on the Boundary Waters, its campers, and the rest of the forest. And while he enjoyed his work and was looking forward to returning to the office, he wasn't planning on doing so until Tuesday, tomorrow being the official holiday. He said, "Well, no one's talked to me, but by the tone of your voice and your question, I'm not sure I want to ask."

Thomas chuckled. And then he began sharing what he knew, which was limited because much of what happened had occurred in remote

124

wilderness. Eyewitness accounts were only beginning to trickle in. From what they could piece together, there had been some kind of event—a large wind event in Northern Minnesota. He thought the Boundary Waters had been affected, but as of now the reports were sketchy, and they didn't have a clear sense of *what* had happened or the extent of the damage.

"Keep me posted," Sanders finally said. "Give me the details as soon as you know more." Thomas assured him he would and hung up.

The Sanders family had been looking forward to the evening's fireworks. It was a beautiful late afternoon and it was going to be a beautiful evening, down near the lake at Duluth's Canal Park. But Jim had heard enough from his MIFC contact to prompt him to reach out to Tom Wagner, his deputy forest supervisor. He conveyed the sketchy report of trouble up north and suggested that later, after the evening fireworks, they should meet at the U.S. Forest Service offices down at Grand Avenue Place to find out what more might be known. Jim suspected whatever had occurred might require some kind of concerted response, and he wanted his deputy there to help him contemplate the best course of action.

After two weeks on the road, Jim had expected he would ease back into his numerous forest supervisor duties. Tomorrow, Monday, he had been looking forward to having the day off to recuperate from his long drive. He had imagined that on Tuesday he would be briefed on the plethora of recurring concerns involved in managing a nearly 4-million-acre forest. When he had left for his two-week vacation out east, no one had any idea that on the day he returned he would need to address cataclysmic disaster. Since neither of the men in charge of the Superior National Forest had a clear sense of what, specifically, had occurred, Jim recognized events had forced him to consider a completely different approach to how he would be spending his first day back at work.

/ / /

In many ways the relatively new leader had been groomed for the Herculean tasks that—unknown to him or anyone else—he was about to face. Born and raised in central Montana, he first began working for the U.S.

Forest Service as a seasonal firefighter in 1972. He was hired on with the USFS office in his hometown, where he started working summers on a ranger district crew. During the school year he attended the University of Montana in Missoula. He completed his bachelor of science degree in forestry in 1975 and soon after began working with the USFS full-time. Over the next eighteen years he worked in a variety of positions in Montana, Washington, and Northern Idaho. During that time, he also applied for and was accepted into the USFS masters in forest ecology and silviculture program. The program was specifically designed to assist selected employees obtain postgraduate education in forest ecology and silviculture that could be applied toward a master's degree.

After completing the program and receiving his certified silviculturist credentials, Jim applied for the assistant district ranger position in West Yellowstone, Montana, on the Gallatin National Forest, a position that would utilize both his experience and his education. Jim worked in that position from 1982 to 1990, most notably during the 1988 Yellowstone fires.

After his eight years on the Gallatin National Forest, Jim applied for a job at USFS headquarters in Washington, D.C., where he worked for six years in a variety of public relations roles, many of which involved working directly on the Hill with congresspeople and senators. His congressional work and his efforts reaching out to numerous individuals and groups with intense, competing interests—particularly involving logging, wildlife, and the environment—would be invaluable training for his work in Minnesota. Finally, midyear 1996, he applied for and was selected to lead the Superior National Forest.

Since then, Jim had taken a crash course on the national forest he had decided to lead. Comprising 3.9 million acres of forest and waters, it is one of the largest national forests within the USFS system. Three-fourths of the forest is considered multiuse, including logging and recreational activities such as hiking, camping, boating, and fishing. The remaining approximately 1 million acres constitutes the BWCAW, a massive tract of forest and water that has been enchanting people for thousands of years.

Jim was just under 6 feet tall with a medium build. He had short-cropped hair parted neatly on the side, and a pair of thick plastic-rimmed glasses were perched atop his nose. He was square shouldered and fit and carried himself erect. But what you noticed most was his direct way of greeting people. His eyes carefully focused on the person in front of him, sincerely interested in what they had to say.

Some leaders are more interested in their own perspectives than they are in hearing the ideas of those with whom they converse. But Jim Sanders was a careful listener. He respected and appreciated the ideas and perspectives of the people he managed as well as those of the countless others with whom he came in contact. In many ways, his demeanor supported his leadership style in a way that, like his history and education with the service, would be extremely well suited to the tasks in front of him.

During his first two and a half years as SNF forest supervisor, Jim realized there were numerous ways to lead and manage, but the one that worked best for him was being on the ground, at or near the front lines, seeing the forest firsthand and speaking with those who were working in and around it. And he wasn't only interested in speaking with USFS personnel whose day-in, day-out jobs were to manage the SNF. Early on he also recognized the 3.9-million-acre tract of forest and waters, including one of the most unusual wilderness areas in the continental United States, touched the lives of many others who would also want and need to be heard. While the USFS was responsible for managing the forest, Jim recognized it did so with the help and assistance of a wide network of private and public, governmental and nongovernmental groups and organizations who also had perspectives about how their public lands were used.

Environmentalists, loggers, county commissioners, state and federal legislators and bureaucrats, wildlife biologists, sawmill operators, recreationalists, paper mill employees, miners and mining companies, and more—all had perspectives about how parts of the SNF should be managed and used. Sometimes these people and the groups they represented had overlapping interests, but often they were competing or at odds. Regardless, Jim realized each of them had a perspective and a voice he needed to hear.

By July 4, 1999, Jim had had two and a half years to develop close working relationships and ties with numerous organizations throughout the state. He said, "We worked with various interest groups, be it

Friends of the Boundary Waters or the timber industry. We've got three large counties in parts of the SNF: St. Louis, Lake, and Cook. I worked to establish good relationships with the county commissioners. And then we worked with the state, because the SNF has that intermingled ownership of private land, county, tax-forfeited land, and both federal and state public land. It was important that we were physically on the ground. You could have national forest on one side of a line, county on the other, state nearby, and all of it intermingled with private land.

"I knew from my previous years working that we each have different roles and perspectives. But together, where we can cooperate, we can accomplish more united than apart."

Given his perspective, Jim Sanders's goal during his first couple years in office was to identify everyone who had a stake in the SNF and to "make sure we could coordinate and work together and that we were only a phone call away. And to meet frequently. Once every other month or once a quarter. Just to establish good coordination and communication."

From Jim's experience, it was easy to bring people together over events like sudden, dangerous forest fires: "Emergencies bring people together—it's easy to rally around that." But during his first two years on the job, he wanted to expand that model of cooperation for many of the nonemergency activities he knew everyone involved with the SNF would be addressing. So, he worked hard to identify and establish good communication and protocol among all the SNF's interested parties.

On July 4, 1999, when the skies began to churn, Jim's extensive network was fully operational and ready to address whatever the SNF might face.

19

MIRACLE

Lake Polly South to Kawishiwi Campground

Mark and Kristina Schwendinger knew they had a long trip in front of them, but they also knew they needed to navigate it in record time. Fortunately, they had traveled to Lake Polly the previous day, so the lakes, portages, and rivers they needed to traverse were still fresh in their mind.

As they paddled down the Lake Polly peninsula shoreline, making a beeline for their first portage, Kristina noticed, "Trees were down all over." When they reached the southern end of the lake, they recognized the start of their first portage south.

Later, Mark would have time to ponder the length, breadth, and intensity of the blowdown. "I remember looking at a map and thinking that the majority of the blowdown area was north of us," he recalled. "I've read other stories where [the forest] wasn't recognizable. This wasn't that. But there were obstacles."

As they traveled across their first 73-rod portage, they definitely encountered damaged country. "It wasn't where everything was blown down and we were walking on top of trees," Mark said. "If there was a tree down and I was carrying a canoe I would use it as a canoe rest and I would hunch down, get the canoe leaned up against that tree that was down, and then I'd either go over or under the tree and get to the other side. Then I'd just stand up and get the canoe and keep traveling south until I got to the next tree."

As they came to the end of that first portage, they quickly entered Townline Lake, the small body of water separating the 73-rod portage from the next 189-rod portage. They dug in with their paddles, crossed Townline in record time, and continued traveling south. Compared to the time it had taken to navigate north, yesterday, on their way into Lake Polly, three factors hastened their paddle and portages south.

First, they had been careful to keep their outfit lean. The only clothes they carried were what they wore. The only food and water they had were granola bars and a couple of water bottles stuffed in a day pack. The previous day, they'd slogged north over portages, needing to cover them twice: the first with their canoe, paddles, and life vests, the second with their packs full of gear. But on the afternoon of July 4, they traversed each portage only once. And kept moving.

Second, Lake Polly and points south are on the southern side of the Laurentian Divide, the north–south continental divide in the center of North America. All waterways north of the Laurentian Divide flow north. All waterways to the south of the divide flow south. Yesterday, traveling north up the Kawishiwi River, they'd been going against the current. On this afternoon, traveling south, the current was with them.

And finally, the storm had dumped several inches of rain on the entire BWCAW area, including Lake Polly and points south. The river that flows from Kawasachong Lake south into Square Lake, along their route, has two low spots where travelers typically portage their canoe and supplies. "When we went in," Mark recalled, "there were places that we had to portage because there were streams that were so small and so low you weren't able to float through. On the way out there was so much rain that we were able to shoot the rapids—it wasn't really rapids, but we were able to paddle those parts without portaging."

It had taken the whole group six hours going in. It only took Mark and Kristina two hours going out.

/ / /

While Mark and Kristina rushed to get to a phone, Ray and Michelle remained beside Lisa, making sure she was comfortable, warm, and conscious. "It was in the manual," Michelle recalled, referring to the first aid pamphlet Mark and Kristina had brought with them. "That was my job. I was trying to keep her awake. It was in the manual—I had to tell her a whole bunch of stuff. Tried to make her laugh. It was tense."

Lisa's recollections help explain why the aftermath of her accident, lying in her tent, may have been filled with more anxiety than laughter. "Michelle was in the tent with me. Ray came in, but most of the time it was Michelle, and she was keeping me talking. And she . . . she'd ask me yes/no questions because the swelling was starting to impact, and I couldn't move my jaw very much. But she was talking to me, and she was asking questions, and keeping me conscious."

People who have just suffered a blow to the head need to be kept awake for fear of brain damage. If they fall asleep, serious symptoms such as small seizures, numbness down the left side of the body, or similar signs of potential trouble could go unnoticed.

"The back of the head was where I felt the most pain," Lisa continued. "It's the most pain I've ever felt. Ever. I don't even really know how to describe it. It kind of felt like somebody just swung a two-by-four to the back of my head."

The left side of Lisa's head was seriously injured. "I kept wanting to lay my head on my left side because it was all numb."

But Michelle knew placing pressure on that side of Lisa's head could lead to more damage.

"She kept me lying flat on my back," Lisa said. "It was really smart on her part. They kept doing that. She kept me going."

/ / /

Finally, Mark and Kristina reached the Kawishiwi campground and entry point 37. They beached their canoe and hurried to their car. Kristina's first action was to plug her phone into the lighter port to charge it and try to call out. While the phone powered up, there was no service. In 1999, cell phone coverage was limited, especially in the woods. She had no bars, so no connection could be made.

"Okay," Mark said. "We have to start driving." As he and Kristina began driving out of the campground, they saw the storm's aftermath, with trees and debris all around them. But as they entered the remote Forest Service road leading into the campground, Mark noticed, "Hey, there's trees that are already cut out of the way. And then we were thinking, like, 'Oh wow—they cleared this really fast.'"

At this time, they were both thinking state or county highway workers had already reached this distant section of wilderness road and begun clearing away the debris. They didn't yet know about the breadth, depth, and severity of the storm, and the extent of its damage.

"Then we caught up to the line of cars," Mark remembered. "It wasn't people who were cutting their way in. It was campers who had chainsaws cutting their way out."

By the time they reached the line of cars, they had already summited a couple of hills. "Luckily, when we got to that line of cars," Mark recalled, "We were up on a little bit more of a hill. And we got a signal."

"It was divine intervention," Kristina said.

"That was the miracle, right there," Mark agreed.

/ / /

Approximately 25 miles to the west-northwest, Forest Service law enforcement officer Chip Elkins and Kawishiwi District ranger Bruce Slover were driving down Moose Lake Road, returning to Ely from their reconnaissance drive. As the pair were heading down the highway, trying to digest the destruction and come up with useful next steps, Chip's cell phone began to ring.

Sometime between 4:00 and 5:00, Kristina Schwendinger dialed and managed to reach the 911 dispatcher. She was anxious to tell her story before losing the connection, so she talked fast. Kristina explained their situation and what had befallen their friend.

"I was trying to describe to the dispatcher where we were," Kristina said. "I remember the 911 operator asked me what county I was in." To which Kristina said, "I have no idea!"

The dispatcher wanted to know the county because search-and-rescue operations were managed by county sheriffs. Regardless, Kristina impressed upon the dispatcher the seriousness of Lisa's injuries.

"I don't remember exactly the words we used," recalled Mark, "but I know we used the phrase 'critically injured.'"

In short order the dispatcher connected them to Chip Elkins. After hearing the seriousness of Lisa's injuries, he assured the pair of paddlers they would be one of the first to be visited by a seaplane carrying an emergency medical technician (EMT). Before hanging up, Kristina and Mark again reiterated the seriousness of their companion's condition and said they hoped to see the seaplane soon. Remembering the shape and size of Lake Polly, and that they had seen other campers, Kristina suddenly realized it might be difficult to identify which campers needed attention. "I remembered an orange tarp. I told them they could use the orange tarp to identify which campsite was ours."

"Of course," Chip said. "We're putting your friend on the top of our list."

He didn't want to tell the paddlers, clearly distraught, that theirs wasn't the only serious emergency. Chip and Bruce both knew that if Chip was getting emergency calls for assistance, other more official channels were probably being inundated.

Near the end of the Gunflint Trail, Mike Prom, co-owner of Voyageur Canoe Outfitters, had spent the afternoon clearing debris, cutting trees, fielding inquiries—though none by phone—and greeting some of the holiday travelers who had experienced the storm and decided they'd had enough of the wilderness, at least for now.

One of his groups had been encamped on Alpine Lake. When the storm blew through, it felled many of the trees around the lake and destroyed the travelers' campsite. Luckily, their canoes were serviceable. The first thing they did was gather their equipment and, as best they could, pack up. Then they got into their canoes and headed down Alpine Lake toward the portage they hoped would be open.

Sometime in the early afternoon they must have been one of the first groups to pass Vicky Brockman, Jan Fiola, and Sue Ann Martinson. Jan or Sue Ann shared their plight with the passing canoes, repeating their plea to tell the authorities that Vicky was hurt and that the only way she could leave the wilderness was by plane. Please send help.

The storm-struck travelers said they would, and continued up the shoreline to portage into nearby Seagull Lake via the river crossing.

By midafternoon the travelers finally returned to Voyageur, where they had rented their canoes and equipment. And they shared what they knew about Alpine and the seriously injured woman.

"They told us someone had been badly injured on Alpine Lake," Mike recalled. "They also told us the Alpine portage was like pickup sticks."

"I didn't have a radio that could tie into the EMS and county dispatch down in Grand Marais," Mike said. "So I went to my neighbor. She had a radio and was on higher ground and a better location to make the call to county dispatch."

Radio etiquette is that you wait your turn to place your call. "I remember sitting there for a while, because of the radio traffic. We waited several minutes while everyone was talking about the storm's aftermath." Finally, there was a brief moment of silence, and Mike said, "This is an emergency." He relayed that a woman was down on Alpine Lake and needed to be medevacked to the nearest hospital.

Back on Alpine Lake, Vicky and her friends had no way to know a call had been made on her behalf, or that the wheels of rescue were turning.

/ / /

After the Ely parade, Forest Service Beaver pilot Pat Loe returned home and received a call from his supervisor at the Minnesota Interagency Fire Center in Grand Rapids. Two campers near Insula Lake, in the south-central part of the BWCAW, had been struck by falling trees and needed medical attention. It was Pat's first medevac of the day. At 3:31 p.m. he took off, flying a straight line due east from Ely to Insula Lake, maintaining communication with the sea base. During his frequent check-ins, Pat reported on what he saw.

"There are some pockets of blowdown here and there," he told dispatch. But he also saw, during his first flyover along the southern boundary of the BWCAW, plenty of trees still standing.

By 4:30 he landed back at the base and dropped off his wounded passengers. He refueled, got his next assignment—to Lake Polly, in the south-central BWCAW—and onboarded local EMT Barb Garrison. Pat nosed his Beaver into the air again at 5:08. He began to understand his day was going to be consumed with medevac missions.

/ / /

As the crow (and Pat Loe) flies, the distance from Ely to Polly is approximately 20 to 25 miles, so it was only a matter of minutes before Pat was circling the lake. Fortunately, he was intimately familiar with the area and its waterways. It only took him a moment to locate the orange tarp he had been told about.

"There were planes flying all over the place," Ray remembered. "We waved that first one down. And they came with two people."

Pat and Barb stepped out of the plane. Barb had her EMT bag and equipment, but nothing else.

"You guys brought your backboard, didn't you?" Ray remembered asking. "The EMT said, 'Well, we need to see how bad it is. And when she came up and looked at Lisa, she said, 'Oh my god. This is way worse than I thought it would be."

Michelle, nearby, cautioned the EMT, "Shhhh. She can hear you."

"I remember hearing the plane come in," Lisa said. "And I remember when the EMT got there and started talking. It was too dangerous to move me without a backboard. I think it was much worse than what she was expecting. I don't think I looked at anything or saw anything. I just kept my eyes closed."

"Barb saw we had her tucked in there real good," Michelle said. "I think we even had her feet elevated. [Barb] put her on oxygen."

In just a few minutes they had assessed the situation and realized they needed a backboard, and more assistance, to be able to secure Lisa and carry her down the embankment and into a waiting Beaver plane.

Barb remained with Lisa, Michelle, and Ray while Pat took off to retrieve a backboard. Unfortunately, as soon as he was airborne he received another emergency call about people needing assistance near Hanson Lake, due north. He said he'd check it out. Then he radioed fellow Forest Service pilot Wayne Erickson, explained the dire situation on Lake Polly, and conveyed that they needed a backboard. He told Wayne he should also take some extra hands—that he would need help getting the young woman out of her tent, across and down the escarpment, and into the cargo hold of his plane.

/ / /

At this point, Pat must have also told Wayne that he should have someone place a call to the Schwendingers, who were waiting for verification
that their campsite, and their friend, had been found.

"This was the kick in the gut," recalled Mark, talking about the aftermath of finally getting word out regarding Lisa. "The only thing we
brought with us was water and a couple of granola bars. We went out
to make the call, and once the call was made, we waited until they contacted us back and said they found the campsite and found them, and
that's when we said, 'Okay, now we have to turn around and go back in.'"

20

RESCUE

Alpine Lake and Seagull Lake

Throughout the long afternoon and early evening of July 4, Jan Fiola and Sue Ann Martinson watched several more paddlers pass their island campsite, searching for the main portage out of Alpine. The stranded islanders shared what they knew about the portage—that it was hopelessly blocked—and that the canoeists they'd seen had opted to try the Alpine River. If someone didn't know about the channel, Jan told them where to find it. And of course, she and Sue Ann explained about Vicky, who was too injured to move. She needed medical attention and to be medevacked to the nearest hospital. Please send help.

/ / /

A little more than 4 miles to the east-northeast, members of the Wilderness Canoe Base were taking stock of the devastation. The base was in the direct path of the storm, and the fallen trees were legion. The damage was apocalyptic.

Gradually, throughout the afternoon, base leader Jen Nagel and the remaining skeleton staff continued assessing the destruction and digging out. It would be a while before they could figure out the extent of the devastation, but eventually they would estimate that on the base's two islands, Dominion and Fishhook, they had lost 85,000 trees. Over the rest of July 4 and the next few days they would determine that forty base buildings had been damaged, mostly by fallen trees. Many had their roofs caved in.

The base was a large wilderness transit station, with groups, wilderness guides, and staff coming and going. Fortuitously, it was a holiday weekend in the middle of the summer, and this weekend marked an unusual hiatus in base activity. Many base staff were using the holiday to take a break. Wilderness guide Joel Rogness had spent the previous evening, July 3, with several other staff members at a Bob Dylan/Paul Simon concert in Duluth. They returned around dawn. Booker Hodges and his fiancée, who also worked at the base, were visiting family down in the Cities. They, too, would return, but later in the day. Camp director Jim Wiinanen and his wife, Rebecca, had been in Grand Marais when the storm tore the world in two.

After accounting for all or most of the base's current residents, the group began to organize and make a plan. Jen had made her way to the mainland and the nearby Gunflint Volunteer Fire Department station to use their radio and let Cook County dispatch know what had happened. Then she began helping others clear the debris from the WCB drive down to the parking lot.

By midafternoon, base guide Cherish Galvin Davis and staff members Maren Olson, Joel Rogness, and Steve Markey commandeered the base's johnboat to venture out onto Seagull Lake to see if they could render assistance. The base used the johnboat, a sizeable flat-bottomed craft with a square hull and 10-horsepower motor, to haul canoes, people and supplies between the islands and the mainland. Maren was an EMT, so she pulled together base medical supplies, and they headed out on the water.

The previous year, the BWCAW regulations governing the use of motorized watercraft on Seagull Lake had changed. Now there were only certain places on the lake, many of them in the Boundary Waters, where the use of a boat motor was allowed. But given the emergency, and the fear there may be people in need out and around the 4,300 acres of Seagull Lake, the base employees decided to ignore the motor restrictions for the next day or two.

As the four piloted the boat down the lake, they passed along Three Mile Island. Before this morning, Three Mile Island had been home to one of the most beautiful stands of old-growth forest in the Boundary Waters. Many visitors paddled along the island just to see its magnificent trees. According to University of Minnesota forestry professor Lee Frelich, the island was also home to the oldest tree in Minnesota, a large gnarled cedar along the island's northwest shoreline.

Fortunately, Minnesota's oldest tree still stood, with a handful of others clustered around it. But the bulk of the island's sentinels had fallen like dominoes.

Not surprisingly, the lake was filled with forest debris. The boaters navigated through the wreckage carefully. When Cherish and her crew approached addled wilderness visitors, they asked three questions.

"Are you okay?"

"Do you know anyone who's hurt?"

"Do you know anybody who may need medical attention?"

It wasn't long before the group passed a campsite on Three Mile Island whose occupants flagged them down. A tree had fallen on a tent, injuring one of the campers. Maren and Joel rendered first aid and decided the camper's injuries were serious enough that he needed to be evacuated. After loading the injured man into their johnboat, they started back to the base.

On their return, they ran into paddlers who told them there was another injured person who needed assistance, on the other side of the short portage out of nearby Alpine Lake. Cherish and her colleagues hustled back to the base and dropped off the first injured camper. Other base employees would get him to the mainland and an ambulance.

From what the paddlers related, Maren and Joel thought it might be prudent to bring a helicopter basket, a kind of stretcher used to evacuate injured people by helicopter. They retrieved the base's basket, turned around, and steered toward the mouth of the river that marked the short portage out of Alpine.

Where the Alpine River emptied into Seagull Lake, the water was wide and deep enough that Cherish could steer the johnboat up the river toward the rapids at the other end. Coincidentally, Maren had been in Alpine Lake with her family several years earlier. On that trip, they had decided to exit Alpine using this river and had shot the rapids in their canoes. Maren had enjoyed the fast paddle, in part because Wilderness

Canoe Base guides were absolutely forbidden to run rapids in a canoe. Regardless, she recalled the river and suspected, especially after so much rain had fallen, that the water would be high enough to enable the john-boat to get up near the part of the river that started out of Alpine Lake. But while they were able to navigate up the river, when they neared the other end, they found no one in need of assistance.

As they contemplated returning to Seagull, more paddlers happened by, exiting Alpine as so many others had that day. When Cherish and her colleagues asked about campers in need of assistance, they told them about Vicky Brockman and her two companions on the island campsite, whom they had just passed. But Vicky was near the start of the long portage out of Alpine, not the short one.

"So, we pulled around into the bay that marked the start of the long portage into Alpine," recalled Maren. "I remember being stunned, because every tree in the woods in front of us was broken off at about 20 feet up. And we all wondered, 'How are we going to get across this portage?'" Especially carrying a helicopter basket.

/ / /

By the time Jim and Rebecca Wiinanen finally reached the turnoff for the Wilderness Canoe Base, near the end of the Gunflint Trail, the road had been cleared. Jim remembered:

> The driveway is a half mile long. We got into the parking lot and could hear the chainsaws. From the parking lot to the lake was a couple hundred feet and the camp staff were just finishing up getting the trees out of that section, so we could get down to the lake. That's when I had my first briefing with program coordinator Jen Nagel.
>
> There were probably twenty staff on site at that point. We had our short briefing on the mainland and headed back over to the island. Just walking from the dock up to the main lodge there were trees down all over. Staff people were saying what normally was a five-minute walk was taking a half hour or so, to climb over all the trees. And then things got really busy.
>
> Some staff had taken a boat to check on people camped on

Seagull Lake. Other general-public groups paddled by the camp and reported on their experience in the storm. Then came the call on the public safety radio asking for help responding to an injury on the next lake south of Seagull, Alpine Lake, where a tree had fallen on a woman, pinning her to the ground.

/ / /

Back at Alpine Lake, Vicky would have answered all three of Cherish's questions with an emphatic yes. She was trying to remain calm. To help distract her, Sue Ann retrieved the book Vicky had been reading, Blind Descent. Amazingly, the book was still in good enough shape to read. Sue Ann settled in beside Vicky and picked up the narrative where she had left off.

Despite Sue Ann's dramatic reading skills, it was difficult for Vicky to concentrate, especially as the clock moved toward dinnertime. She had been in the same position, prone on the ground, for the last six hours. And since the balmy dawn, the day had cooled considerably, especially on the ground. Vicky felt a deep chill. As she watched the light change from late afternoon to early evening, she began to worry about spending the night here, on the ground, unable to move. She had an understandable fear of hypothermia. The wilderness at night, even in the middle of summer, could get cold. And she was still wet. The possibility of shivering to death was real.

Her friends were also concerned. For most of the day, after the storm, the skies had been cloudy with occasional light rain. It appeared there may be more rain and bad weather coming. And they could sense darkness, like a shadowy hand in a bad horror movie, beginning to creep across the devastated wilderness.

Sue Ann reflected on all the people who had passed by, trying to remain optimistic. To every passing traveler they repeated their request for help: "We need a plane. We have an injured person. Send help."

The canoeists affirmed they had heard and would pass along their requests. Then the stranded islanders watched them paddle north, their eyes lingering on the distant silver glint of canoes until they disappeared around the point, heading toward the channel. None of them had returned.

Unless they had all capsized, Vicky, Jan, and Sue Ann surmised, the paddlers had made it into Seagull Lake and alerted someone, anyone, to their predicament.

/ / /

On July 4 in Minnesota, the sun sets shortly after 9:00. Technically, the U.S. Forest Service seaplane pilots can fly only from dawn to dusk, and pilot Pat Loe had been busy all afternoon. Earlier, after leaving EMT Barb Garrison with Lisa Naas on Lake Polly, he had received a radio call from dispatch about an injured person on a small body of water off Hanson Lake. He knew Hanson Lake, which was more than 10 miles due north of Lake Polly, and thought he recognized the small lake off Hanson being referenced. He remembered it as a much-too-small patch of water on which to land his Beaver plane. Pat returned to the sea base to pick up another medic team and a canoe. He was going to drop them off on Hanson, where they could portage into the smaller lake and check on the injured. After refueling and loading up, he nosed his plane off Shagawa Lake at 7:12 p.m.

/ / /

Late in the day on July 4, Cherish, Maren, Joel, and Steve were examining the start of the long portage from Seagull into Alpine, wondering how they were going to traverse it while hauling the helicopter basket. "We pulled our boat up on the shore and decided to just try and scramble across it," Maren said.

They spent at least the next hour climbing, bending, dropping, and threading their way across the wreckage. "I remember laughing about it afterward," Maren said. "Because we climbed on trees the whole way across. It was insane! But we were on a mission, and so . . . off we went."

Maren managed to reach the Alpine Lake side of the long portage first. Her colleagues were close behind. When she peered across the lake she could see two groups of campers, one on the nearby mainland, and another on the nearby island. She turned to the mainland group and yelled over to them. "Do you need any help?"

"We don't," one of the campers yelled back. "But they need help over there." He pointed across the water to the island.

/ / /

On the island, Sue Ann was taking a break from reading to Vicky. In the struggle to get out from under the fallen tree, she had twisted her ankle, and now she hobbled down to the water's edge, fretting. It was getting late. Pretty soon it was going to be dark. And it was getting cold. The skies were overcast, and they still could not move Vicky. The direness of their situation gnawed at her. It was one of those moments she feared for the future and for the well-being of her friend.

"It was almost sunset," Sue Ann remembered. "I was down at the water, and I looked up across to the portage and saw this young woman there, slender and blond, standing across from us."

"Do you need any help?" Maren called across the water to Sue Ann.

After a pause, Sue Ann said, "We already sent for help."

Maren suddenly recognized how it must appear: a young woman alone, standing at the edge of a fallen forest with no canoe. But Sue Ann's comment still made Maren smile.

"That's us," Maren said.

"Are you alone?" Sue Ann asked.

Before Maren could answer, she was joined by Cherish, Joel, and Steve. At that point, Sue Ann must have realized the four were there to help them.

Knowing there was little time to waste, and the four rescuers were without a canoe, one of the mainland campers paddled over to give them a lift to the island.

/ / /

After dispatching fellow pilot Wayne Erickson to Lake Polly and picking up the medical team with a canoe so they could paddle into the small body of water off Hanson Lake, Pat Loe got word of a woman needing to be medevacked out of Alpine.

"I dropped off the medic team on Hanson Lake with a canoe," Pat recalled. "And then I proceeded to Alpine Lake, which is at the end of the Gunflint Trail off of Seagull." It was 7:44 p.m.

At this point, all Pat knew was that "a woman had been in her tent and a big tree came down and I think broke both of her legs." Because the injury sounded severe, another medic with the necessary equipment accompanied Pat to Alpine.

The pilot's flight from Ely all the way to Hanson Lake and then onto Alpine was more startling than anything else he had seen that day. His northeasterly trajectory took him along the same path as the blowdown, over the exact middle of the most severe damage.

Approximately two-thirds along the length of that route, his trip took him over Kekekabic Lake, in the middle of the Boundary Waters.

"Kekekabic had a little administrative ranger cabin in there," Pat explained. "Historically, before the blowdown, the Kek cabin was really hard to see by air. There were just two little islands out front." Normally, the cabin was so hidden by forest it was difficult to spot, unless you knew where to look and what you were looking for. On Pat's flight to Alpine on July 4, however, he peered ahead and saw flattened forest clear out to the horizon.

At that moment he made a radio call—to the sea base and the Minnesota Interagency Fire Center, but also anyone else who had access to his radio channel, which was public and open.

"The Kek cabin looks like the Little House on the Prairie," Pat commented.

Many were listening on that channel and heard Pat's remark, including fire management officer Jim Hinds. Anyone familiar with the remote Kek cabin would have had a hard time imagining how wilderness, once covered by dense, mature forests, now looked like a "prairie."

/ / /

As soon as the four rescuers stepped onto the island campsite, EMT Maren began examining Vicky while the others explained to Sue Ann and Jan that their message had gotten out and a plane should be arriving, but they could not say when.

The news that a plane was hopefully in their near future was an incredible relief. The rescuers, and the plane news, caused Vicky, Jan, and Sue Ann to begin reevaluating how the rest of the day might unfold. Prior to seeing Maren across the water, all three of the survivors wondered whether they would be spending another night on the island. They didn't want to think about it, but prior to Maren's news, they believed enduring another night in the wilderness was likely. Now they realized Vicky might well be in an Ely hospital by nightfall. That meant they would be left to find their own way out of the woods, and eventually to Vicky's car.

While the day had evolved quite differently and been more traumatic than any of them could have imagined, they still had enough common sense to consider logistics. If Jan and Sue Ann exited the wilderness the way they had planned, they would eventually arrive at the parking lot where Vicky had parked her car. They hoped it was unscathed, but regardless, they wouldn't be able to open or drive it without Vicky's keys. Fortunately, Vicky remembered the pack pocket in which she'd stowed them, and now Jan made sure she had the Camry's keys.

/ / /

A few years after the July 4 blowdown, the Weather Channel produced an episode of the series *Storm Stories* about the event. "By the time we reached Vicky," Cherish said in the episode, "we needed to act as quickly as possible. Not only because of the severity of her injury, but because we would be operating in the dark very soon."

"All of a sudden this plane," commented Jan, "this little red and white boat plane came from the sky, and it was like a miracle."

Unfortunately, the sky was still overcast, and the sun, though they could not see it, was settling into the western horizon. Trying to find Vicky on Alpine Lake at dusk from a cloudy altitude of more than 1,000 feet, among twenty campsites and numerous coves, islands, and peninsulas, was not a simple task. Joel knew they needed to somehow signal Pat. He looked around, noticed the lipstick-red outfit Jan was wearing, and asked whether he could borrow her jacket.

Of course she agreed.

In moments, Joel found a clearing and began waving Jan's red jacket like a flag. Fortunately, it was still light enough for Pat to see the signal. He banked the plane into position, put the Beaver down, and taxied to their campsite.

The relief of all concerned was palpable, especially Vicky, who began to realize she would not need to suffer the dark and stormy night in the cold, on the ground. But at the same time, she also began to wonder how this group, albeit strong, would be able to get her off the ground and into that small plane—especially considering that every time she moved, shooting pains ricocheted through her body like electric jolts.

Pat brought the plane in close to the island's edge. He knew he would need to be as near the shoreline as possible, given that Vicky would need to be carried on a backboard stretcher and somehow shuttled through the door of the small plane and laid in the rear cargo hold.

Over the next few minutes Pat managed to bring the door side of the plane adjacent to the shoreline. The Beaver's left wing jutted several yards out over the campsite's bank, and the wing spanned over several fallen trees. Obviously, the shoreline here was not ideal, given the downed trees. The rescuers would need to step very carefully to maneuver Vicky into the plane. Thankfully, there were six able-bodied people—three to each side of the stretcher—who could help manage the load.

While Pat was bringing the plane in close, the others worked to stabilize Vicky and figure out how best to get her onto the flat device. Fortunately, the stretcher was thin enough that they could slide it under her with minimal movement. They spent several minutes making sure she was in an optimal position for transferring. They bent her legs and placed bunched towels and clothes under her knees to relieve pressure on her lower back.

Every time Vicky moved, the effort was painful. But there was no other recourse. As carefully as possible they shifted her body and eventually got her settled onto the stretcher. Once she was properly positioned, they used the stretcher's straps to stabilize her. One of the rescuers didn't think the existing straps were sufficient to keep her stationary, so he pulled off his belt and used it to further secure Vicky to the stretcher.

Jan noticed the gallant gesture, which must have reminded her of an old movie in which the rugged male lead makes a sacrifice to assist a damsel in distress. Later, whenever she and Vicky remembered this moment, they laughed about the handsome rescuer who used his belt to secure Vicky in her time of need. While she was clearly in pain and incapacitated, she was at least well enough to recognize humor in the moment. In the future, it would, for the two friends, become a cause for shared mirth.

Their campsite was in disarray. Sue Ann and Jan had done everything they could to clear space around Vicky and make her as comfortable as possible. But fallen trees and branches covered the site. Now Pat, the medic who traveled with him, and the four Wilderness Canoe Base employees took up positions on either side of Vicky's stretcher. Daylight continued to bleed out of the sky. They needed to hurry, but they also needed to tread the campsite's debris with care. Tripping or falling was simply not an option.

Somehow, they managed to traverse the fallen trees and branches and thread Vicky and the stretcher into the plane's rear cargo hold. Beaver flights can be rocky rides, especially when taking off and landing, and even more so when the atmosphere is as troubled as it had been this day. The group made sure the stretcher and Vicky were fastened tight, and then Pat climbed into his pilot's seat and started the engine. In moments he was airborne, winging his way toward Ely and the medical attention Vicky had needed for the past several hours.

It was 8:43 p.m.

Pat Loe did not yet know it, but before he could return with Vicky to the Shagawa sea base, his flight would be interrupted by another plea for help.

21

A BROKEN NECK?

Lake Polly, South-Central BWCAW, and Ely

"It was nice that Barb was there and got her onto oxygen," Michelle said. "And that we knew that reinforcements were on the way. Earlier, Barb had shared her concern that they were having trouble getting choppers out and having enough people to help. I remember them agreeing Lisa had to be prioritized, but when the pilot left, he wasn't sure how long it would take because of a lack of resources and the inability to fly. I believe more storms were on the way."

Fortunately, pilot Wayne Erickson, back at the Shagawa Lake Seaplane Base, was able to procure a backboard and recruit a sheriff and a deputy to help him with the delicate load. They were airborne by 6:09 p.m.

"I remember when I heard the plane again and felt relief just hearing that," Lisa recalled. Wayne easily located the campsite and taxied to shore. Equipped with the backboard, Barb and the others worked to get Lisa onto it and secured. "I remember being strapped to the backboard," Lisa said. "You're strapped, including your head. You really do get immobilized. And I remember there's more people and more men. And they're going to take me down the rocks to get to that plane."

Once Lisa was secure, Michelle and Barb remained on the top area of the campsite while each of the four men took one side of the backboard. "We walked down that rock embankment," recalled Ray. "It was 15 foot of rock going pretty much straight down. We all held on to Lisa and climbed down to get her in."

"It was quite harrowing to watch," Michelle recalled. "It was not designed for a medevac situation. We chose the campsite for that rise of rock, and that is exactly where they had to go down."

Not only was it a 15-foot drop of rock to reach the waiting plane, but the storm had downed trees and covered the entire campsite with debris. The men had to carefully pick their way around the debris and down the rock side. At one point, the sheriff and the deputy joked that it was a good thing Lisa was small.

For Lisa, it felt like she was being twisted and turned in every direction. "I was sideways and nearly upside down and I was upright and then I was to the other side. Feet down and head up. As they were moving me around, I remember at one point saying, 'Stop stop stop stop stop.' I can't remember how I said it. And I couldn't have said it with a lot of words, but I said, 'This really, really hurts.' And as long as they knew that, then I was okay, and we went the rest of the way."

Finally, the four men managed to get Lisa into the Beaver plane. Once she was secured, the sheriff, the deputy, and Barb boarded the plane and Wayne took off.

/ / /

By now it was after seven o'clock. Wayne managed to land with Lisa and the others at the sea base at 7:28 p.m., when Lisa was placed into a waiting ambulance and driven to the nearby clinic. Finally, after more than six hours of pain and semiconsciousness, she was examined by a doctor. Thankfully, she was immediately put on an IV and given some drugs to assuage her pain. But after she was examined, the rest of the news was bad.

"They thought my neck was broken," Lisa remembered. The clinic had x-ray equipment, but not the type needed to x-ray a patient fastened to a backboard. And the team did not want to move her, for fear they could do more damage. The obvious next step was to get her to the level-one trauma center in Duluth, which had the proper equipment and necessary expertise to address her more serious injuries. Before arranging an ambulance, the doctor also conveyed to Lisa the seriousness of her situation.

/ / /

After Lisa's parents retired, they had moved from Wisconsin to Arkansas. In the hospital, she was reluctant to contact them until she knew more about her condition, particularly whether her neck was broken. She knew a broken neck was serious, but she still wanted to wait to let her parents, and a brother in Colorado, know about what had happened to her in the wilderness.

But the doctor was adamant: they needed to be contacted, immediately.

When Lisa had first been struck by the falling tree, she knew something seriously bad had happened. Subsequently, she felt the worst pain of her life and had drifted in and out of consciousness. One of her eyes was swollen shut. She could not feel the left side of her head, and the back of her head felt as though someone had struck her full swing with a two-by-four. She could see out of her right eye, but because of the pain she had largely kept it shut. Until now, she had been painstakingly focused on each step of her journey: letting others get her dry, warm, secure, moved, loaded into the plane, flown to Ely, transported to the clinic. There had been so much to do she had only been focused on the next task in front of her.

Now, the doctor's vehemence about her need to contact her family, immediately, was like a trigger that suddenly brought the full impact of her condition front and center. If she had been ignoring it, now it could not be ignored. What if she were partially or fully paralyzed? Wasn't there a chance she could die?

For the first time since the accident, Lisa's anxiety surfaced like a runaway freight train, and she began to hyperventilate. Fortunately, she was in the right place to have a panic attack. The medical attendants, familiar with these kinds of episodes, eventually managed to calm her down, in part by having her breathe into a paper bag.

But the evening was far from over, and her survival was still uncertain.

Lisa's parents and her brother were finally notified. Given the dire reports, her brother booked a flight from Colorado to Duluth.

It was late in rural Arkansas, and Lisa's parents were obviously alarmed. They determined the quickest way to reach their daughter was to pack a bag, get in their car, and start the long drive to Duluth.

22

A DESERTED CAMPSITE

Prairie Portage, the Canadian Border, and the U.S. Side of Basswood Lake

"It was hot, and I was sweating like crazy," Pete Weckman said. He, Duane Whalen, and several stranded boaters were clearing away fallen trees and debris from the mechanized route along Prairie Portage, near the Canadian border. The portage manager, Jeep, was using his tractor and front-end loader to help clear a path through the fallen forest.

"It took us more than an hour," Pete recalled. "Thankfully, we had lots of swampers and Jeep's tractor." Once the portage was finally cleared, the boaters were happy they could get underway. In their exuberance, some began hugging Pete, Duane, and Jeep.

At this point, it was around 7:00 p.m. "I just talked to a few people briefly," Pete said. "Of course, everybody had a story of how that wind affected them. Either they were out fishing and their boat flipped over or they were camping and trees came down on their tents, and everything else. But they all said, 'That's it. We're getting out of here.'"

Given the stories he was hearing and the destruction he'd already seen, Pete feared the worst: "I didn't know if we were going to find dead bodies, or what to expect." The boaters waiting on the Basswood side of the divide were anxious to get hauled across the truck portage and be on their way home. "There were literally hundreds of people exiting the wilderness right in front of me. They were going to get out because now Prairie Portage was open and they were going to get to their vehicles."

Pete related what he knew about the roads—that they might be blocked. But at least, he told them, you'll be headed in the right direction.

Until now the Forest Service radio in Pete's boat had had spotty reception. While they were coming into Basswood Lake's Inlet Bay they had tried to call out a few times but could only reach static. They had heard the Forest Service Beaver planes periodically going over. Now they heard another, headed on a search-and-rescue run, and as it passed over they heard some radio chatter from the pilot.

Pete got on and talked about the destruction he'd seen, the clearing of Prairie Portage, and that visitors were starting to stream out of the wilderness. The pilot told Pete that back at dispatch and the Ely Service Center they had received numerous emergency cell phone calls from people with potential first aid issues.

The pilot said there had been some calls from the Washington Island area on Basswood Lake. Pete said he and Duane were headed that way, checking campsites and portages along the way to make sure campers, if they found any, were still alive.

As they continued through Inlet Bay and then turned their boat west-southwest down the length of Basswood Lake, they passed Green Island, to the north, and continued down the long waterway toward the distant Washington Island. Along that route they checked numerous campsites, and at one, Pete ran into one of his Ely neighbors, a man who spent a lot of time in wilderness. They stopped to make sure he was okay.

"That's the worst storm I've ever been in," Pete's neighbor said.

"Fortunately, he didn't have too much damage," Pete recalled. "A few rain flies that were ripped. But overall, he was doing pretty good."

Of course, like everyone else, he wanted to share his perspective on the storm's ferocity and the havoc it wreaked. Pete told him they needed to head farther down the lake, to check on others.

"You had to cut people off," Pete explained. "We told them we were heading west to make sure other folks were okay."

It was getting late in the day, but at this time of year Pete Weckman knew sunset was around 9:00. He still had time. "Besides," he said, "I know all the rock piles and islands and potential hazards. My comfort level being out on the water was still there. And I knew I had a ways to go to get to Washington Island."

Pete and Duane continued to make their way in a west-southwesterly direction down the length of Basswood Lake. There were plenty of islands and campsites along the way. "So we continued checking on people and parties, and it was more or less an exodus back out of the wilderness," Pete said. "It was starting to get to that dusky darkness out, where you know it's getting close to the time to head back and report."

At this point, from what Pete had seen, he knew the destruction was so extreme it would trigger some level of incident management response. He knew there were probably people still in the wilderness, some possibly in need of medical attention, some possibly stranded because their canoes or boats had been smashed, and some possibly dead. He and Duane had been busy checking as many campsites and other locations as possible in the few hours of light allotted to them.

Given the waning daylight, Pete figured he would check nearby Granchee Island, which was northwest of Norway Island, west of Lincoln Island, and near Washington Island. He knew two men were camping on Granchee, which was a small island with a natural cover and a sand beach. One of the men had a golden retriever. Two days earlier he had visited the two fishermen. He knew one of the men, Pat, who worked for a local outfitter. They had chosen Granchee Island to camp on because it was also populated by beautiful Norway and white pines, covering the top of the island like a natural cathedral. Once he checked on the two fishermen and their dog, he could quickly swing up to Washington Island and see whether there was anyone in need of assistance.

When Pete motored up to the island he was shocked by the scene. "I get to the campsite and it was totally, totally devastated."

The fishermen had two boats. Pete found one of them secured in an island bay and largely untouched and intact. The second was missing. The island was so choked by fallen trees, Pete told Duane he had to try to get up to their camp, near the top of the island, and see whether they were okay.

"Pat!" Pete yelled, as he climbed over trees toward the nearby summit. "Hey! Anybody here?!"

His calls were met with silence.

By now it was after 9:00 p.m., and while there was still light in the western sky, in another hour it would be dark. "I got up to the campsite," Pete said. "There's a big screen tent with a table and stuff and everything is totally smashed." He could see a little farther into the mayhem of huge fallen trees. There was a sleeping tent, also crumpled beneath the trees.

"Nobody was answering. And there's no dog."

Pete figured the fishermen should be at their camp. It was going to be dark soon. He couldn't find any trace of them and feared the worst.

"I had this bad feeling," Pete remembered. "It's almost dark, and I didn't have any more time in the day to search. I knew I was going to run into more stuff on our way back, so we had to leave."

At this point, he decided that as soon as he made it back to the Forest Service center in Ely, he would contact the Lake County sheriff. He would request that the first flight tomorrow morning, which happened at first light, be a flyover of Granchee Island to see whether the men had returned.

Pete knew that long before they returned to their Moose Lake dock, it would be dark. But it was familiar territory. Or at least, it had been, prior to the blowdown. Still, Pete felt certain he could navigate the way south of Prairie Portage in the dark.

But there was one last site he needed to check, up on Washington Island. Full throttle, the two men swung up to the campsite.

"I'm going up that way and I see two people on shore waving for help," Pete said. He and Duane approached, and they saw it was a man and woman in their late twenties.

"Everything okay?" Pete said, nearing the couple.

He learned that when the storm came up they had been in their canoe with all their gear. They had not been wearing their life jackets. When the wind, rain, and waves started, they capsized and almost drowned. The canoe was swamped and they lost all their gear, but they managed to hold on to the canoe and, once the weather subsided, made it to shore. The only items they were able to save were the clothes on their backs and their canoe.

At that point Pete suggested they get into the boat with him and Duane. The man had rented the canoe from an outfitter; Pete told him not to worry about it, that he could pick it up tomorrow and tow it back.

The two happily boarded the boat, and Pete turned up the lake toward Prairie Portage, the engine once again at full throttle.

It took a while for him to navigate back through the portage and then down through the chain of lakes into Moose. During the ride he learned the couple had just gotten married and this was their honeymoon!

By the time they arrived at the Forest Service dock on the southwest side of Moose Lake, it was after ten and dark. Fortunately, people had been busy clearing debris in their absence. They started up the truck, and the four of them were able to get down the cleared Forest Service Road to Moose Lake Road and on to the Fernberg Road.

Since the two newlyweds had nowhere to stay, Pete dropped them off at the Grand Ely Lodge, a fitting venue to spend at least part of a honeymoon.

"She gave me the biggest hug," Pete said, recalling the thankful new bride. "That was a very good way to end that day."

23

THE LONG RIDE

Ely and Duluth

When Vicky Brockman lifted off the waters of Alpine Lake, she felt thankful to be airborne. She would soon be at the Ely hospital, where they could tell her what, exactly, had happened to her. There, she assumed she would receive the medical attention she needed and begin to mend.

But as daylight continued to fade from the eastern horizon, Vicky's passage to her ultimate destination was just beginning. En route to Ely, pilot Pat Loe was cruising above Knife Lake, near the U.S.–Canada border, still awestruck by the devastation, when something below caught his attention.

"It was getting late in the day," remarked Pat. "It was getting toward dark."

He was looking down at the flattened forest when he noticed a flare over Eddy Lake, just south of Knife Lake. He flew lower for a better look.

"I could see people in canoes waving," he recalled. "I circled around. It was a group of Boy Scouts. Adults and a few kids."

Pat quickly determined he had just enough daylight to land, render assistance, if needed, and still return to the sea base before dark.

According to the flight logs he would later share with the Minnesota Interagency Fire Center, he landed on Eddy Lake at 8:48 p.m.

"I thought if it was something severe, I could drop the EMT off and continue on. So, we dropped in there. The scouts were pretty shook up,"

Pat recalled. "They thought they were the only ones who had been hit, so they wanted immediate attention."

Pat quickly explained how widespread the event had been, that their group was not the only group affected. Further, he explained, he already had an injured person—Vicky, who lay in the cargo hold with something seriously wrong—so he could only provide help if someone needed immediate attention.

In the end they determined one of the boys had a broken collarbone. "So," Pat explained, "we grabbed the kid and one of the adults and took off for Ely."

It was 8:58. Thankfully, Pat's stop on Eddy Lake had taken only ten minutes.

He landed on Shagawa Lake with his passengers at 9:17 p.m. "By then it was right on the edge of dark, so we were done for the day."

/ / /

At the sea base a full contingent of passengers deplaned: the EMT who had accompanied Pat to tend to Vicky Brockman; Vicky; the scout with a broken collarbone; and one of the troop's adults. Vicky was still strapped to a backboard stretcher, and it took some work to extract her from the cargo hold and carry her into a waiting ambulance. She was joined by the scout and troop leader.

The Ely-Bloomenson Community Hospital has been serving the Ely area since 1958. In the wake of the blowdown it was busier than usual. Vicky was quickly examined and sent off for an x-ray. "They were getting people to slide me off the gurney," recalled Vicky. "I was surprised to see three young women attendants were given the job." Specifically, all three women had smaller statures. "I didn't think they would be able to lift me." But after getting her unstrapped and sizing up the task, they were more than equal to the effort.

After examining the x-ray, the attending doctor saw that Vicky's injuries required more extensive attention than what could be provided in Ely. She would need to be transported to the region's nearest level-one trauma center, St. Mary's Medical Center in Duluth.

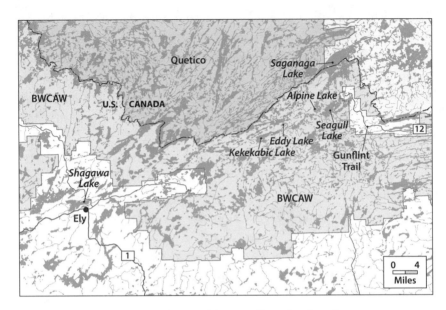

"Finally," Vicky said, "I was able to call my husband."

Somehow, they got a phone to her and she was able to call down to Dinkytown in Minneapolis, where her husband was hosting several neighbors for a Fourth of July celebration. Mike was surprised to hear from Vicky, who wasn't expected out of the woods until the following day. The most severe damage from the midday storm had happened in the Boundary Waters, and because phone lines were down, very little was known about what transpired in the remote wilderness—local news coverage of the storm had been nearly nonexistent. When Vicky told her husband what had happened, and how she had been hurt, and that her injuries were so extensive she needed to be transported to the region's level-one trauma center, Mike was stunned and understandably upset. "He basically got in the car and headed toward Duluth without packing anything," Vicky recalled. "He was pretty panicked at that point, not knowing the full extent of my injuries."

If there could be any comfort in Vicky's words, it was that she had never lost consciousness, and even though they weren't exactly clear yet what had happened or been broken, she was alert and relatively comfortable, albeit in some pain. And she was heading to a medical center where there would be specialists who could give her the attention she needed.

The quickest route from Ely to Duluth is down Highway 1, almost due south for approximately 25 miles until travelers can turn right onto Highway 2, which makes a straight line south into Duluth. That route is approximately 100 miles and takes two hours to drive—at least in daylight when the weather is good. But cover it in darkness, when a second storm was hammering through the area, and it was quite a different ride.

Anyone who has ever driven Highway 1 south of Ely will probably recall the road's most memorable attributes: hills, curves, and drops that make it seem more like a roller-coaster ride than a drive down blacktopped highway.

On this night, Vicky was being shuttled in an ambulance to Duluth. And she wasn't alone. "There was a woman with a concussion in the ambulance with me," Vicky recalled. "I don't know who she was, but she didn't look like she was doing well."

The woman was Lisa Naas, and she was not doing well. She was in and out of consciousness, and there was a chance her neck was broken. There was a chance she could die.

/ / /

As if the state of their health weren't dire enough, on their way to Duluth the two drivers and Vicky and Lisa were hit by another intense storm. "It was dark," recalled Vicky. "And it was scary again because it was another fierce storm. I remember it was raining so heavy that the ambulance drivers struggled to see the road. It was a second wave of that earlier storm, and it was scary."

For the moment, all anyone could do was slow down, drive with care, and hold on. After a while, the weather eased and they continued down the road.

"I was really happy when I made it to the hospital," Vicky said.

Since Vicky's husband had left Minneapolis as soon as she called from Ely, he arrived in Duluth at about the same time as she did. Mike was happy to see her at least conscious and in the care of a level-one trauma center.

With the help of Mike and the hospital staff, Vicky got cleaned up and put to bed. She was given a morphine pump for the pain. The attending doctor at St. Mary's determined her pelvis was crisscrossed with several hairline fractures. When the tree fell, she had been lying on her side with her left arm covering her head. She had extreme bruising along her left arm and her left leg—the latter had a huge, ugly bruise that swelled the tissues in the area to twice their normal size. The physician was as worried about potential clotting from the bruise as about mending the fractures in her pelvis. For now, they decided the best solution was to keep Vicky quiet and let her body heal.

/ / /

At this point the day was, needless to say, beginning to wear on Lisa. Not only was her consciousness still intermittent but the painkillers were strong. "I remember being put in the ambulance. I remember being put in or taken out. I don't think I was the only person in that ambulance. I remember looking and seeing the back window and seeing the rain on the back window."

What Lisa didn't know was that unlike Vicky, she was going to require more treatment than the course of healing prescribed to her ambulance companion. Lisa Naas needed surgery.

24

DEPARTURES

Alpine Lake and Seagull Lake

In the waning light of day, Jan Fiola and Sue Ann Martinson gathered their supplies. Cherish Galvin Davis, Joel Rogness, Maren Olson, and Steve Markey helped the two women pack up their campsite.

Having struggled through the long Seagull-to-Alpine portage, Cherish and her companions knew it would be impossible for the six of them, with their equipment and supplies and especially Sue Ann's ankle, to return through that kind of blowdown. Even though night was coming on, they decided the only viable route for returning to Seagull Lake was the Alpine River.

The base employees were all seasoned wilderness guides. Base rules forbid them from shooting rapids in a canoe, so they were all familiar with tying canoes with a line on the bow and stern and then wading, as best they could, along shoreline shallows. If the forest was clear enough and they could find a path, they could also try portaging along the riverbank. Regardless, once into Seagull, they planned to crowd onto the johnboat and motor back to the Wilderness Canoe Base and the safety of Pinecliff Lodge.

At this point, the mainland campers across the way generously loaned the group one of their three canoes. Since Sue Ann and Jan's canoe had been pulled up on the beach between two boulders before the storm, it was largely unscathed. Now, outfitted with two canoes, the six of them divided their gear and shoved off. Joel and Maren were in one canoe with Sue Ann in the middle, and Cherish, Steve, and Jan paddled across the water in the other, crossing the lake toward the entrance to the Alpine River.

"By the time we got down to the place where we went through the channel, it was not yet totally dark," Sue Ann recalled. "But it was getting dark. The young women had those flashlights that they put on bands on their heads, and they were in the water."

Because it was growing dark, all four base employees affixed headlamps and turned them on. The six travelers, with the four lights piercing the inky stillness of the poststorm wreckage, made an eerie assemblage across the black water.

"So we end up with these two canoes and we get to the top of the rapids," recalled Maren. "We're well-trained wilderness guides. We weren't about to run those rapids in the dark." The six of them moved their canoes with their gear to the side of the river.

"We were just going to hold on to the bow and stern lines and walk our way down the side of the rapids," Maren said.

Now it was nearly full-on dark. The riverbank was thick with fallen trees. The massive rain dump had swollen and deepened the Alpine River.

"It became very clear, very quickly," Maren recalled. "There were so many trees down and the brush was so thick and there was so much water, and it was too deep for us to line the canoes." They could see the riverbank choked with downfall.

"And so"—Maren paused—"we made what was probably an idiotic decision."

Truthfully, in the gloaming, there was no other decision to make. They could not walk the shoreline and they could not wade in the water.

Maren said, "I have been quite cautious my whole life. My forty-something-year-old self realizes how ridiculous running the rapids in the dark was. But that is what we did."

Somehow, the six of them found a steady spot along the shoreline and climbed into the canoes. By now the darkness must have swallowed up the circumference of their headlamps. Squinting down the rapids they presumably saw vague outlines of the torn riverbank on both sides. Maren, who had been on this stretch of water before, must have recognized the waterway she had previously paddled. Obviously, it would have been a radically larger torrent, twice its prior size.

"I suspect we must have had enough of a view of the river that we knew we were okay to run it," Maren said. "Because I don't think we would have done it otherwise."

Cherish, Steve, and Jan set off in one canoe, digging in to aim and steady their craft. Maren, Joel, and Sue Ann pushed off in the second canoe.

"Jan fell going through the rapids," Sue Ann recalled. When she watched Jan fall out of her canoe, she was instantly worried and said so. But Joel, maneuvering the canoe from the stern, told Sue Ann not to worry—that the rapids were shallow enough that Jan could stand and recover. And she did.

"We ran that section of river," Maren said. "And we didn't touch a rock. Which was great, because I don't know what we would have done if we had swamped with [Sue Ann] in our canoe."

When the paddlers reached the bottom of the rapids they were surprised to find Tamara Jackman, one of their base colleagues, waiting for them. Having heard her four friends had embarked on a rescue down on Alpine Lake, Tamara figured they might need some assistance. She had secured one of the base's fishing boats, revved up its 10-horsepower motor, and sped as fast as possible to the place where the Alpine River emptied into Seagull Lake.

"We didn't know Tamara was coming," Maren said. "But that was incredible."

They were all happy for Tamara's timely assistance because they knew piling six people and their gear into one johnboat would slow their return to the base to a crawl.

"We took the canoes and stashed them back in the bay where the start of the long portage is," Maren said. "And then we all got into our boats."

The trees were down along the shoreline of the Seagull Lake bay in which the rescuers stashed their canoes, but they were still near enough to block their view of the broader horizon. When the group finally managed to exit the bay, the view opened up. As if their day had not already been filled with enough challenges, they were unnerved by what they saw.

"There was lightning in three directions," Maren recalled. "Which made us quite nervous. Normally, we would get off the water." But they had seen the damaged forest. Earlier they had climbed over a 105-rod portage and never touched the ground. They had witnessed firsthand how dangerous and unstable the fallen forest could be. So, they decided their only recourse was to head out over the open water and hope they could outrun another round of dangerous weather approaching from the west and south.

/ / /

Fishhook and Dominion Islands are at the far northeastern end of Seagull Lake, approximately 3 miles from the Seagull-to-Alpine portage. The lake is dotted with more than 130 islands. In broad daylight it is difficult water to navigate. Now Cherish had to thread her way along dark channels and shadowy islands in a fully loaded johnboat.

"We started going, but we were so loaded down with people [and gear] we were making really, really slow progress," Maren said. "So after just a little bit we decided we were going to jettison some of our gear."

The group began searching along the shoreline for an opening where they could stash some gear. But it was dark and difficult to see details along the shoreline, especially with all the fallen trees. Finally, Cherish spotted an opening in the forest debris, and the two boats quickly pulled over and began tossing out gear, knowing they would come back for it tomorrow.

Now the night was black. The sky, when they could see it amidst the lightning, was filled with ominous clouds. Behind them the flashes and thunder continued approaching. Though Cherish and her companions had paddled this lake countless times, everything appeared different when they were able to see the nearby shoreline. Prior to the midday storm, a cluster of huge white pines might have marked a particular point along Three Mile Island, a recognizable landmark. Now those trees were gone, or at least lying on the ground. The storm had altered everything, obliterating familiar terrain and along with it the landmarks that had once been their guides.

Fearing that at any moment they might be overtaken by the approaching bad weather, they motored the two boats from island to island.

"Right before we were about to cross a big section of open water," remembered Maren, "we cut the engines and listened for thunder, to try and get a sense of how close the storm was. And then we'd go across the next section of open water."

Eventually, island hopping toward the canoe base, they reached Miles Island. They remembered where some acquaintances were camping and pulled into their site to both check on them and listen for the thunder—to see whether they should stop or continue boating across potentially dangerous water. Their friends had been, like them, counting the seconds between lightning and thunder, and they assured Cherish and the others they still had time to make it.

"And so we kept going," Maren said. "But we were terrified to be out."

While they sensed they were nearing the base, they also recognized the storm behind them was getting close.

Suddenly Cherish, feeling overwhelmed and frightened but still at the johnboat's helm, started singing.

"This young woman began singing 'Kumbaya,'" Sue Ann Martinson remembered. "To calm herself. And she had a nice little voice. It calmed us all."

The boat riders kept looking over their shoulders. They assumed the storm was accompanied by rain. They all knew it was foolhardy to be out on a lake in lightning—the aluminum johnboat and the speedboat skipping over the water were like giant lightning rods.

But they had to keep going, heading in a direction they felt certain would get them in the neighborhood, if not home. It was a race to safety, trying to outrun the weather that was again threatening to overwhelm them.

Suddenly, in the late-night darkness ahead, the sky was illuminated with fireworks. It was, after all, the Fourth of July. Someone on Fishhook Island must have had some skyrockets, and now, whether in celebration of the holiday or in anticipation of their friends and colleagues needing a signal to lead them home, the sky was momentarily lit with a colorful blast that looked like the blossom of a surreal chrysanthemum. The bright flash was like a lighthouse lantern, and Cherish steered toward the welcome beacon.

Within a few minutes, she managed to find the base and pull into the dock. Everyone scrambled out of the boats.

"She did it," recalled Sue Ann. "She did it. She got us there."

The absence of electricity on the base had plunged the area in darkness. It took a while to climb the stairs to Pinecliff, particularly for Sue Ann, who after keeping the pain from her injuries at bay during their tumultuous return to the edge of civilization was now beginning to feel her body's numerous aches. Meanwhile, the storm they had been trying to outrun finally caught up to them.

Maren noted it arrived "within minutes" after they entered the lodge. "It was crazy, how fast the storm hit."

Fortunately, they were inside Pinecliff, where most of the island's inhabitants were spending the night, before another deluge struck.

When they walked into Pinecliff they were greeted by worried director Jim Wiinanen and several others. Jim asked them about the plane, and they all explained about Vicky Brockman being medevacked to safety.

Since the disaster, which according to Sue Ann's broken watch had happened at 12:30 p.m., she and Jan had had little to eat, let alone a moment to think about food. Now that they were safe and inside, they realized they were famished. Staff members had prepared food in the Pinecliff kitchen, which they now shared with the thankful campers. They topped off the satisfying meal with a slice of homemade blueberry pie.

"I think there were also cream puffs," Maren recalled. "I suspect they were trying to use up all the refrigerated food, knowing that we had lost power."

"We were hungry," Sue Ann recalled. "And it was very, very good."

Although there were dozens of base people staying in Pinecliff, the staff found two couches for Sue Ann and Jan, who did not have any spare clothes or equipment, their packs having been left back on a distant shoreline. They settled in for the night, exhausted.

"We were still wet, and there were people all over the floor, sleeping," Sue Ann recalled.

But, as Jen Nagel noted, "It was one of those days when everything's off-kilter and you're not sure what's happening and what time of day it is."

She added, "I have a lot more memory of lightning afterward and all through the evening and I think into the night. It's such a surreal thing when the power's out, even in the woods, in a building that you're used to having power in. I remember we all slept in that building that night. And I remember the building being dark, and at that point the systems, like for fire . . . there probably was an override. You know, things started to beep. It's just a weird thing when buildings that are meant to be powered aren't powered. It's very strange. I know there were a couple of emergency lights that would go on whenever we lost power. That kind of stuff."

"I remember it stormed off and on all night," recalled Maren. "I kept waking up and hearing it storm and thinking, 'I am so glad that we decided to run, to try to get across the lake, because if we hadn't we would have been out there worried that trees were going to fall on us in this storm.'"

As the evening wore on and tilted into the next day, everyone was understandably discombobulated. July 4 had been unsettling for everyone, to say the least. But in the end, most people slept. Especially Sue Ann and Jan.

As Sue Ann recalled, Pinecliff "felt like heaven. It was dry and we were safe."

25

EPIDURAL HEMATOMA

Ely and Duluth

Sometimes the longest journeys happen because there is no other alternative than to keep going. It is difficult to imagine how fatigued Kristina and Mark Schwendinger must have felt after paddling and portaging at breakneck speed to get to their cell phone and find enough coverage to make their call for help. Once the call was made and they were assured Lisa was being treated, they only had one real option: return to their campsite on Lake Polly. Although they could have stayed in their car overnight, they had no food, little water, and no way out given fallen trees were still blocking the roads. Besides, they had told Michelle and Ray Orieux they would return, and their friends had assured them they would have a hot meal waiting. The thought of hot food cinched it, so they returned to their canoe and began paddling north.

Fortunately, there was still plenty of light, and because they had no extra gear they only needed to cross each portage once. They left the Kawishiwi campground around dinnertime. By around 8:00 p.m. they paddled up to their campsite, exhausted.

/ / /

After Lisa had been evacuated by plane, Michelle and Ray busied themselves around camp. "There were trees everywhere," Ray recalled. "You could hardly get to the latrine. It was chaos. Our tent had a branch

168

through it—I put a tarp over it for the night. We moved everything up onto that rock, so we weren't in the woods or by any more trees that could potentially fall on us."

"Trees came down on either side of Mark and Kristina's tent," Michelle recalled. "But it didn't ruin their tent or their fly. We moved them up to the rock, too."

When Mark and Kristina paddled in before sunset, all of them were happy to be reunited. And obviously there was much news to share. But first, Mark and Kristina were anxious to quell their hunger.

Fortunately, Ray and Michelle had prepared a pot of macaroni and cheese, which Mark and Kristina hungrily devoured, washing it down with wine. "We had given them so much grief for hauling that box of merlot into the Boundary Waters, because it had to be heavier than hell," Michelle laughed. "But I was so glad they brought it." And so were Mark and Kristina, who remarked that it was the best mac-and-cheese meal they had ever tasted. Possibly the best merlot, too.

While their campfire burned down and the four survivors finished their last drafts of wine, the adrenaline high that had sustained them for more than eight hours finally began to ebb. Each of them must have felt the onset of heavy weariness. Thankfully, mostly dry tents and sleeping bags awaited them, and before long they had all retired.

"I was tired," Ray confirmed.

"As soon as he lay down," Michelle remembered, "he was out."

Of course, the weather had not yet finished with them. In the middle of the night the same storms that beset Lisa Naas and Vicky Brockman in the ambulance also struck them. The storms were heavy with rain, and the night sky flashed with lightning and pounding thunder.

"My memory was none of us got much sleep that night," Michelle said. "Because of the storm and the lightning and the absolute horror of the day." One apparent exception was her exhausted husband, Ray, who snored loudly beside her.

/ / /

By the time Lisa reached the trauma center in Duluth, it was late and dark. The painkillers and pressure on the inside of her skull were having an increasing effect on her consciousness.

"I really didn't know where I was," Lisa said. "Then I don't remember anything until I was on the operating table. And the anesthetist was trying to put the mask on my face, and I felt like I was in a nightmare and I was trying to push it away. I remember she won. And then I don't remember anything until waking up in ICU."

Lisa was diagnosed with an epidural hematoma on the left side of her brain. The doctors needed to operate immediately in order to relieve pressure on the inside of her skull. After regaining consciousness, and gradually some awareness and memory of what had happened, Lisa remembered her parents and brother had been called. But none of her family had yet arrived.

"My brother was flying in, and of course, because of the storm, he had been rerouted and delayed in Des Moines," Lisa recalled. "My parents got the call maybe seven or eight at night. It was a shock. They got all their stuff together and they probably started driving at midnight." This was before cell phones were ubiquitous, so whenever Lisa's father stopped for gas he would use a pay phone to call the hospital and check on Lisa's status. "One of the times he called, the nurse at the nursing station told him she was sorry, but there was nobody who could come to the phone right now to give him an update."

At that point, Lisa's dad—frustrated, worried, and anxious—requested with dread, "Just tell me if she's still alive."

"Yes," the nurse assured him. "She's still alive. She's in surgery."

26

A TEAM STARTS TO ASSEMBLE

The BWCAW, Western and Eastern Zones

When Kawishiwi District ranger Bruce Slover called Jim Hinds, he said, "Something has happened. I don't know what exactly, but you need to come in to work and help figure this out." Bruce recalled making that call later in the day, after he had listened to Pete Weckman's transmissions, as well as others—and after he had seen first-hand the extent of the damage out on Moose Lake Road.

"I met with District Ranger Slover at his office in Ely," Jim recalled. "We had had little information but began to implement a plan to coordinate with the Lake and St. Louis County Sheriff's Departments and to determine the true nature of the storm incident."

Perhaps it was while Jim was with Bruce that he heard Pat Loe's comment over the radio that the Forest Service Kekekabic cabin looked, as he flew toward it from the west, "like the Little House on the Prairie."

Since it was right on the edge of darkness, Jim knew Pat either would be in for the day or was already docked at the sea base. Hinds wanted to talk with him face-to-face, just to be certain he clearly understood what the pilot had seen over the eastern wilderness. "As Pat pulled the Beaver aircraft up to the dock, I walked out to meet him."

Pat's final flight of the day landed at 9:17. He deplaned Vicky Brockman, the wounded Boy Scout and the scout leader from Eddy Lake, and the EMT.

"We were standing on the dock as he tried to tell me what he had just seen on his flight to the east over the Boundary Waters. While I had a lot of respect for Pat's abilities, I could not grasp what he was telling me. I told him he had to be a little more clear, because if it was really that bad, we would need to order an incident management team."

At this point, Pat put his hand on Jim's shoulder and said, "Starting at Basswood and then to Saganaga and beyond, there are no trees left standing."

"If you know the area," Jim explained, "you can understand the incredible scale of damage he was describing."

At that point Jim returned to Bruce's office. In his absence, Lake County sheriff Steve Peterson had also arrived. "The three of us agreed that an incident management team, IMT, should be ordered," Jim concluded.

/ / /

"The way we found out about the extent of the damage was through Pat Loe, the Beaver pilot," confirmed east zone fire management officer Tim Norman.

After the Tofte holiday parade it had taken a couple hours to get Tim's daughter's and her friend's horses trailered and back to their paddock. Tim and his wife, Diane, were then entertaining guests, so for most of the rest of the day he had been offline, enjoying his holiday. What he didn't know was that electricity and phones were out from midway up the Gunflint Trail (at Trail Center) to its end. "And there was no cell phone coverage in the area, especially back then," he said.

At some point, however, Tim heard word about Pat Loe's last flight of the day, picking up Vicky Brockman on Alpine Lake. "I don't remember how many flights he did that day. But what I do remember is that nobody believed Pat Loe. He was a fairly new pilot at that time. I think he'd started the year before."

Perhaps Tim and others did not know the extent of Pat's background and experience, and the fact that he'd grown up in the area. Pat knew the Boundary Waters, much of it by canoe and on foot. "I don't know if we just didn't take Pat seriously or what. But he came back to the dock in

Ely and said, 'Everything's blown down between here and the Gunflint
Trail.' None of us had any idea of the scale of what he was talking about.
We've talked about that ourselves, many times afterwards, where . . . Pat
had to say it three to four times before people would listen. He'd say,
'No, I'm not kidding. Everything's blown down between here and the
Gunflint Trail.'"

Pat's colleagues' inability to immediately accept his description of
the disaster doubtless had more to do with what he was telling them
than who was saying it. Of everyone on this day who had experienced
some aspect of the disaster, no one had his eyewitness view of it. Beginning at 3:31 in the afternoon he had been flying medevac missions: to
Insula Lake, near the western edge of the wilderness; to Lake Polly, in
the south-central BWCAW, from 5:08 to 6:00; then due north to Hanson
Lake from 7:12 until 7:36. Crisscrossing the Boundary Waters at these
points, he had seen a lot of damage. But it wasn't until his flight to Alpine Lake, from 7:44 until 8:43, that he followed nearly dead center the
storm's path of destruction.

Fellow pilot Wayne Erickson had gotten called up late in the day and
had flown the final mission to evacuate Lisa Naas from Lake Polly from
6:09 to 7:28. Wayne would fly many more missions over the next week
or more.

But on the afternoon and evening of July 4, the only person to have
seen the full breadth and scope of the destruction was Pat Loe. Not surprisingly, it was hard to believe the scale of destruction he was describing.

The Kawishiwi Ranger District headquarters in Ely was large enough to
have a conference room (Room 28, which would subsequently be designated as the incident command headquarters, or IC HQ) and several
other offices. During the evening of July 4, Jody Leidholm met with fellow air support supervisor Pete Tentinger. They had both been called up
by the Minnesota Interagency Fire Center about the same time, earlier
in the afternoon, and Pete had driven over from Bemidji. Now they were
joined by Steve Jakala, the designated Type II operations chief, who had
also been called up earlier in the afternoon. "The initial briefing from

SNF personnel gave us a rough idea of the extent of the blowdown and the probability for serious injuries or fatalities of campers within the blowdown area," Steve said. "So, a rapid, systematic search of the blowdown was paramount."

Steve, Jody, and Pete knew the best way to accomplish that was to get more planes in the air. The wilderness area where most of the storm's destruction had occurred was large, with thousands of campsites and portages on hundreds of lakes. They all needed to be searched.

The aerial search-and-rescue effort would be executed by the Superior National Forest Beaver aircraft that had already been flying missions. With MIFC's assistance, they were also able to call up two state patrol helicopters and five Civil Air Patrol planes, all of which would be onsite in the morning, in Ely and in Grand Marais.

Steve Jakala was in charge of determining the strategy and tactics they'd be using in the air. Pete Tentinger was in charge of air operations on the ground. Jody Leidholm was to coordinate the effort in the air. As the three colleagues discussed what they knew about the extent of the destruction, they began formulating an air search-and-rescue plan. Given what they knew about the storm's aftermath and the extent of the damage, they decided to divide the air attack between the Superior National Forest's western and eastern zones. Steve and Pete would remain in Ely and manage air operations for the western zone, while first thing in the morning, Jody would fly to the Grand Marais airport and lead the aerial search effort from the eastern zone. But they still needed to determine the best way to proceed once they got up over the wilderness.

"I decided that the best way to do the systematic, rapid search of the area was to utilize Fisher maps assigning aircraft to each map area," Steve explained.

> We developed a three-tiered approach. Each CAP [Civil Air Patrol] aircraft with pilot and observer was assigned a Fisher map area to do a systematic, gridded search to identify campsites or portages which may require a closer look for campers needing assistance, injured campers, or fatalities. If a site was identified for a closer look, the second tier of aircraft, a helicopter, would be dispatched to assess rescue needs and nearby helispots to insert rescue person-

nel and if possible evacuate injured. In reality, it would be highly unlikely to find a safe helispot for a helicopter to land due to the amount of blowdown. Finally, if rescue personnel were needed, a Beaver would fly in a saw team, or teams, consisting of a sawyer and swamper and medical personnel. The Beaver would also be used for evacuation of the injured. We also maintained aircraft availability for immediate dispatch if specific information was received regarding reported injuries and location.

"Steve came up with using the Fisher maps with the campsites on them," Jody said. "We decided we would base our search on those maps, checking each site and portage from the air." There was a pause while Jody recalled what happened the next day. Then he added, remembering their initial plan, "Or so we thought."

But for the evening of July 4, it was decided. In the morning, early, all Forest Service employees and others who would be part of an as-yet-to-be officially sanctioned IC Type II team, either as team members or as contractors, would attend a briefing, where they would cover what they knew and what the plan was for July 5. After that meeting, Jody would catch a ride with his pilot, Larry Diffley, to the Grand Marais airport.

"So, at the end of our first meeting the evening of July 4, Jody, Pete, and I had developed a plan to systematically and rapidly search the blowdown area utilizing a three-tier aviation concept that in theory would rapidly evacuate the injured over the entire blowdown area," Steve concluded.

/ / /

Jennifer Rabuck had been at home in Monroe Center, Wisconsin, during the storm on July 4. Monroe Center is in south-central Wisconsin, approximately 80 miles east-northeast of La Crosse. "We didn't have it nearly as bad as they did farther north, but it was still impressive—trees down, tourists and vacationers toyed with, power outages," she said. "Regardless, it wasn't long after the storm blew through that we began hearing accounts of how bad it had hit Minnesota."

Jennifer began working as a park ranger for the U.S. Fish and Wildlife

Service in April 1998 and was stationed at nearby Necedah National Wildlife Refuge. Interested in taking on additional duties, she enrolled in the public information officer (PIO) training course in February 1999 in Duluth. Her first PIO assignment was the following month.

According to the Federal Emergency Management Agency (FEMA) Emergency Management Institute, the "PIO training program is designed to provide PIOs with the essential knowledge, skills, and abilities to support proper decision-making by delivering the right message, to the right people, at the right time." In practice, it can be a tricky business. PIOs act as crucial gatekeepers of important information. As information officers, their role is to collaborate with key officials and government entities working on a disaster, decide what needs to be shared with the public when, and disseminate it using whatever methods make the most sense for the intended audience.

By early evening on July 4, the storm that had decimated the Boundary Waters was still raging north and east into Canada. But enough was already known about its path of destruction in northeastern Minnesota to suggest the need for a Type II IC team to manage the event. Determining the extent of the destruction was still a work in progress, but early accounts indicated the storm had been significant, and to communicate that significance to the public the team and local authorities would need the help of trained professionals. They were already starting to get inquiries—from interested media and relatives and friends of people who were in the Boundary Waters. Word was just starting to spread that some kind of wind event had happened up north, but the public was unclear about what, exactly, had occurred. Consequently, someone—probably at MIFC—requested a PIO.

MIFC was unable to fill the need for another PIO using a Minnesota resource, so staff called the sister organization in Wisconsin, which contacted Jennifer. "I was told to go to Ely as soon as possible and get an in-brief," Jennifer explained. She had just enough time to alert her workplace of her pending temporary reassignment and pack a bag. Before first light, she would be on her way to Ely.

/ / /

By the time Pete Weckman and Duane Whalen returned to the Ely Service Center, it was nearly 11:00 p.m. While Duane headed home, Pete got word of a meeting being held at the nearby Forest Service HQ. Pete decided he would pay whoever was there a visit and share what he had seen that day. Also he knew pilots would be heading out at first light. He wanted to make sure they checked Granchee Island on Basswood Lake, where he knew two men and a dog were missing.

"Of course, there were quite a few people starting to file in with incidents," Pete said. Present were Ralph Bonde, Bruce Slover, Jim Hinds, Steve Peterson, Steve Jakala, Chip Elkins, and others. They were beginning to develop a plan for the following day.

After Pete shared details about his day, he requested that the next morning the first flyover include a check of Granchee Island, to see whether they could spot anyone alive. They assured him they would.

/ / /

Late in the day on July 4, Ralph Bonde et al. knew a Type II team would be formally called up. In response, someone retrieved their documentation regarding incident briefings, the *Agency Administrative Briefing*. It was mostly a form with nine pages of questions and blanks that needed to be completed. "The document . . . is part of a standardized-format briefing package that an agency would provide to an incoming Type II team," explained Jim Hinds.

This evening, the document was completed by hand. But it's unclear who the authors were. "Who filled out the form?" Jim wondered after viewing a copy of some of the pages of the completed form. "While I have filled them out several times, I did not do this one. In this instance, there appears to be two or three sets of handwriting, so . . ." Regardless of who completed the Agency Administrative Briefing, when a Type II team was formally summoned, they wanted to be ready.

The top of the form began with a few brief instructions, indicating the document should be completed "as soon as possible after arrival of all *General Staff* members on the fire team." The typical incident for northern Minnesota almost always involves a forest fire, hence the reference to the "fire team." But the same briefing form is used for any kind of incident—in this case, a meteorological event.

The first items on the list were under the heading "General" and included "Incident Name," "approximate size of incident," "name of local Incident Commander," "incident camp location," "other incidents on forest," and a few other subheadings. For the incident name, someone wrote "Lake Co S&R." There were nine pages to complete, and it was presumably late in the day—likely they could not think of a more appropriate name. But they also clearly knew "Lake County search and rescue" was probably not the best name for the incident, so they added "need a new name" next to this temporary name. The local incident commander was listed as Jim Hinds, while the incident camp location was the Ely Service Center. One of the people filling in the blanks penned "Cook Co." after "Other incidents on forest."

"For the blowdown incident," Jim Hinds recalled, "I was listed as the incident commander in the briefing package since that was essentially my role from the beginning of the incident up until the point that a Type II team would assume responsibility for the incident. It was obvious from the beginning that a lot was involved. In other words, someone is the IC until the team arrives, regardless of complexity."

The responses written on this initial report's pages reflect what little was known about the event. For example, for the approximate size of the incident (in acres), someone wrote "100,000 +/–." Eventually, it would be determined that the size of the impacted area was approximately 500,000 acres. At this point officials knew it had impacted St. Louis County as well as Cook County to the east. Lake County sat between those two counties, and its absence on the form must have been simple oversight. Another section of the report identifies the agency representatives as Steve Peterson and Bruce Slover. Obviously, whoever completed the form knew Lake County had been affected, because they knew Steve Peterson had already been working on search and rescue in his county, in and around the BWCAW.

There are plenty of other sketchy details in this initial report, including under "Priorities for control." Here someone wrote, "1—S&R— a) campsites b) portages c) entry pts, 2—portage & campsite cleanup, 3—road cleanup." Throughout the next two weeks of the more official

Type II team daily incident plans, these control objectives would be more formally stated but remain largely unchanged.

/ / /

When Steve Schug, the wilderness program manager for the Tofte and Gunflint Districts, was pulled from his Tofte Fourth of July celebration to start answering calls at the ranger station, he didn't have any idea what was happening. A rough storm with rain and wind had blown through Tofte earlier, but it paled in comparison to what had happened farther north. Of course, with no cell phone coverage in the wilderness or along the Gunflint Trail, and with the land lines and electricity knocked out, word was spreading slowly.

"I tried to get as much information as I could," Steve said, recalling the afternoon and evening of July 4. "One thing I became aware of quickly . . . all roads leading up to the wilderness had been impacted by the storm." Throughout the day, as accounts trickled out of the impacted areas, it became clear that deeper into and near the wilderness, trees were down on all the roads. That was true from Trail Center to the end of the Gunflint Trail as well as the western parts of the Sawbill Trail out of Tofte and the other Forest Service roads feeding the south central BWCAW. "People couldn't get there," Steve recalled, "and people couldn't get out of there."

As unbelievable as the accounts were, one thing was apparent: people in the wilderness needed help, and the roads leading up to and into the wilderness needed to be clear.

"I talked with Brian Henry, our timber manager," Steve said. "Within a few hours we had local loggers out on the roads with their clamshells picking up logs and getting roads open."

/ / /

East zone fire management officer Tim Norman was occupied with family the afternoon and evening of July 4. He was on holiday. "I still didn't know there was anything going on in the BWCAW," Tim recalled. "Although I vaguely remember something going out over the pager."

Later, after dark, a second storm blew through Tofte and the surrounding region. This one had plenty of lightning, thunder, and rain. "That hit Tofte the hardest," Tim said. "We got 8 inches of rain. Later on that night. It pretty much took down the highways around here. It took out the Caribou River bridge. Highway 61 was shut down. Carlton Creek between us and Sawtooth Outfitters ended up going right over the road, washing out big rocks and gravel. It took out some 10-foot-diameter culverts on some of the roads. It took out a whole section of FS road 166."

Tim was a member of the Tofte Volunteer Fire Department. As part of his volunteer role, he "got paged out in the middle of the night to block off Highway 61." The massive rains washed bowling-ball-sized boulders and other debris over the road. Until it could be cleared, it was a serious traffic hazard. "We took our fire truck and put all our lights on and parked it across the highway in front of Bluefin Bay Resort."

The resort manager hopped into a skid loader and began pushing debris off the road. Water was still running over the highway.

"While we were down there a flatbed trailer came barreling through. It couldn't quite see all the debris. There's a low spot in the road in front of Bluefin." When the truck ran over the boulders, "you could see sparks fly," Tim remembered. "The cab was twisted one way and the flatbed another way. But eventually he got it back under control."

/ / /

Sometime in the middle of the night Steve Schug, Tim Norman, and their boss, Jo Barnier, all got word—either by pager or phone—that they should be at the Grand Marais Forest Service office by 6:00 a.m. There was going to be a conference call about what had happened (at least what they knew of it) and what needed to happen next with the wilderness. Information was still sketchy, and plans were evolving. But as darkness settled over the storm-ravaged wilderness, everyone hoped that anyone still trapped in the fallen forest and in need of assistance was at least for the moment safe, and that they could hold on until first light.

27

MAKING A PLAN

Duluth, Minnesota

After the fireworks in Duluth's Canal Park ended, Jim Sanders met deputy supervisor Tom Wagner at Superior National Forest headquarters. It was well after dark. They made the call to Jim Thomas at the Minnesota Interagency Fire Center, but he was only slightly more informed about what, exactly, had happened. Secondhand accounts suggested a catastrophic wind event had seriously impacted the Boundary Waters and other parts of the Superior National Forest. At this point, after dark, the U.S. Forest Service Beaver planes had been grounded, but they had flown several missions throughout the afternoon and early evening, almost all involving medevacs. The pilots reported massive destruction in the wilderness. And they would return to the skies at first light—there were still injured parties that needed to be airlifted out. They should know more tomorrow. In response to what they were hearing, Kawishiwi District ranger Bruce Slover had arranged to fly over the area at first light. He would base next steps on what he saw from the air.

Because details were still sketchy, there had not yet been an official determination of how the SNF, county governments, and others should respond to what had happened in and around the Boundary Waters area. Obviously, several SNF wilderness rangers and other employees, as well as county law enforcement, were already engaged. But Jim Sanders knew an official declaration would be needed if they wanted to address whatever happened in a concerted, organized, and resource-appropriate manner.

/ / /

The primary responsibility of MIFC, which was part of the National Incident Command System (NICS), was to coordinate responses to forest fires and other emergencies.

One of the most important duties of a forest supervisor like Jim is determining the level of resources that should be brought to bear on a disaster like the one that had just happened in the BWCAW and surrounding forest. To address many of the issues arising out of the catastrophe they would need people, equipment, financial support, and numerous other resources. They would also need an experienced team to organize and lead the effort. For Jim, that meant being guided by the Incident Management System.

The organizational approach to addressing incidents involves five possible levels. A Type V incident might involve dousing an untended campfire or some similar low-level emergency, while a Type I incident involves major disasters such as hurricanes, tornadoes, forest fires, and the like. Type II and I incidents need to be managed by professionals with the experience, education, and certifications required to lead large responses to significant disasters. A Type I incident is organized, staffed, and managed at the national level. Only Jim Sanders, or someone higher up in the USFS, could call up a Type I response. A Type II incident could be managed at the state level, leveraging existing state resources, and could be requested by district rangers like Bruce Slover.

"We had three Type II teams available right here in Minnesota," Jim explained. "We knew we had a large event. We knew we had injuries. We knew it was extensive. So, it was easy to make the call for a Type II team, one of which was local to the area. Once I got on-site and we knew more about the magnitude of the event, it would be easy to scale the team accordingly."

MIFC let Jim and Tom know the current Type II team on call was led by Ralph Bonde in Ely. Jim knew this team would be perfect. Ralph was one of his most senior SNF employees in the Ely Forest Service office—he had been an agency employee for thirty-five years, working in a variety of capacities throughout the service.

The Type II team's duties would be divided into six categories: command, finance, logistics, operations, planning, and safety (CFLOPS). Staffing a Type II incident requires certified professionals to lead each of these areas, and these professionals in turn have personnel and equipment resources on which to draw, some more than others, depending on their roles.

Fortunately, most of the people who would occupy the various CFLOPS positions already worked out of the Ely offices or were near enough in the state to be marshaled on short notice. "They're trained to work together," continued Jim. "They know each other well, and they're trained with the objective of bringing organization to a chaotic setting. So, having Ralph call up his team was an easy call to make. It was an investment of time and money. But given that they were local, in northern Minnesota, it was easy to spool them up and have them in place without making a large investment of money."

By the end of Jim's meeting with Tom, back in SNF headquarters in Duluth, they had formulated a plan. Tomorrow they would begin the day with a 6:00 a.m. conference call between MIFC, people on the ground in Ely and Grand Marais, and whoever else needed to be included. The call would be an informal incident command team briefing for all prospective team members. They would cover what they knew and what they were anticipating for the day, July 5.

After that early-morning meeting Tom and Jim were going to split up. Tom would remain in Duluth, at the SNF offices, and manage whatever came up. Meanwhile, Jim was headed to Ely. He knew he had to get on the ground, meet with his district ranger and other potential members of the Type II team, and begin hearing firsthand what those nearest the disaster had seen. Once he was elbow deep in the incident, he would have a clearer sense of what was needed and how he could help.

/ / /

Back near the end of the Gunflint Trail, Gunflint Lodge and Outfitters owner Bruce Kerfoot had spent the afternoon making sure his mother, Justine, could get out of her cabin and doing a safety check of his employees, guests, and others on Gunflint Lake. He and his lead guide, Kevin Walsh, had split up and taken two boats in either direction on the lake, checking on cabin owners and any recreators who might have been caught in the storm. "Most of the summer homeowners were up over the Fourth of July," recalled Bruce. "And the resorts and outfitters were full. So, we made the rounds, and much to our surprise we assisted very few people. I mean, yes, we found canoes sailing down the lake empty and we freaked out a little bit, but then it turned out everyone had gotten to shore."

People shared their stories with Bruce and Kevin, explaining how they would hunker down under a tree, and then the tree would break off or be pulled up by the roots and toppled. Then they would move to the next tree, and the next, and so on. Some people reported that their canoes had been picked up and sailed off into the air, sometimes as much as a quarter mile before they toppled back to the lake's churning surface.

"We found people shivering on barren points with all the vegetation completely flattened, and they were just standing, kind of in shock," Bruce said. They checked on all the cabin owners, and while all had trees down, many having fallen on their cabins or other nearby structures, they found no one seriously injured. They found owners who were stunned, amazed, and still struggling to understand what they had just endured. But otherwise, they were okay.

By the time Bruce had finished doing safety checks, retrieving and bailing out boats, digging out his mother, assessing his 50 miles of trails, and more, the day was getting late. Obviously, he had seen enough to know he needed some serious help. Somehow, he still had access to an operational phone.

Gunflint Lodge and Outfitters is a large resort, with plenty of structures, septic systems, roads, and other types of property needing to be built or maintained. Over the years Bruce had struck up a partnership with a local contractor, David, in Grand Marais. David had access to bulldozers, trucks, all kinds of logging gear and other types of equipment, and employees who knew how to use them.

Bruce knew that every Fourth of July, David hosted an informal family reunion at their house in Grand Marais. "Multigenerations of an old Scandinavian family would come back to Grand Marais for the confab with the relatives," explained Bruce. The entire extended family would gather and have a huge picnic and later in the day watch parades and fireworks.

Fortuitously for Bruce's contractor friend and his reunion, the day in Grand Marais had been fine. And because almost everyone at the end of the Gunflint Trail had their electricity and phone service cut off, there were only a handful of people in town who had any idea about the catastrophe that had happened northwest of them.

Late in the day, Bruce managed to get his contractor friend on the phone. "I chased him down and I said to him, 'I need every piece of equipment you own up here as soon as you can bring it tomorrow,'" Bruce recalled. "He said, 'You're just jazzin' me up. It's a nice sunny day down here.' And I said, 'David, I'm serious. Dead serious. I need everything you've got.' Finally, I was able to convince him, and he agreed that first thing tomorrow, he would bring everything he had."

PART III

JULY 5-19

SEARCH, RESCUE, AND ASSESSMENT

28

LIFTOFF

July 5, 1999
Ely, Grand Marais, and the BWCAW

On the morning of July 5, 1999, the sun rose over northern Minnesota at 5:21 a.m. Numerous people awoke at or before dawn. Since the U.S. Forest Service Beaver pilots could take off after first light, Pat Loe and Wayne Erickson were doubtless among them. On one of their first flights of the morning they would carry district ranger Bruce Slover, law enforcement officer Chip Elkins, and Lake County sheriff Steve Peterson over the forest to get a bird's-eye view of the damage. While Superior National Forest supervisor Jim Sanders, Bruce Slover's boss, would be coming to Ely later that morning, Bruce and Steve had the authority to confirm the call-up for a Type II Minnesota Incident Command Center team.

"Search and rescue is a county responsibility," Bruce explained. "It was important to get the Lake County sheriff airborne to see the extent of the damage. My recollection is that Chip arranged that. We needed to encourage the sheriff to request an incident command team."

By now the Minnesota Interagency Fire Center had already summoned several members of the eventual Type II team, and others. And people all over northeastern Minnesota were rising to address the needs of a dramatically damaged world. While many were awake in Ely, others were rising in the Superior National Forest's eastern zone, including Tim Norman, Steve Schug, and Gunflint District ranger Jo Barnier. Well before 6:00 a.m. Tim, Steve, Jo, and others were on their way to the Forest Service offices in Grand Marais.

"I ended up going into the office about 5:30," Tim Norman recalled. "And there was that truck broke down on the side of the highway." He had seen the truck barrel through a boulder-strewn low spot in front of Bluefin Bay Resort the night before. Sparks had flown from the truck's undercarriage. "He busted up good underneath that truck. Highway 61 looked like a war zone with trees down and boulders. I just barely made it into the Gunflint office in Grand Marais." But, Tim remembered, "At that time all the significant damage was up the Gunflint Trail."

Because of the trajectory of the storm, Grand Marais had largely been spared. The town on the edge of Lake Superior had experienced some momentary bad weather, but nothing extreme or unusual for that time of year. In fact, because of the lake effect, July 4 had been a pretty nice day. Except for Cook County dispatch and others who had been notified, like Jim and Rebecca Wiinanen, most people had no idea of the destruction that beset the Gunflint Trail from Trail Center to its end, 57 miles northwest of Grand Marais.

For the morning's conference call Tim Norman, Steve Schug, Jo Barnier, probably wilderness rangers Duane Cihlar and Tom Kaffine, and others took over a large conference room in the Forest Service Grand Marais office. Since the team assembling in the Ely office had already heard from pilot Pat Loe, rangers Nicole Selmer and Pete Weckman, and others, people there had more awareness of the breadth and depth of the damage than those gathered in Grand Marais. During the call the emphasis was undoubtedly on brevity and the immediate need for search and rescue. They must have shared their perspectives on the extent of the damage and discussed the likelihood of Ralph Bonde's Type II team being formally called up later that day. If Jim and Tom were both on the call (very likely), Jim probably mentioned he would be up in Ely later that morning. Because of the phone calls Steve Schug had fielded the day before, he was already working to dispatch loggers and road crews up the various roads in and around the SNF east zone to continue and intensify the cleanup.

Typically, these meetings are led by the operations chief, which for the time being was Steve Jakala, at least informally. On the other hand, because the formal team had not yet been called up, it could have been led by the eventual incident commander, Ralph Bonde. Regardless, any of the de facto division heads—air attack supervisor Jody Leidholm, safety officer Bob Brittain, information officer Tom Kroll, planning chief Mark Carlstrom, logistics chief Dennis Cameron, finance chief Sharon Karr, or any of several other incident leaders—could have discussed what they knew and, most importantly, what they planned for the day.

Again, they needed to be brief because they knew people were still in harm's way. They would have quickly covered what they knew about what happened and the steps that had already been taken to clear roads, assess damage, and perform search and rescue. They would have stressed the need to get into the wilderness as soon as possible to make sure anyone who needed help could get it, and to make sure no one had died.

/ / /

Bruce Slover, Chip Elkins, and Steve Peterson missed the early-morning conference call. By approximately 5:30 a.m. the three were headed to the Forest Service sea base on Shagawa Lake. There they met Wayne Erickson and spent time getting situated for their flight and talking about what section of the forest they should fly over to get the best sense of the storm's aftermath. They all agreed that if they headed straight out toward the Gunflint Trail they would have a good sense of what happened to the heart of the BWCAW.

First, remembering Pete Weckman's request for an early flyover of Granchee Island on Basswood Lake, they decided they would make a reconnaissance flight of the campsite. They hoped to glimpse two men, two boats, and a dog.

By 6:29 a.m., Wayne, carrying Bruce, Chip, and Steve, nosed his Beaver plane down the length of Shagawa Lake and was soon airborne. Within minutes they were viewing plenty of forest destruction. When they flew over Basswood Lake, Wayne angled over Granchee Island. As they swung low over the island they saw two boats, a dog, and two men waving from the devastated shoreline.

/ / /

"I was out before dawn," Pete Weckman recalled about the morning of July 5. Pete was making the same circuit he had made the previous day. This time he had a different partner, and they had chainsaws. They were heading up the Moose Lake chain, crossing the portage, and then would boat down into Basswood to search more campsites and find out what happened to Pete's two acquaintances whose Granchee Island campsite had been destroyed. He hoped they somehow survived and were alive.

Pete's boat had access to a Forest Service radio. "I was in radio contact when they flew over Granchee Island," he said. "I have a headset that I can listen to when I'm operating the motor. And I made contact with our pilot and he said, yes, there was a boat there, and there were two people with a dog. And I said, 'Thank you. I will be heading to the island to find out what the story is.'"

/ / /

Once Bruce, Chip, and Steve confirmed the safety of the two islanders, they continued in the Beaver plane down Knife Lake toward the Gunflint Trail. "What I saw was utter devastation from horizon to horizon," recalled Bruce. "I called the flight off prior to hitting the Gunflint Trail. I had seen all I needed to, to start the process of initiating a team request and to brief my boss, forest supervisor Jim Sanders."

On their return flight to the Ely sea base, Wayne was flying over Knife Lake when someone spotted people below waving the plane down. The group was encamped near Knife Lake's Thunder Point. Wayne set down the plane and they taxied to the group to see whether they could assist. It was 7:02.

"We set down on Knife Lake and picked up an injured man," Bruce recalled. "He was ambulatory, but I later learned that he had a cracked vertebra. His friends had repaired a squashed canoe by lashing branches across the gunwales and thwarts. They were packed and were getting ready to paddle out." They took a while helping the injured man and getting him into the plane. By the time they returned to the sea base it was 8:33.

Bruce, Chip, and Steve had all seen enough to know a Type II team was definitely warranted. Official determinations and paperwork still needed to be completed, but later in the day, when Jim Sanders arrived, Bruce and Steve knew what they were going to tell him. The destruction was unimaginable. Not only would they recommend a Type II team be officially called up, but eventually they would suggest the Forest Service ease its restrictions on the use of motorboats, chainsaws, and other mechanized equipment in the wilderness. The destruction they had just witnessed convinced them they would need all the resources (and people) they could possibly muster.

/ / /

The previous evening, operations chief Steve Jakala, air support group supervisor Pete Tentinger, and air attack supervisor Jody Leidholm had met in the Ely Forest Service conference room and figured out the all-important air strategy for July 5. Steve had finalized the strategy, which he referred to as a three-tiered approach involving Fisher maps, the Civil Air Patrol, state patrol helicopters, and Beaver planes. Jody would be managing the effort from the air in the eastern zone, out of the Grand Marais airport, while Pete would manage the west zone search and rescue from the ground in the Ely offices. Consequently, immediately after the Monday-morning briefing, Jody headed to Grand Marais.

Since Jody would be managing the effort from the air, he needed his own pilot and plane. "My aircraft came out of Bemidji—a Beechcraft Baron, 4016A—and the pilot was Larry Diffley, the owner of Bemidji Aviation." Jody had flown with Larry before. "Larry came over bright and early, and when we were done with the briefing in Ely we got airborne." They arrived at the Grand Marais airport around 8:30 a.m.

For their important work over the wilderness, MIFC had called up six aircraft from the Civil Air Patrol. Four would be in the air at all times during the day, at least initially, while two would be held in standby. "The state patrol brought us two helicopters," Jody remembered. "The DNR brought its Beaver plane over and landed it on Devil Track Lake. The game warden's Cessna 185 was also at Devil Track. The plan was to brief everyone in the morning and get the search underway on a lake-by-lake basis with an assignment for each aircraft. There would be four CAP flying at any one time over the entire blowdown area. Two worked out of

Ely and two would fly with me out of Grand Marais." Pete would brief the people out of Ely, and Jody would be in charge of briefing the pilots out of Grand Marais.

After landing at the Grand Marais airport, one of the first people Jody met was Cook County sheriff Dave Wirt. "I could tell he was distressed over the slowness of the response. He thought we should have been going since the break of dawn. He was a little frustrated and understandably anxious."

Sheriff Wirt also told Jody he wanted a deputy to go up in each aircraft, to assist with the search and, if necessary, the eventual rescue. Of course, Jody knew county sheriffs had the primary responsibility for search and rescue. Because much of Cook County was designated federal wilderness, the lines of search-and-rescue responsibility were slightly more ambiguous, but Jody understood the sheriff's concerns, and also why he would want deputies going up in each plane.

"That's no problem," Jody told Dave. "But where are they? They need to be briefed."

"I don't know," Sheriff Wirt said. "What do they need to know?"

"Well, they have to be given a passenger's briefing on the airplane. Do they get airsick? It's windier than heck out there. And it's actually a little outside our operations limitations for a Cessna 172." The Civil Air Patrol was flying single-engine Cessnas. "I'll need to speak with the pilots. Crosswind limitations are borderline for takeoff and landing right now, and that's a pilot's decision. I'm assuming they'll let them go, but there are a few things we need to sort out."

Soon thereafter, the deputies arrived. Jody began speaking with them and discovered none of them had ever been up in an airplane.

When he found out they didn't know whether they got airsick, he suggested they head back to town and pick up some Dramamine from the nearest pharmacy. "I told them it was going to be rough. We had 30- to 40-mile-per-hour wind gusts. We were still in the aftermath of the storm and were on the back side of that low coming around." The deputies took Jody's advice, and one of them headed back to a Grand Marais pharmacy. As Jody was briefing the deputies and getting them squared away, he could feel the sheriff's tension rising. But as the air attack supervisor, Jody's main job was to make sure the search was carried off in a safe fashion so that everyone in the sky was flying in coordinated airspace and no one was running into each other. "And like I said," Jody explained, "weatherwise, we were already pushing the limit. Maybe on a normal flight a pilot might say, 'I'm going to wait for the wind to die down.' But that's why we needed the briefings. To make sure everyone understood their roles. And to make sure the deputies knew the emergency procedures."

Coincident with the deputies' arrival, the CAP pilots and support staff were setting up. Jody had never worked with the Civil Air Patrol. They had set up a communications van to keep in radio contact with their pilots after everyone got airborne. One of the pilots' primary skill sets is search and rescue, which was the main reason they'd been recruited for this effort.

Jody was introduced to the CAP leader and began telling him about the three-tiered strategy he, Pete, and Steve Jakala had come up with the previous night for searching the wilderness. "So I'm talking to him," Jody recalled, "and I'm telling him what the plan is, and he said, 'Nope. Nope. We don't do it that way. We do a grid search.'"

A grid search divides an entire area up into quadrants. Each of the CAP planes has designated quadrants to search. They follow a patterned flyover of each quadrant, searching for anyone who may be in need of assistance, or for any other signs of distress—in this case, smashed campsites, canoes, overturned boats, people trapped on portages, and so forth. When Jody understood what they wanted to do, he said, "But nobody's gonna be in the woods. They're gonna be on the shores of the lakes. At campsites, or . . . there's not going to be anything to look for in between the lakes. Are you sure you want to do that?"

The leader affirmed that they were going to do a grid search: "That's what we're trained to do, and that's what we're going to do."

Jody got on the phone with Steve Jakala and explained that the CAP didn't want to do a lake-by-lake search using Fisher maps. He told Steve they wanted to do a grid search. "Yeah," Steve said. "We're finding that out over here, too." Presumably, Steve and Pete had been told about the grid search by the two CAP pilots flying out of Ely.

"Just go ahead and do the grid search," Steve said.

The deputy returned and Jody spoke with all of the deputies about searching from the air. It's not easy to spot people from the air, especially in a forest with as much blowdown as they were going to see. Jody told them to divide the flyover areas into segments, or pie pieces that they could see. Examine that area as well as you can, and then move to the next segment.

Finally, by around 10:00 a.m., they were ready to lift off. Unfortunately, Sheriff Wirt's patience had run out. "He had some words to say to me," Jody recalled. "I told him we're doing the best we can. We can't have another accident. We gotta do this the right way. He'd had plenty of training, too, so he knew I was right on that. But, you know, they'd already been dealing with search and rescue for several hours. It was understandable that he was anxious."

Jody explained how his air attack supervision unfolded: "We had two CAP aircraft in Ely and two in Grand Marais, and we had frequencies for air to ground . . . if we did have somebody to talk to on the ground. We had an air-to-air frequency for flight coordination. And we had what we call a flight-following frequency, for the CAP leader, for anything they needed, to announce their arrival or landing. And we had state patrol helicopters—trooper five was over in Ely and trooper seven was with me in Grand Marais."

The purpose of the helicopters, Jody explained, was to speak with anyone who needed help on the ground. The helicopters had public address systems. They would land, if possible, or more likely hover low and let stranded people know help was on the way. "They would ask them to signal if there were injuries," Jody said. "Or if there were any fatalities. They didn't come out unless we requested them. We didn't want them flying around because they only had about one and a half hours of fuel onboard. So they were to stay on the ground unless we had a mission for them.

"I took off first, and then the two CAP took off and they roughly penciled out how they were going to do the grid search. When I got in the air, I radioed Ely and told them I was airborne and told them to launch their aircraft. I wanted them to report every fifteen minutes, at a minimum, to me. I think they flew straight north and south grids in the blowdown. I also asked them to call me at a checkpoint when they were turning. They'd call in, like, 'We're at Brule Lake.'"

Each plane had a deputy, and Jody had created manifests for all of them, so he knew who was onboard each aircraft in case any problems arose.

They commenced the search, and over the next ninety minutes Jody fielded calls from the pilots or their onboard deputies. They didn't find much, but occasionally he would make notes about four people down on a particular section of the wilderness, or reports of canoes washed up on shore, with no people around. There were a few instances where they saw overturned boats.

"Believe it or not," Jody said, "within an hour and a half, doing the grid search, we had apparently searched the entire BWCAW. And I thought, that just can't be. We can't have done that."

Everyone landed, and Jody called Steve Jakala over in Ely. "We just searched the whole BWCAW in about one and a half hours," Jody said, incredulous. "That's not adequate. I want to go back and do a lake-by-lake search, like we originally planned."

Steve and Pete Tentinger concurred, and a second search commenced. This time they searched lake by lake using the Fisher maps and found some people who required the assistance of the state trooper helicopters and the Beavers piloted by Pat Loe and Wayne Erickson.

It was an incredibly busy day for Pat, Wayne, and the other pilots in the air. The flight logs turned in to MIFC at the end of the day show Wayne flew over the wilderness ten times on July 5, three flights involving medevacs, and Pat logged five flights, two involving medevacs. In total, they flew 1 hour over St. Louis County, 6.7 hours over Lake County, and 6.1 hours over Cook County, to the east.

Before dusk on July 5, Jody, Pete, and Steve were confident they had made a pretty thorough search of the entire BWCAW and bordering blowdown areas. They had helped some survivors, and they knew in the next day or two they might find others. But for now they felt good about the day's air efforts.

Most important, so far, they had not found a single fatality.

29

EXODUS

July 5, 1999
Lake Polly and Duluth

"The next morning it rained so hard," Kristina said, recalling Monday morning, July 5.

The group on Lake Polly had always planned on departing their campsite and heading home that day. They had jobs and not much vacation time and needed to return to work. But none of them had ever expected they would be leaving in conditions like these, or without their close friend Lisa Naas. All of Lisa's gear remained behind and needed to be portaged out, including her damaged canoe.

"Her canoe still floated," Kristina added. "We just had a line tied to it and we pulled it behind. Then we portaged out." But there was much more to the morning and day than just "portaging out."

"We had to pack Lisa's gear and move all the stuff," Ray said. "Everything. And it was all soaking wet, because it had rained so much . . . like a foot of rain. And on the way out, on every portage, we were walking through a foot of water."

When Ray had first told his friends about portaging into Lake Polly, he explained the portages were marshy and low. Normally, that was a good thing, because parts of it were dry and easily traversed. "But now," Ray said, "it was brutal. We had our boots on and all our gear. Our gear weighed much more than it should have, because now it had like 5 gallons of water on it."

"I remember falling back like a turtle several times," Michelle added. "And then I couldn't get up because the packs were too heavy and it was so wet."

On Monday, everyone was trying to get out of the Boundary Waters. Everyone who had been through the storm had been affected. Even if visitors had originally planned to stay longer, the storm's force and wake of destruction convinced them it was time to leave.

The Schwendingers and the Orieux encountered others on the portages. "There was one guy who helped carry Lisa's canoe," Ray remembered. "He was running back and forth on the portage and he ended up coming and helping us. And making a couple trips, because on the portages we had to double back two or three times because of all the extra gear."

It took a few hours to reach the Kawishiwi campground and their cars. Unfortunately, then they needed to contend with the wilderness roads. "The storm flooded a lot of roads," Ray said. "Even for us leaving a day later, most of the roads were flooded or there were still trees down over a lot of areas."

They affixed Lisa's damaged canoe to the top of her Corolla. Fortunately, they had her keys. Michelle got in behind the wheel, and the three vehicles started down the road in a caravan.

"Ray had that truck, so he would go first," Kristina said. "There were a few other cars watching Ray as the lead car to determine if we could all make it through. We all turned around a few times because some of the roads were impassable."

By early to midafternoon the four weary travelers reached Tofte, on the North Shore. They returned Lisa's damaged canoe to Sawbill Outfitters. "We had to ask forgiveness for it, because it got damaged in the incident," Mark remembered. "The guy at Sawbill Outfitters let us off. He was very nice."

Before leaving Tofte they turned into the local Holiday gas station. Here, they bought much-appreciated snacks, and Michelle made some calls. She found out Lisa had been medevacked to Ely, then taken by ambulance to the level-one trauma center in Duluth and been operated on, but she was apparently okay and recovering.

"We'd been in wilderness for a few days and we were dirty and smelly," Mark said. "And Ray bought Cheetos. He had orange fingers. And he thought, 'What am I going to do with these orange fingers?' And then he thought, 'Eh'—and wiped them on his shirt." At that point they all agreed, after what they had endured for the last twenty-four hours, they could not look any worse, and it did not matter.

Eventually, they arrived at the hospital in Duluth where Lisa was recovering from emergency surgery. She was in ICU but well enough to see visitors. Amazingly, the four not-terribly-clean-friends were allowed in. "We'd just come out of the Boundary Waters after four days," Ray said. "We hadn't showered."

"Yes," Michelle agreed. "We needed to be fumigated. But everyone in the ER was so nice. They let us see her, and it was amazing."

"Her head was shaved," Ray remembered. "And she had this huge question-mark stitch on the side of her head."

"She looked like Uncle Fester from the Addams Family," Michelle laughed.

"The visit," Lisa remembered, "was awesome. I don't know who said it, but someone said, 'Oh, I like your hat.' And I said, 'I have a hat?' And I reached my hand up and yes, there was a hat there. I had a hat that they put on newborn babies. They had put it on my head to keep me warm."

30

FIRST DETAILS

July 5, 1999
Ely and the BWCAW

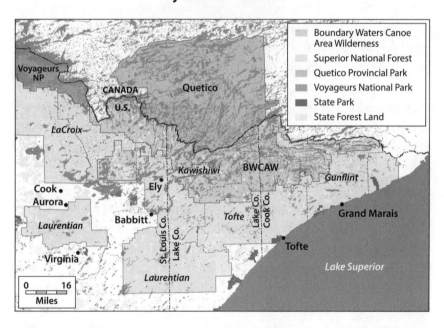

S uperior National Forest supervisor Jim Sanders had risen early on
July 5. The Duluth morning was shrouded in light rain. Northern
Minnesota can be cool in the morning, even in the middle of summer, and the temperature at 5:00 a.m. was just 64 degrees. When Jim
arose, he could feel it was going to be a seasonally normal day. Indeed,

in Ely it would be cloudy, warm, and a little breezy, but more or less typical for this time of year, belying the catastrophic wind event that less than eighteen hours earlier had devastated northeast Minnesota, southern Canada, and hundreds of miles east, all the way into Maine.

Jim and Tom Wagner participated in the 6:00 a.m. briefing call. Afterward, even though it was a Forest Service holiday, Jim managed to commission a car from the vehicle pool. He was on the road early, eager to get north to where he could begin to acquire a sense of what, exactly, had happened. He knew that it was a large event and that there were people in the woods with injuries. The wounded would need to be medevacked out, and that meant the Ely air base and Grand Marais airport would be busy. He understood a concerted air attack was already in process, and as part of that effort the Forest Service Beavers needed to answer their emergency calls. But Jim knew that once the injured were evacuated and cared for, flying over the wilderness in a Beaver would be the best way to get an extensive bird's-eye view of what, exactly, had occurred.

Ely is known throughout the state and country as the gateway to the west and north sections of the BWCAW. The small town is home to numerous outfitters, hotels, restaurants, retail stores, museums, and more, almost all of which reference the wilderness in some way, shape, or form. When Jim arrived, he would be checking into the Paddle Inn and possibly having a meal at the Chocolate Moose.

On his drive north Jim had time to consider his day. He had been the SNF forest supervisor long enough to have a clear understanding of the size and scope of both the 3.9-million-acre forest and the 1-million-acre BWCAW inside it. The SNF is divided into five ranger districts: from west to east, the LaCroix, Laurentian, Kawishiwi, Tofte, and Gunflint. Each of the districts is managed by a district ranger, who in turn has a staff of administrative personnel, and several wilderness rangers, each responsible for patrolling specific parts of their ranger district.

The BWCAW stretches nearly 150 miles along the international border with Canada, and sizeable sections reside within four of the SNF's five ranger districts. The far northwestern side of the wilderness sits in the LaCroix Ranger District. Details about the breadth, intensity, and impact of the storm were still sketchy, but in time Jim and the others would come to understand the LaCroix District had incurred damage in and around the Trout Lake area but was otherwise unscathed. The storm had apparently skipped over a large forest section, returning to the ground near Moose Lake. As it moved east, the Kawishiwi, Tofte, and Gunflint Ranger Districts had been severely impacted. In the south-central BWCAW, the Laurentian Ranger District had also sustained intermittent damage.

Even though the BWCAW is wilderness, it contains plenty of infrastructure for which the SNF is responsible. Within the 1 million acres there are more than two thousand designated campsites, twelve extensive hiking trails, and at least 1,200 canoe routes, all connected via a series of rivers, lakes, and portages. From a civil government perspective, the BWCAW also resides in the northern sections of St. Louis, Lake, and Cook Counties. Each county is in part managed by elected county commissioners.

Jim knew, as time permitted and he learned more about the storm remnants, he would need to reach out to both his SNF district rangers and the relevant county law enforcement officers and commissioners. He knew some of them would be joining him today in Ely. To begin, they all needed to get much more information about the event. Whatever Jim and his team decided would be based on what they learned today, tomorrow, and through the next few weeks.

During this time he also contacted his superiors in the USFS Region 9 office in Milwaukee. Since it was a holiday, he spoke with the on-duty deputy regional forester, Ruth Voltz. Fortunately, she had some knowledge of, and experience with, wind events. At this early stage, Jim let her know that something significant had happened in northern Minnesota and that a Type II team might be called up to address it. He said he would keep the regional office informed. Jim also contacted the primary county commissioners in each affected county and let them know what was being done.

The beauty of the incident command system was its flexibility. If Jim discovered the event to be less disastrous than preliminary reports, he and his team members could decide a smaller Type III team could manage the incident. If his team recommended a more robust Type I incident response, the forest supervisor, who was the only person in the SNF senior enough to authorize that level of response, would be on hand to do so.

/ / /

By late morning Jim climbed the stairs to the second floor of the Forest Service district offices. Several of the Kawishiwi District leaders were assembled, including Bruce Slover, as was Gunflint District ranger Jo Barnier. Throughout the rest of the day Jim asked questions, listened, watched, and took copious notes.

Gradually, information about the event trickled in, none of it good. Bruce, Chip Elkins, and Sheriff Steve Peterson shared what they had seen during their early-morning reconnaissance flight. The concerted air attack, involving Civil Air Patrol and other aircraft, was getting underway. The Beaver planes were running medevacs. When the pilots returned, they reported breathtaking devastation, with extensive parts of the boreal forest leveled, as though a massive sickle had swept across the land and felled several million trees. Even more troubling, every time the pilots returned from a mission, they reported seeing more people needing help.

"At this point," Jim said, "we were trying to identify and locate all our wilderness rangers and figure out where they were located and how they could best be deployed into the affected areas. If we could get them in there, they could survey the damage and help coordinate a response for people on the ground."

As the day progressed, Room 28 of the Kawishiwi Ranger District became peopled with many of the representatives necessary to make some early key decisions. Jim was joined by Dave Wirt, Ed Lerer from the Department of Emergency Management, several other members of what would become the Type II overhead team, and a representative from the Civil Air Patrol.

By 4:00 p.m. the obvious decision was made to formalize the call-up of a Type II team to manage the response to the disaster. The original request was made by the Lake County Sheriff's Office. The proper documentation was drawn up, giving Ralph Bonde the authority he needed to summon and begin working with his team. The temporary name, "Lake Co S&R," that had been written on the previous day's administrative briefing, was now changed to "4th of July Incident."

DELEGATION OF AUTHORITY

Ralph Bonde is assigned as Incident Commander on the 4th *of July Incident*. You have full authority and responsibility for managing the fire suppression activities within the framework of law, agency policy, and direction provided in the attached Overhead Briefing Direction and Guidelines.

Your primary responsibility is to organize and direct your allocated resources for efficient and effective operations. You are accountable to me or the designated representative listed on the guidelines sheet.

Specific direction for the incident covering management and environmental concerns is listed:

1. Conduct a site-by-site review of the campsites and portages for injured parties
2. Assess and open roads and facilities
3. Assess and open wilderness portages
4. Assess and open wilderness campsites
5. Maintain wilderness values
6. Low level flight operations in support of search and rescue is authorized
7. Mechanized equipment use (saws, boats) in support of search and rescue is authorized

Bruce Slover, Forest Service, and Jo Barnier, Forest Service, will represent me on any occasion that I am not immediately available.

The delegation was signed by Cook County sheriff Dave Wirt, Lake County sheriff Steve Peterson, and forest supervisor Jim Sanders.

The document was important for a few reasons. First, the immediate concern was the welfare of everyone in the wilderness in the wake of the storm blowing across them. Everyone in this meeting already knew many injured people had been medevacked to safety. They also knew those search-and-rescue flights were ongoing, and they would find more injured people needing assistance. At this point everyone also felt certain they would find bodies, though none had yet been found.

Again, county sheriffs were responsible for search-and-rescue in Minnesota, so the initial responsibility for calling up the Type II team logically arose from county sheriffs—in this case, Steve Peterson and Dave Wirt. Both had been up in planes over the wilderness and had glimpsed the extent of the damage.

Also, everyone in the room was familiar with the Forest Service regulations prohibiting the use of mechanized saws and other equipment in the Boundary Waters. When wilderness rangers like Nicole Selmer worked on campsites and portages, they traveled to those sites using paddles and canoes, and the tools they used to repair those wilderness areas were primitive—hand saws, shovels, buckets, and the like. But desperate times called for desperate measures. Jim Sanders had heard enough throughout the day to make a momentous decision. It was not an easy one to make, and it would ultimately be reviewed by Jim's superiors in Region 9, and perhaps in Washington, D.C. But what he had heard throughout Monday, July 5, convinced him they needed to relax the usual regulations governing the use of power tools and mechanized vehicles in the wilderness, at least for the time being.

The decision is important enough to require some kind of official documentation. Accordingly, Jim penned a letter on SNF letterhead to the leadership team and Ralph Bonde, incident commander. In part, it read:

> This letter is to document my decision to allow the use of motorized equipment and airplanes within the Boundary Waters Canoe Area Wilderness for emergency aerial and ground search and rescue efforts. This search and rescue effort is necessary in response to the large wind and rain event that occurred in northern Minnesota on July 4, 1999. I have authorized the following activities to occur because of the critical need to respond in a timely manner and minimize potential for possible loss of life or severe injury:
>
> 1. Use of aircraft to fly below 4,000 feet to identify potential rescue needs, and if necessary, landings within the wilderness to extract injured or trapped individuals. Use of aircraft to fly search and rescue

personnel within the wilderness to allow for quicker response to potentially injured or trapped parties.

2. Use of chainsaws and mechanized winches to facilitate ground search of the affected portages and campsites. The objective of these tools is to allow for quick access to the affected areas, and provide a safe environment for search and rescue efforts and evacuations.

3. Use of motorized boats on lakes within the wilderness to allow for more efficient search and rescue operations.

4. If you have other needs for motorized equipment that I have not outlined, they should be discussed specifically with me or Deputy Forest Supervisor Tom Wagner, for review and possible authorization.

I believe these actions are the minimum tools necessary to respond to this large-scale emergency situation and allow the County Sheriffs of Lake, Cook and St. Louis Counties to carry out their jurisdictional responsibilities for search and rescue operations. This authorization will remain in effect until such time that I believe the search and rescue emergency has been addressed. I will make this determination through consultation with the respective county sheriffs. If you have any concerns or needs for clarification, please contact me or Tom Wagner.

By the end of the day, Jim had learned enough to know the full, robust resources of a Type II team were the appropriate response to the disaster.

Unfortunately, the Beaver pilots were so busy it would be at least two more days before he would be able to get up over the forest and view the destruction for himself. By the end of July 5, Jim managed to get supper, then checked into his room at the Paddle Inn. Tomorrow, he knew, would be another busy day.

31

A RETURN TO CIVILIZATION

July 5, 1999
Seagull Lake, the Gunflint Trail, and Duluth

The morning of July 5, Sue Ann Martinson and Jan Fiola awakened to the sound of chainsaws. The buzz was accompanied by worry over Matt Bliefernich, one of the base's wilderness guides. Jen Nagel, Jim Wiinanen, and others had determined Matt had been the only base employee in the woods when the storm blew through. He had left the base on July 2, leading a group of five recent high school graduates from Chicago who were having one last adventure before leaving for college. Jim, Cherish Galvin Davis (who was Matt's girlfriend), and the other base employees were understandably concerned. They had seen what happened to Vicky Brockman, and of course witnessed the destruction firsthand, so they were anxious for news of their colleague.

/ / /

Before Jan and Sue Ann could return to the mainland and Vicky's car, they needed to retrieve their gear. Of course, Cherish remembered the island shoreline where the previous night, fleeing the oncoming storm, they had stowed their canoes and supplies to lighten their load. But for the time being, Cherish was too preoccupied with Matt's fate to think about heading down Seagull Lake. Until they got news about him and his group of graduates, everyone at the base would work on cleanup and wait.

Pinecliff had the kitchen, so while they waited, Jan and Sue Ann ate a camp breakfast with the other employees. There was no want of work to be done, and there was so much destruction it would be a long time before the chainsaws fell silent.

Jen recalled that her first venture out of Pinecliff the previous day felt "alien and otherworldly." When she visited the mainland, it wasn't much different. "I remember getting to the Cove and realizing how high the trees were stacked on the driveway," Jen said.

As this day began, Jen and everyone else at the WCB were starting a cleanup that would last days, weeks, months, and—though no one could yet fathom it—years. But it was difficult for the base employees to focus, knowing their colleague was still unaccounted for.

"So," Sue Ann said, "we had to wait until they were sure Matt was okay and the kids were okay."

Before noon, several miles away down the Gunflint Trail, some of the high schoolers made it out of the woods to a BWCAW landing with a pay phone that was miraculously still operational. They let the authorities know there had been an accident: Matt and another member of their party had been struck by a falling tree in the middle of the blowdown. They both had head injuries, possibly concussions, but were otherwise okay.

Word was immediately relayed for a medevac, and Forest Service pilot Wayne Erickson got the call. He departed the air base at 11:58 and landed on the BWCAW's Owl Lake, where Matt and the injured teen waited. After lifting off Owl Lake the pair of injured young men were flown directly to the Duluth trauma center.

Finally, by early afternoon, the remaining members of the group arrived at the Wilderness Canoe Base, where they let everyone know what had happened to Matt.

The news was enough.

Cherish took the johnboat, headed down Seagull Lake, and retrieved Jan's and Sue Ann's packs and gear. She let them know she, or someone else at the base, would retrieve the canoes and return the rented one to Way of the Wilderness Outfitters. "Then they took us over to the landing with our packs and supplies," Sue Ann recalled.

Fortunately, by midafternoon, Jan and Sue Ann found Vicky's car in the lot, unscathed and operational. But they were stunned by the fallen forest. Their day had already involved a series of shocking observations. They had awoken to chainsaws, and while they waited at the base the chainsaws never ceased. The area was choked with downfall. The toil of clearing it had just begun.

/ / /

From the parking lot near the End of the Trail campground, the Gunflint Trail was the only way to drive out of the woods—at least, what was left of them. As they drove down the two-lane blacktop, most of it with only one lane open, they were amazed by the breadth and depth of fallen trees. Everywhere the forest had been flattened. There were occasional scraggly trees that were twisted and partially denuded but still standing or leaning at a 45-degree angle over the ground. The ditches and shoulders were stacked high with cut or bulldozed forest debris.

"It was very impressive," Sue Ann recalled, "the way it had been cleared. The wires were all down, but you could see places in the road where they were very, very careful. We had to go around them. But they had done a very good job of clearing the highway."

The sky was at least calm after the previous day's storm. As the pair of survivors carefully traversed the Gunflint Trail, heading toward Grand Marais, they could not help but pause periodically, either to steer the car through particularly dicey, tight spots or to consider the extent of the destruction.

Sue Ann again got out her camera and began taking photographs. One showed a single lane of blacktop covered with fallen trees, their frazzled tops lying across the center yellow dividing line. There was just enough space in the remaining lane to steer the car around the wreckage. To the side of the fallen trees several others were angled out over the debris. They had not yet completely fallen, but in time they would, or would need to be cut down.

They spent more than an hour threading, pausing, and occasionally stopping along the next 30 or so miles of tree-covered blacktop. Eventually they arrived at the Laurentian Divide overlook, a few miles from Trail

Center. Because the Laurentian Divide is an important geographic point, the Superior National Forest created a small parking lot off the highway and erected a sign explaining the site's significance. "You are looking at Birch Lake located on the Laurentian Divide," the sign reads. "Water at this point flows northward into Canada's Hudson Bay watershed and eastward into the Saint Lawrence watershed." Over the past twenty-four hours, the parking lot had been cleared. Sue Ann and Jan parked and stepped out of the car.

Standing in the parking lot, visitors can look north down a steep slope to Birch Lake below, and then across the lake to the opposite ridge and beyond. Jan and Sue Ann were again astonished. Traveling along the Gunflint Trail, they'd seen massive destruction on both sides of the road. But they hadn't yet had an extensive vista like the one at the top of the divide. Now they stood in a place where the forest to the north stretched before them . . . or what was left of it.

"We looked across that body of water," recalled Sue Ann. "You could see for miles this huge panorama of downed trees."

The damage had been terrible back at the Wilderness Canoe Base, and all up and down the end of the Gunflint Trail. Now they saw it was more extensive than they could have possibly imagined.

After a few more miles the forest destruction began to thin. The two-lane blacktop opened up. By late afternoon they arrived in Grand Marais, and then continued down Highway 61 on their way to Duluth.

Sue Ann kept taking photographs. While Highway 61 had only been partially impacted by the kind of devastation they'd seen during the first part of their return to civilization, the creeks and rivers along the highway were torrents. An estimated 7 inches or more of rain had fallen the previous day. The north shore of Lake Superior rises several hundred feet to the plateau above the lake, and the water that had fallen the previous day was cascading off the plateau. Creeks that were sometimes dry were now juggernauts. Rivers were swollen out of their banks. The scenic waterfalls that characterize the North Shore, one of the reasons many people visit the area, were now thunderous.

Sue Ann took a photograph of a raging Cutface Creek. As they continued down Highway 61, she snapped a picture of the Temperance River, its turbid waters as wide as they had ever been. The power of the torrent was dumbfounding. They drove down the blacktop, stopping at Gooseberry Falls, which now looked like a mini Niagara.

Finally, they arrived in Duluth. From a restaurant where they stopped to eat, they called the hospital in Ely and discovered that Vicky had been transported to Duluth. The day was getting late, and the two travelers were weary. But they tried to find Vicky. "We tried to figure out where she was," Sue Ann said. "But we couldn't find her." Eventually, they resolved to spend the night, checked into a motel, and decided they would try again in the morning to locate their friend.

Sue Ann was anxious to read the local news coverage of the catastrophe. She figured the local paper would run numerous photographs and devote several column inches to what had happened in one of Minnesota's most popular wilderness areas.

"Well, I found a paper," Sue Ann recalled. "On page three there was a short little article about some kind of blowdown or something happening in the Boundary Waters." The two women, like every other storm survivor, were shocked. "They didn't yet know the seriousness of it."

Sue Ann and Jan finally lay down to rest on normal beds for the first time in days. Even though they were sore, they felt glad to be under a roof again. And they suspected that in the next day or so the world outside the Boundary Waters would begin to awaken and become aware of the fickle, overpowering destruction wielded by nature's hand.

32

ON THE EDGE OF THE BLOWDOWN

July 5–6, 1999
Fourtown Lake and Environs

Nicole Selmer awakened to a changed world. Overnight, there had been—amazingly—more storms. In addition to more heavy rains, the night sky flashed with more unnerving thunder and lightning. Nicole, second in command Pam Kubichka, and her group of volunteers had cobbled together two tents from the salvaged parts of those damaged in the previous day's storm. They'd huddled into those makeshift shelters, trying to stay dry and warm. But it was a long and fitful night.

Now the morning dawned clear and warm, with a return of the pestilential bugs, as though the previous day's events had never occurred. But it was hard to put a storm like that out of their minds, especially when their radios had crackled into the evening with accounts of others farther south, who had been in the middle of the worst weather, calling for help.

The radio reception from their camp on the south side of Fourtown Lake was poor. They could receive static-filled messages, but they were unable to call out. Nicole needed higher ground. She and another team member paddled out to a rock island near the center of Fourtown. From its peak Nicole was finally able to make contact with the Kawishiwi Ranger District.

The district confirmed that there was extensive damage all over the Boundary Waters but that they were still in assessment mode. For the time being the office wanted Nicole to enlist another team member and

paddle into some nearby lakes, both to determine the extent of the damage and to make sure no one was hurt or in need of other help. The rest
of her crew should return to district headquarters back in Ely, where they
would be reassigned.

When Nicole returned to camp and shared the details of their new
mission, everyone pitched in to break down and pack up their equipment and supplies. "After the storm," Nicole explained, "Pam led the
rest of the crew out of the Boundary Waters, and I asked for a volunteer to
come with me to complete the search and rescue. I really wanted to bring
Pam with me, as I didn't know what I was going to find, but she needed
to bring the rest of the crew to safety." Pam was the only one besides
Nicole who was a Forest Service employee rather than a volunteer, so she
had to stay with the rest of the group.

Their four canoes were undamaged, so six of them would paddle and
portage back to their pickup point on Mudro while Nicole and Lindsey,
the volunteer who had agreed to go with her and assist, went to check out
the lakes to the east and north of Fourtown.

"It was basically a paddling mission," explained Nicole. "At that
point we just had our crosscut saw with us, so anything that was over the
trail that could be easily cleared, we cleared. But it was really more of a
search-and-rescue mission. We were assessing damage and making sure
people were okay."

From Fourtown they had a short portage into Boot Lake, to the east.
Boot was a long lake that angled north. From Boot they paddled into
Gun Lake, and then into Gull. From Gull Lake they had a long portage
into Thunder Lake, followed by a shorter portage due west into Beartrap
Lake. They encountered blowdown on portages, but not enough to slow
them down. As they passed through each of the five lakes, they searched
the designated campsites and found everyone to be safe and secure.
They also noticed that the farther north they paddled, the less damage
they saw. "People were fine," recalled Nicole. "Everyone thought it was
a big storm, and people were amazed by the rain and wind, but most of
them had sustained little or no damage."

When the rest of Nicole's team returned to Ely, they were given other
assignments. "Most of them were volunteers," Nicole said. "We had one
woman who was sixty-three years old. She became a driver and went all

over the place, including the Gunflint. They went from being volunteers to being paid to do whatever job they had out there for them. Because of the emergency they hired them as ADs." AD means "administratively determined": the Forest Service could hire and pay them for whatever tasks were needed, provided they had the necessary skills and qualifications. Admittedly, for the work they would be doing, the requisite qualifications usually meant good health and a strong back.

/ / /

After Pete Weckman heard from Wayne Erickson about having seen the two campers and their dog on Granchee Island, he was curious. He continued down the length of Basswood Lake, and not long after Wayne's overflight, he motored up to the island.

"Pete," one of the men said. "What's going on?"

Pete told them about visiting their campsite the previous evening. "At 9:30 at night, you weren't here," Pete said. He told them how he found their place destroyed, and how with both of them and their dog missing, and one of their boats gone, he had feared the worst. Which is why he had requested the early-morning flyover.

"They were very, very appreciative," Pete said. "After they got done telling me that, I said, 'Now I want to hear the story. Where were you?'"

The men had brought along so much gear to the island, they had taken two boats. They also had a canoe.

"For a day trip," Pete explained, "they took the boat with a canoe rack over to the Quetico. They paddled on the Canadian side into Merriam Bay for a day of walleye fishing."

"The storm hit, and it mostly stayed on the American side of Basswood Lake," one of the fishermen explained. "We hunkered down in a cedar swamp, pulled in our canoe, and stayed pretty safe, watching the storm go by."

After the worst weather had passed, they returned to their canoe and, with nearly a half pound of leeches left for bait, they continued fishing. "One of the men, Pat, was a guide," Pete explained. He was familiar with the area and knew where to fish and what to use for bait.

"I've never had fishing like that," Pat told him. "We were catching

8- and 10-pound walleyes on this sunken reef. The fish were going on the feeding frenzy of a lifetime." Pat explained that neither of the fisherman could resist it. They remained fishing until after dark. Eventually, they made their way back to camp and found it totally destroyed.

"I'm sure they lost everything," Pete concluded. "So it was very good to see that they were alive."

"As the whole day went on," Pete continued, "it was constant talking to different parties. I was going into campsites where I was finding smashed tents just left there. It was the unknown of not knowing if people were somewhere else. It was this eerie feeling of not knowing what you were going to find. All the time you expected to find a fatality."

But he never did.

/ / /

After Nicole and Lindsey checked the campsites on Beartrap Lake, the next-nearest stop would involve an extremely long portage to a lake farther north. Since damage north was less than it was to the south, and since there were other places in the direct path of the storm that needed to be checked, they were instead called back to the incident command center at the Forest Service offices in Ely. They ended up spending only one night getting from Fourtown up to Beartrap and back again before arranging to be picked up midmorning on July 6.

"We went back into the office," recalled Nicole. "They'd all been in crisis mode for a few days, and there were a lot of things happening. People were coming and going, supplies were being stockpiled, everyone was running all over the place. We were coming back to a very different office. We were called into the command center, and they had maps on the wall and Jim Hinds gave us our next mission."

The large maps showed the three counties that covered northeastern Minnesota: St. Louis, Lake, and Cook. The map delineated a clear BWCAW border, with dots marking campsites and lines illustrating portages between lakes. Green dots and lines meant the campsites and portages had been visited and checked. Red dots and lines meant they still needed to be assessed. Many more portages and campsites were marked in red than green. Jim explained that they were still in search-and-rescue mode, so they needed to get into the hardest-hit areas to make sure everyone was okay. The cleanup could happen after they made sure everyone was safe.

"We're sending you into Spoon Lake," Jim told Nicole, pointing out the lake on the map. She knew the area and had been there before. Jim wanted her and Lindsey to start in Spoon and then portage in a west-southwesterly direction into Dix Lake, Skoota Lake, and then Missionary Lake. "I want you to check each campsite, if you can find it," Jim said. "Look for things like tents. See if there's anyone or anything there. You might need to clear parts of the portage to get through it, but if you can get through a portage without clearing it, do that."

"They just wanted to make sure people on those lakes were okay," Nicole said. "Then, once the lakes had been checked, we would go into the next phase."

33

A PUBLIC INFORMATION OFFICER FOR THE EASTERN ZONE

July 5–7, 1999
Monroe Center, Wisconsin; Ely; Grand Marais; and Environs

On the morning of July 5, park ranger turned public information officer Jennifer Rabuck was dressed in her U.S. Fish and Wildlife Service khaki browns, heading across state lines in her U.S. Fish and Wildlife Service tan pickup. By the afternoon she was in Ely and, like everyone else, was introducing herself, trying to figure out what exactly had happened and how she could help. "The first twenty-four hours when you get on any incident is pure chaos," Jennifer noted. "That first afternoon I was trying to figure out what was going on. What do we know? What don't we know? Who are the players? How are we going to set ourselves up? We're trying to identify our goals and objectives. Frankly, we really didn't have a good sense of the size of the affected area or extent of the damage. And at this time, 1999, there weren't a lot of best practices regarding how to deal with extensive blowdown events. At least not events at this scale."

The good news, Jennifer recalled, was that the damage had already been done. It wasn't like a fire or hurricane, which can be live and raging and changeable. This event had already happened, and now they were trying to determine the extent of the damage and how to proceed. The first several days were considered the search-and-rescue phase of the response. "We were trying to figure out who was still stuck, and who might be injured. Or killed. There was definitely a sense of urgency. We knew people were out there in wilderness. Anyone who has been in the Boundary Waters knows you need to bring your resources with you. You might have an extra day of food. But if your canoe or your paddles or both are gone, how are you supposed to survive? What are you going to eat? Especially if your fishing gear is obliterated. And what if you're hurt?"

As the team continued to learn more about the scope of the event, their sense of urgency intensified. They knew there were numerous BWCAW visitors in vulnerable situations. "We felt a deep sense of responsibility to prevent the disaster from getting any worse than it already was," Jennifer added.

By all accounts the derecho was the most massive and extensive windstorm to ever hit the Boundary Waters and surrounding area. Evacuation and medevac flights were in the air from dawn to dusk. The Civil Air Patrol did not have the kind of aircraft that could land on lakes and rescue or help survivors, but its pilots could perform reconnaissance and other important emergency air activities.

Firsthand accounts of the damage had convinced the Type II leaders that the destruction during the search-and-rescue phase of the mission would be best addressed on two fronts: a western zone headquartered in Ely, and an eastern zone headquartered in the U.S. Forest Service offices in Grand Marais. From the western zone, flights could be dispatched to all parts of the Boundary Waters and vehicles up to the wilderness's edge as far as roads could take them. And from the eastern zone, flights could be dispatched from the sea base on Devil Track Lake and the Grand Marais airport. Perhaps more important, the eastern zone first responders could get vehicles and supplies into the heart of the Boundary Waters via the Gunflint Trail, the Sawbill Trail, and other nearby roads and trails (providing they were cleared).

Several Gunflint side roads support cabin and resort owners and outfitters. The Sawbill begins in Tofte, farther south on Lake Superior, and provides access to the southeastern BWCAW. Like the Gunflint, the Sawbill also feeds several side roads into the forest and is a main road for many cabins, resorts, and outfitters, most particularly the well-known Sawbill Outfitters at its terminus.

The numerous businesses surrounding the Boundary Waters were important for a variety of reasons. First and foremost, they may have outfitted wilderness travelers who were now wounded or stranded in the woods, possibly without paddles or canoes. These outfitters would become key participants in identifying who was in the woods, who was missing, and who might need assistance. They were also on the front line. Many of them had been damaged, some severely. And since the wilderness was an area on which their business depended, all of them were interested in what was happening.

/ / /

By July 7, Jennifer was stationed in the conference room overlooking a parking lot at the USFS offices in Grand Marais. While she and her colleagues who were addressing the search-and-rescue needs of the disaster's eastern zone were not considered their own Type II team, for all intents and purposes, they were. Like Ralph Bonde's team in Ely, the Grand Marais team had an operations chief (Mike Wurst), a logistics chief (Les Miller), a PIO (Jennifer Rabuck), and several others who were slotted into various roles: Tim Norman, Steve Schug, Tom Kaffine, Duane Cihlar, Jo Barnier, and more.

In some ways, PIOs are on the public front lines of the incidents on which they work. In the case of the blowdown, Jennifer's office was a kind of gatekeeper. Anyone seeking access to the rest of the east zone team needed to pass her office to get there. "If media outlets were coming in, we could catch them and answer their questions without them getting into the inner workings of the team and potentially hearing or seeing things that we were not ready to release. We'd hate for someone to stumble into a conversation about a fatality before we'd gotten notification to the next of kin or permission from the sheriff to announce those sorts of things. In that way, PIOs are the folks guarding the door. We're not security, but we want to make sure that we're paying attention when media or other folks come in, so they're not wandering haphazardly around the incident command post."

Today social media plays a key role in distributing important information. But in 1999 the process was much more traditional. One of Jennifer's first duties was to set up traplines, which are still used today. "A trapline is a series of locations where we share information in the community. We pick businesses, busy intersections, or places where entry is restricted for safety due to the incident. We post information literally on two pieces of plywood on a sandwich board placed in a high-traffic area," Jennifer explained. She worked with others on the team and in the Grand Marais, Gunflint, and Sawbill communities to determine the best locations for the traplines. In Grand Marais, boards were posted at USFS headquarters and other locations around town. Up the Sawbill and Gunflint Trails there were sites established at Sawbill Outfitters at the end of the Sawbill, the Gunflint Lodge near the end of the Gunflint, and similar locations.

Traplines serve as vehicles for conveying all kinds of information, but they need to be well tended and maintained, ideally on a daily basis. Some of the items Jennifer posted and frequently updated were maps conveying BWCAW damage areas, a list of closed entry points, phone numbers for all kinds of information (including a number to call to report or check on missing persons), Type II team press releases, quotes from the incident commanders, operations chief, and other relevant team members, and so on. Traplines, and the people that work them, quickly become the source of accurate, timely information and help build trust relationships in a community hit by a significant event. "And occasionally people would post their own stuff, like missing persons or lost dog notices," Jennifer added.

Since traplines typically focus on gathering places, one of Jennifer's duties involved exchanging information with whoever might be present. Informal conversations were excellent ways to both convey and hear about storm-related issues.

A day or two after Jennifer arrived in Grand Marais, she was joined by another PIO, Patti Hines, whose day job involved working for the USFS. Patti's uniform was the standard army green, while Jennifer's brown uniform and truck were sometimes mistaken for UPS.

With regard to traplines, "The important part is the networking and communication and adding fresh information and insight and being able to answer people's questions," Jennifer explained. "So, Patti and I went together that first day to try to figure out the best places to put the traplines."

As they spoke to people, Jennifer noticed that many of them were "borderline rude." At the time, she attributed the attitudes to the catastrophic nature of the blowdown—Gunflint and Sawbill residents were severely impacted by the event. "Whether it's a fire or a blowdown people are going to say things, and they might not be careful with their words. It's not personal, it's just them trying to make sense of a terrible incident."

That first day they drove Patti's green USFS truck up the Gunflint Trail. The next day, Jennifer drove her tan USFWS truck, updating the traplines by herself. "I was shoring myself up for some tough attitudes, reminding myself to keep smiling and listening. And I was astounded," remembered Jennifer. "It was like these were completely different people. I mean, people were giving me fresh-baked cookies and cup after cup of coffee. Everywhere I went people invited me in to sit down. And you know, the first couple, I did. But pretty soon you realize you're not going to be able to finish if you keep doing this at every stop."

Jennifer was surprised by and wondered about the changed perspectives. "But sometimes," she recalled, "I heard comments from folks about the Fish and Wildlife Service, and how we do things differently from the Forest Service. It was the first time I began to understand what you wear and what you drive matters." Jennifer was quick to add that in terms of being a PIO on a major incident, there was no difference between her and Patti's roles or responsibilities. Some people simply had a different perspective about the work of the two agencies. "Many of them were outfitters or business owners concerned that the integrity of the Boundary Waters was going to be forever lost. When they looked out their windows it looked like things were never going to be the same again."

/ / /

From the outset, everyone wanted to know how many visitors had been in the BWCAW on July 4. Unfortunately, that number was frustratingly difficult to compile. Everyone entering the Boundary Waters is supposed to complete a permit, but while Jennifer and others on the IC team had access to the permits, it wasn't always clear how many visitors each permit represented. As previously noted, in 1999, only one member of a party needed to complete a permit. Most parties involved more than one person, even though the permit provided only one name. A party could have up to nine people, only one of whom might be listed.

As a PIO, one of Jennifer Rabuck's most important duties was to answer calls from the public. From the moment she first sat down in her office to the end of her assignment around July 31, some of the most common calls she fielded involved missing persons. People called wanting to know whether their spouse, relative, or friend who had been in the BWCAW when the blowdown happened was okay or had made it out alive. But Jennifer and others in incident command struggled to identify specific missing people. To the best of their ability, they began compiling a list. Whenever they received an inquiry, they double-checked their list—which was always changing—and shared what they knew.

If the caller knew which BWCAW entry point the visitor had used, Jennifer noted the information and let them know they'd check on it as soon as they were able. Knowing the visitor's entry point, she and other members of the team could visit the area—if and when they were able to get to it—and take down the license plates of all the vehicles parked there. With the assistance of law enforcement, they could run the plate numbers and see whether a vehicle matched a person on their list and/or a person of interest. But that process didn't always lead to the identity of a specific permit holder. In fact, in numerous instances, it resulted in more confusion than clarity.

"Let's say my mom loaned us her car to drive to the Boundary Waters because it was a better vehicle for hauling a canoe," Jennifer explained. "In those instances, we wouldn't find a permit name associated with the vehicle, and we wouldn't find the name of the vehicle owner on any permit. Similarly, I'm sure there were instances when someone completed a permit and then decided, for whatever reason—maybe they got sick—not to enter. We had a name, but there was no one in the Boundary Waters associated with it."

Trying to find and check on everyone was an important part of the poststorm effort. Considering the destructive force and extent of the blowdown, everyone guessed they were going to find fatalities. Identifying who went in and who came out was a huge group effort. "Initially, some of the hotshot crews clearing portages and campsites helped out. They'd find cars at entry points, record the information, and get it back to us at ICP, the incident command post, so we could update our inventory. Then we would either give the license plate numbers to law enforcement or see if we knew who they were. There were some cases where we—information staff and other team members—were actually making calls and telling whoever answered that we'd found a vehicle at a specific entry point, and did they know who went in? Who was using the vehicle? Eventually, as people came out, we tried to keep a list of their names. But of course, some would come out and leave without telling anyone. So, we never actually had a full, comprehensive list."

34

FLYOVER

July 7, 1999
Ely, Minnesota, and the Boundary Waters

On the morning of July 7 Jim Sanders met Pat Loe at the hangar on Shagawa Lake. Over the past three days Loe, Wayne Erickson, and recently returned fellow Forest Service pilot Dean Lee had been busy flying approximately sixty missions over the length and breadth of the BWCAW. While Wayne and Dean were heading out again on more missions, Pat's morning flight would involve taking Jim up above 4,000 feet, where they would circumnavigate the entire million-acre wilderness and some areas stretching beyond. This was the morning Jim Sanders was going to acquire a comprehensive, bird's-eye view of the destruction that until now he had only heard about.

July 7 was a clear day—definitely clear enough to get Jim the unobstructed view of the forest he wanted. As Pat taxied to his takeoff position, Jim turned to his pilot and said, "Looks like a good day for it." Pat agreed. Over the past three days he had made dozens of passes over every corner of the BWCAW. But while he was familiar with the extensive damage, there was no growing used to it.

When flying over the BWCAW even the Forest Service Beaver planes needed to follow the rules. Flying was restricted over the wilderness. While Jim had earlier signed an official letter granting permission for pilots to fly beneath 4,000 feet, planes allowed to fly over the wilderness needed to stay above 4,000 feet whenever possible, which was fine by Jim, who was determined to get a visual perspective of the storm's remnants.

As soon as they were in the air, Pat started gaining elevation. As he did so he turned north over the Echo Trail. Out of Ely the 70-plus-mile trail turned almost due north for 20-odd miles before bending due west to Orr. Pat followed it on its trek north, just out of town.

When the blowdown happened, it tracked in an east-northeast direction, coming out of the west-southwest. While its trajectory was mostly in a miles-wide straight line, it gradually angled north. As they tracked the Echo Trail, Jim began to see some of the storm's first touchdowns, sections of forest that appeared flattened by a fickle hand. Fickle, because for quite a distance Jim could see the forest was healthy and intact. Then he would see a wide swath of flattened trees that stretched west to east, mostly lying in an east-facing jumble. Then, after a short distance, the flattened landscape would again give way to healthy standing trees.

As they traveled north out of Ely and then east over the Fernberg Trail, Jim said, "Well, this doesn't look too bad."

Pat Loe kept his eyes on the horizon, climbing higher over the trees, knowing this was only the start of the damage. "Just wait, Jim."

As Pat continued gaining elevation and traveling east he worked his way back in toward the eastern edge of the blowdown. He was navigating toward the Moose Lake area because Jim had told him he wanted to get a full "contextual picture." He wanted to see the full extent of the damage and how it fit into the whole Boundary Waters area, as well as to the borders beyond, even up into Canada. Pat, who now had a clear sense of where the most intense destruction lay and where the storm had passed over the forest without causing damage, knew exactly the route to take.

Jim Sanders had been in the Forest Service long enough to be familiar with blowdowns and know what to look for. Historically, windstorms strong enough to cause blowdown events happened every year around the United States. In the Upper Midwest they were a familiar enough weather event in the Dakotas, Iowa, Wisconsin, and in Minnesota. But derechos, severe windstorms with a length and path of destruction exceeding 100 miles or more, were rarer.

As they entered the eastern edge of the BWCAW, Jim could see several blowdown patches across the forest, similar to what he'd seen elsewhere. "That doesn't look too bad," he repeated, glancing north and south to see more patches of fallen trees. "Not too terrible over there."

Pat kept the nose of the plane aimed in a mostly eastern direction, toward where he knew the worst damage lay. "Just wait, Jim," he said again.

The Beaver was ideal for their purposes. At 4,000-plus feet, the plane was high enough to afford an extensive vista, but low enough to glimpse forest details. Beavers don't travel fast. They are reliable and in many ways the perfect aircraft for a wilderness area crisscrossed by lakes and rivers.

As Pat continued east, Jim kept his eyes fastened on the distant horizon. So far, he had seen extensive damage, but much of it was in patches, much of the forest below still green. Then, as Jim peered ahead, he began to see a dramatic borderline where the color of the forest changed to taupe.

"What's that?" he asked.

Pat knew what it was, but words were insufficient to describe it. So again, he could only tell Jim to wait, that he'd get a better view shortly.

And then in a few more minutes they were at the edge of it, an area of complete forest destruction unlike anything Jim had ever seen. What he saw now forced him into silence. He was known as an uber communicator, not the kind of leader who was typically at a loss for words. But as they approached and then passed over the border of total destruction, it was hard to do anything but stare in mute observation.

The area of the worst blowdown stretched in front of them approximately 30 miles to the eastern horizon. As they came upon it, the north–south spread covered at least 4 miles, sometimes stretching as far as 12 miles. Across the massive area the destruction was almost total. Occasionally, there was a solitary sentinel left standing, some lucky, strong tree that had somehow managed to remain upright. But for every tree left standing there were thousands lying on the ground in a straight line, facing east. From 4,000-plus feet in the air the flattened trees looked like giant toothpicks laid out in a row.

For the next hour Pat and Jim flew over the center of the worst section of blowdown, as far east as the Gunflint Trail corridor. Then they traced the northern perimeter of the fallen trees along the U.S.–Canadian border. Eventually, Pat turned south, traveling to the lower eastern section of the BWCAW. They traced the southern perimeter of the blowdown, finally turning east, navigating back toward the Shagawa Lake air base.

"That was when I got a full contextual view of the blowdown," Jim said. "Truth is, I was speechless, looking at it all and getting a sense of what we had in front of us."

/ / /

After Jim Sanders's overflight with Pat Loe, he had a much clearer idea of the scope of the disaster and what must now be done. They had already located and evacuated approximately sixty injured people. Incredibly, there were still no reports of fatalities. The destruction was so widespread that attending to the health and safety of everyone who had been in the impacted area when the storm hit at midday on July 4 would take at least several days. They needed to be certain they had canvassed the entire region and helped everyone who needed it.

"After that," Jim said, "we would need to turn our attention to infrastructure protection: repairing the roads, trails, and campgrounds outside the BWCAW and the portages and campsites inside the wilderness." Thinking about the scale of what had happened, Jim realized the health and safety segment of the storm response would constitute his team's efforts for at least the first seven to fourteen days. After that, infrastructure protection would take the rest of the summer into the next couple years.

"Your final concern with a disaster of these proportions is resource protection." Jim could already see, as could everyone else involved with the event, that forest fires would be inevitable. In the span of one July afternoon, the windstorm had arguably created one of the largest tinderboxes in the world.

35

THE HEART OF DARKNESS

July 7–11, 1999
Center of the Boundary Waters

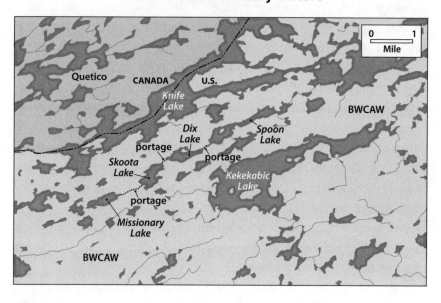

y the afternoon of July 7, ranger Nicole Selmer and volunteer Lindsey had been resupplied by an Ely outfitter. Then they made their
way to the seaplane base on Shagawa Lake, where Forest Service
pilot Wayne Erickson would fly them into Spoon Lake.

Nicole was happy to be flying with Wayne. "He was always taking me
to my best work trips ever," she recalled. "Whenever I got on a flight with
him, I knew it was going to be something good, because he was a lucky

charm for me." If "something good" meant seeing and experiencing a dramatically changed wilderness, Nicole was about to get her wish.

For this trip, the flight covered approximately 20 miles in an east-northeasterly direction out of Ely. Nicole was looking forward to getting a bird's-eye view of the wilderness. From the first eyewitness accounts, it sounded as though they'd be heading into some of the worst damage. But as they gained elevation out of Ely she wasn't seeing much. "Taking off from Ely you're seeing trees, and maybe a little bit of damage," she recalled.

As they crossed into the BWCAW she was watching out one side of the plane and could see periodic places where the forest had been struck. But looking out the other side, there were still large sections of forest standing. Then a few miles from their destination the change in what she saw startled her. There was a sudden demarcation where the forest beyond a certain line was flattened. They could see trees, but the entire forest was lying on the ground, facing the direction they were headed. "I remember looking off one side of the plane and seeing normal forest. And then looking out the other side and it was like an animal laid down, like when you have long grass, and a deer lays down and you can see the flattened remnants of its bed. Some people described it as taking a weed whacker to the trees. That's how dramatic it was, because it was all raw and had just happened. You could only see the remnants of trees, and the whole forest was flat."

Wayne put them down onto Spoon. Nicole wasn't sure she should thank her lucky-charm pilot, but she could not deny he had carried her into a wildly changed wilderness.

Spoon Lake stretches for approximately 2 miles in a west-southwest to east-northeasterly direction. It was the largest of the four lakes they were going to visit, and Nicole had maps indicating the locations of five campsites on the lake. Once they were on the water, paddling and searching for the campsites, the immediate, changed nature of the forest was eerie.

"There was nothing standing except for these little, teeny trees," Nicole said. "And there were no birds. It was eerily quiet. You didn't hear the normal wood song—squirrels and birds and the wind blowing through the trees. Normally, the wood sound is constant. But here, nothing. So we began to pay attention to the silence, and eventually we heard some loons. But they sounded weird. I remember them sounding different, as though they were maybe looking for each other or their chicks."

The portage from Spoon into Dix is 20 rods, or approximately a football field. But by the time they found it and put ashore, "it was like stopping at a wall. We couldn't get through it because there were so many trees down."

Normally, cutting through the debris could have only been done with crosscut saws. But for this trip, Nicole carried a Stihl 044 chainsaw. She had been trained and certified in its use and had used the tool countless times in the past. "But even with my 044 it was a massive job for two people to cut a path through that portage," she said. "We ended up camping on the portage itself." There were so many trees down all they could find was a narrow opening on the ground, approximately one-half of a tent pad in width, to make camp. They managed to pitch a tent to protect themselves against the mosquitoes, but the cramped quarters made for a difficult night sleeping.

/ / /

The forest in the chain of lakes Nicole and Lindsey were traveling comprised a mix of deciduous and coniferous trees, but mostly large, mature aspen. The trees were laid flat in an east-northeasterly direction, and so for the most part, they were lying parallel along the portages. But not always. Consequently, cutting a path through them, even with a chainsaw, was difficult and slow.

The wall of felled trees was 10 feet off the ground in most places. To begin clearing enough of the fallen trees to get through the portage with a canoe and their supplies, Nicole needed to climb partway up the downfall.

"It was like climbing a ladder," she recalled. "I had to climb at least 4 feet off the ground to get to a vantage point where I could cut the trees above me. It was tricky, but I never felt scared to cut or that it was out of my scope. I just needed to be focused on safety. You're climbing up 10 feet of fallen aspen, and I remember figuring out where exactly I was going to cut. Then I'd make the cut and then hand the log down to my partner and move on to the next cut. And we were only cutting exactly what we had to, the narrowest amounts that would allow us to get through to the next spot. It was dangerous work, but you're in the moment and know you need to get into the next lake, so you keep moving."

Sometimes the portages would include a turn, and the trees would be lying perpendicular to the trail, rather than parallel to it. "Sometimes that was easier," Nicole recalled. "Because you could cut the lower stuff and leave the upper stuff and tunnel through. When the trees were laying down the trail you had to cut everything."

Nicole Selmer is 5 feet 4 inches tall. Though she was a seasoned 044 user, she was not used to wielding a 20-pound chainsaw up and down fallen trees for twelve straight hours. "It's a larger chainsaw, and it's heavy," Nicole noted. The 044 uses a pull cord to start. "If I turned the chainsaw off, after a while it was too hard to pull the cord to get it started again, so I would leave it running while we cleaned what we had just cut." That said, Nicole recognized when the chainsaw needed to be turned off so they, and their equipment, could take a break and recuperate. "You'd reach a point where you'd say, 'Okay, maybe I should sit down and rest for a half hour.' If the chainsaw goes off and you can't restart it, maybe it's a sign."

The next day they managed to cut a path into Dix. Nicole pulled out her map with the campsite locations and they began searching. She was a seasoned wilderness ranger, and one of her jobs was maintaining BWCAW campsites. "Usually, it's really obvious where a campsite is. Usually there's a lot of bare ground and you can see a fire grate. And then from the fire grate you look for the latrine. But I remember we couldn't find any of the campsites. All the trees were down, so I'd try to locate the campsite by the map and then we'd land and walk around and see if we could find anything. I remember my partner saying, 'Oh, I think I found a fire grate.' Okay, that's the fire grate, and so the latrine is somewhere back here. We were trying to keep records of what needed to be repaired because they were hit by trees. But there were so many trees down."

At that point Nicole remembered one of the primary purposes of their paddle into these lakes: to make sure any campers who had been in the area were safe and accounted for. "And then I remember thinking, 'How am I supposed to know if there's a tent here?'" Nicole continued.

"There was so much destruction, how do we know if there were people here or not? Because if there were tents, they would have been smashed and their remnants would have been buried under the trees. There was no way anyone would have survived."

Nicole recognized this wasn't a search-and-rescue mission. It was really more about search and recovery—searching to see whether there were any survivors on these lakes, to see if there was any life.

/ / /

By July 9 they had made their way from Spoon to Dix to Skoota Lake, checking as best they could the campsites along the way. Fortunately, they found no stranded or hurt campers. If anyone had been on those lakes during the storm, they had somehow already made their way out of the fallen forest.

The portage from Skoota Lake into Missionary Lake is 177 rods, or more than a half mile. By the time Nicole and Lindsey arrived at the portage, they were not only tired but facing another wall of fallen trees. Fortunately, another group led by wilderness ranger Dan McLaughlin was cutting a path through the portage from the opposite direction, Missionary to Skoota. "So we were going to meet each other in the middle," Nicole said. "And I remember when we heard what was happening, we felt incredible relief. We felt like we were being saved, because we had spent two to three days cutting and hauling logs, and we were exhausted."

Dan's group had set up a home base at the cabin near Kekekabic Lake. At this point the two groups joined forces. Nicole reported, "It was great, because we had more people. It makes a job so much easier. As I recall they had three or four saw teams, each with a sawyer and a swamper. With teams of sawyers and swampers you can leapfrog, and there's more rest. Finally it wasn't just Lindsey and me and the trees. Everything got easier. I was able to clean my saw and get a break."

After a couple nights encamped near the Kek cabin, they were finally flown back to Ely and the service center. The focus at this point was still search and rescue. They, and fellow wilderness rangers and others across the entire BWCAW, would spend the next few weeks heading out on more missions, widening portages, clearing campsites, and of course checking to make sure there were no missing persons or fatalities. Despite the massive destruction, they never found anyone in need of special attention or a medevac.

"Within the course of six to eight weeks it gradually went from search and rescue to search and recovery and finally to just rehab," Nicole said.

36

THE MANAGEMENT INCIDENT REPORTS

The Boundary Waters, West and East Zones

Whenever an incident management team is in place, like the Type II team getting underway in the BWCAW on the afternoon of July 5, the team releases a daily plan, or progress report. Sometimes this is referred to as an incident action plan (IAP), or shift plan. The IAP records what is known and unknown about an event and outlines the key objectives and directives for the following day.

In the waning hours of July 4, everyone knew the Boundary Waters had been impacted by a serious meteorological event that included wind and rain. But on the morning of July 5, there was still more unknown than known. What exactly had happened? Hurricane? Tornado? How much of the forest was impacted? More tangibly, who needed search-and-rescue support? Was anyone in need of medical attention? What had been done the afternoon and evening of July 4, and what was the team planning to do on Monday, July 5?

The first formal IAP was prepared late in the day on July 5. This and every other daily report appearing through July 19 would follow the same format. Across the top of the first page were the incident name (now "4th of July") and the date and time the report was prepared. The first page also listed "General Control Objectives for the Incident," "Weather Forecast for Period," and "General Safety Message." Obviously, the all-important weather changed from report to report. But for each of the reports from

July 5 through the last IAP on July 19, overall objectives remained the same:

1. Conduct a site-by-site review of campsites and portages for injured parties and facilitate the rescue operations.
2. Assess and open roads and facilities.
3. Assess and open wilderness portages.
4. Assess and open wilderness campsites.
5. Maintain wilderness values.

Similarly, the general safety message didn't change, at least until July 15, when this part of the report was finally left blank. From July 5 through July 14, the safety message in each daily briefing was ominous and reflected the belief that fatalities were expected to be found. The preface to the complete safety message read:

What to do if you discover a fatality.

1. Confirm that the individual is deceased.
2. Notify the Sheriff via the command channel. No names on the radio!!
3. Secure the area, don't move or touch anything!

READ THE SAFETY MESSAGE ON THE NEXT PAGE

These daily reports were also important for identifying team members and tracking who was responsible for what. They were used to conduct a briefing for all participants as early as possible in the morning, often right after dawn. In addition to listing all the key incident command players, the IAPs also articulated everyone's marching orders for the day (hence incident *action* plans, or shift plans).

Several people listed on the July 5 report remained in the same position throughout, but personnel changes did occur. Ralph Bonde remained the Type II incident commander until July 19, when the serious and substantial forest recovery efforts were continued under the normal operating procedures of the Superior National Forest and all other agencies and organizations involved. The planning chief (Mark Carlstrom), the logistics chief (Dennis Cameron), and the finance chief (Sharon Karr) likewise remained on the team until it disbanded on July 19. The agency representatives were Cook County sheriff Dave Wirt, Lake County sheriff Steve Peterson, USFS Kawishiwi District ranger Bruce Slover, and USFS Gunflint District ranger Jo Barnier.

The other command, finance, logistics, operations, planning, and safety (CFLOPS) personnel included information officer Tom Kroll, safety officer Bob Brittain, operations chief Steve Jakala, and liaison officer Osten Berg. At this point the organization assignment list also included division/group supervisors for Ely (Jim Hinds), St. Louis County (Rob Bryers), and Grand Marais (Tim Norman). The all-important air operations branch supervisor was Pete Tentinger.

For the first report, compiled midnight July 5 for the use the next day, Tuesday, July 6, what was surprising was that so many people were already identified and out in the field, mostly in search-and-rescue and assessment, in and around the Boundary Waters. After the organization assignment page, the report includes a division assignment list for air operations, engineering, inside BWCAW, outside BWCAW, staging, and St. Louis. Over these seven or more pages approximately thirty to fifty people are listed, along with subareas of assignment. For example, the "Inside BWCAW" sheet contains a list of nine two-person teams of primarily wilderness rangers who either were being dropped off in wilderness areas or had already been dropped off. The IAP states, "Crews are checking campsites within assigned areas, checking on campers and doing clean-up/cutting."

Pete Weckman entered the wilderness at Wind Lake with fellow rangers Hall and Landers. Presumably they began checking on portages and campsites on Wind Lake and nearby areas, clearing as much as they could as they went. Nicole Selmer and her volunteer, Lindsey, headed up the Angleworm Trail. Similar to the others on the list, these teams' primary purpose was to make certain there were no bodies in the area or people who needed help. They were clearing as they went, but the real purpose was search and rescue. Six of the nine teams, including Pete's and Nicole's, were going to be in the wilderness just two to three days, expecting to be picked up on July 7, though that was only an estimate. Two teams (Koschak and Gegorich, and McLaughlin and Backe) were heading to Knife Lake and the Kek cabin, respectively, for "5 days food out 7/10" and for "6 days food out 7/11." Those areas were both in the Kawishiwi Ranger District, on the far eastern edge of the BWCAW's western zone.

According to the "Inside BWCAW" list, additional teams were taking to the air, going into the eastern zone of the BWCAW, and heading into the Trout Lake area of St. Louis County, north of Lake Vermilion. Much of the Trout Lake area is in the BWCAW, but it is northeast of Ely. That area had sustained significant damage, but much of the forest surrounding it was largely unaffected.

Surprisingly minimal in the coverage of this first Type II report were any search, rescue, and assessment efforts in the Tofte and Gunflint Ranger Districts (the eastern zone of the Superior National Forest). In time, it would become clear both of those BWCAW eastern zone districts had sustained significant damage, possibly the most extensive of the blowdown. In particular, the northwest edge of the Gunflint Ranger District, which included the Gunflint Trail, was one of the hardest hit and would require the most significant concentration of the Type II team's resources. But in the beginning, almost all of the reports coming in chronicled forest damage so extreme that none of the numerous members of the Type II team and its workers in the field needed to search very far to find widespread destruction, all of it in need of their attention.

/ / /

In addition to each daily report's safety messages about what to do if a fatality was found, safety chief Bob Brittain included a more detailed, handwritten safety message in each daily briefing. The message he penned for the July 6 Type II team kickoff meeting was typical and sobering.

MAJOR HAZARDS:

1. Sprung, leaning, and hanging trees.
2. Hanging limbs (widow makers).
3. Washouts on roads outside the BWCAW.
4. Downed power lines.

DISCUSSION

Every one of these trees under stress is a potential killer, so
extreme caution must be used when cutting each one!!
There probably are many limbs torn off trees and just hanging,
waiting to fall with little or no warning.

Heavy rains have caused some washout, so don't drive into water
unless you are sure it is safe!!

There may still be some live downed wires, so treat every wire as if
it is still hot.

Keep your eyes and ears open at all times!!

PPE is required for all people in the field.

As the Type II team, stationed in Ely, got underway, they focused
most of their efforts on their immediate area. Even though USFS pilots
Pat Loe and Wayne Erickson had flown over and seen the forest to the
east, almost all the initial players on the Type II team were from the
Ely area. They had heard Nicole Selmer's accounts of damage and the
more intense damage chronicled by Pete Weckman. Understandably, the
team's initial emphasis was on assessing the damage and cleaning up
the area nearest them, with which they were most familiar. The engineering work documented in this first report was almost entirely focused
on cleaning up nearby roads.

The July 6 report contained two crude maps, essentially copied
from local commercial maps. One map showed the western zone of
the BWCAW. The other map showed the eastern zone. Someone used a
magic marker to outline the impacted areas on both maps. A sticky note
on the top of the map says "7/6/99, Approx. Search Area, Scale ¼" = 1
mile." By this measurement the damaged geography was massive.

/ / /

What becomes clear in reading the reports, which were compiled late
each day for release (and to give all Type II team members their marching

orders for the following day), is that every day brought new understanding of the extent of what had happened, and the breadth and depth of the damage.

The second official report was compiled at 10:00 p.m. on July 6 for release on July 7, covering the operation period from 7:00 a.m. through 9:00 p.m. July 7. In the twenty-four hours between reports, much was done. The July 6 report was fifteen pages long, while the July 7 report was twenty. The additional pages primarily captured an uptick in activity in the eastern zone of the incident—the Gunflint/Tofte area. The "Road Cleanup Summary" in this report contained two additional sections for Grand Marais and Tofte. For Grand Marais, the report notes, "5 crews will be clearing roads in the Gunflint area, with 3–4 logging trucks." For the Tofte section, it reads, "Three crews will be working in the Tofte/Isabella area with 3 logging trucks. Work will proceed on FR 369, FR340, and the Little Isabella River Campground."

The entire area continued to be mapped by air, and search-and-rescue missions were flown by the Forest Service, Department of Natural Resources, Minnesota State Highway Patrol, and Civil Air Patrol pilots. Additionally, fifteen wilderness ranger crews were heading out into wilderness areas in the eastern zone, up and around the end of the Gunflint Trail. Twelve of these were two-person crews, while three were four-person crews. All of them were set to go into the woods on July 7, assess the damage in the area, check on as many portages and campsites as possible, assist anyone who needed it, and cut and clear out as much of the blowdown as needed to complete their assessment.

Similarly, other wilderness ranger crews were headed into the western zone for search-and-rescue and assessment. All of these crews consisted of two rangers and planned to be in the woods for anywhere from one to five days, except for one: wilderness ranger Mark Ringlever was leading an eight-person crew into the Ensign Lake area to assess damage and begin the cleanup: "Trident Lake is a priority. CLOSE UNSAFE SITES THAT CANNOT BE REHABBED." This group was going out for eight days. As the days passed and more areas were cleared of campers, larger crews like Mark's would go into the woods for longer periods to focus on cleanup, rather than search and rescue.

/ / /

Sometime after July 19, Ralph Bonde completed a summary report of the first fifteen days of the incident, chronicling the callup of the Type II team and its work. "I was asked by the forest supervisor [Jim Sanders] to provide him with a brief summary of daily events for the entire incident," Ralph recalled. For the most part, he documented the work on a daily basis, when the day's numerous activities were fresh in his mind.

For each day of the event beginning on July 4, a half page or more of single-spaced text covers the key activities and important statistics for the day. For example, the July 4 page states, in part, "Between the end of the storm on 7/4/99 and close of business 7/5/99 a total of 20 injured personnel were medivaced from the BWCAW. . . . Injuries ranged from bad bruises/cuts to broken leg, back and chest injuries." The report of this day's details concluded, "It had now become apparent just how massive and destructive this windstorm was. On the afternoon of 7/5/99 it was decided to mobilize a MNICS overhead team to manage the incident."

While the daily incident management plans identify who was doing what, in terms of personnel and areas being assessed and cleared, the summary information for each day of the incident contains more detailed and prosaic information about important happenings each day. The summary for July 5 talks about the IC callup, its authorization, and Jim Sanders granting permission to use "aircraft, chain saws, motorboats, mechanized winches and other motorized equipment within the BWCAW for the emergency search and rescue efforts." It also began to track three key incident statistics.

> Estimate size of Incident: 200,000 acres.
>
> Personnel on Incident: Approximately 114 including 22 overhead.
>
> Cost to date: Not yet calculated.

Ralph's summaries for each day of the incident tell a progressive story. They record a growing awareness within the IC team and in the larger public about the severity of the windstorm. For example, the July 6 half-page summary states, in part, "Phone ringing off the hook at district office with people seeking information about situation or friends/relatives." The report for that day also notes, "Aircraft begin to arrive for aerial search. . . . Affected area in Lake and Cook County set up in grids and aerial search begins. . . . Osten Berg to Grand Marais to act as liaison with Cook County Sheriff. Ordered up 2 more PIO's for 1800 today." These comments reflected the dawning awareness of the extent of damage in the eastern zone, the end of the Gunflint Trail and surrounding area. The summary concludes, "Based on information available it is estimated that 800–1000 campsites (50%), 60 miles of portages (33%) and 125 miles of trail (50%) have been affected."

> Estimate size of Incident: 200,000 + acres
>
> Personnel on Incident: 120 including 36 overhead
>
> Cost to date: $20,000

Quoting key sections from each of the following daily summaries conveys the chaos of each day and, again, the evolving understanding of the windstorm's destruction—and cost.

7/7/99

Phone calls and media continue to be major challenge. . . . BWCAW portages and campsites being loaded into GIS. Will be used to track progress. Hope to produce updated map at noon each day. . . . Concerned with lack of resources (overhead help) on Cook Branches. . . . 1245—fly to Grand Marais to spend time with Berg, Wirt, Barnier and other personnel. . . . Attended Cook County Board meeting at 1500. Board declares county a disaster area. . . . Entire grid area has now been covered 2½ times from the air. . . . 2000—attended public meeting at Ely District Office hosted by PIO. . . .

> Estimate size of Incident: 250,000 + acres
>
> Personnel on Incident: 174 including 44 overhead
>
> Cost to date: $25,000

Like the summary from July 6, the one from July 7 conveys a growing sense of the extent of the eastern zone damage, as well as the need for more resources to address the needs of that area. The reference to GIS mapping represents the first effort to depict what was happening on a map. These maps would note which campsites and portages had been reviewed and/or cleared and which still needed to be cleared. They would be posted for everyone on the team to see and would become important pictorial representations of each day's progress.

The summary comments also convey the busyness of not only Ralph Bonde, flying west to east and back again to attend public meetings, county board meetings, and the like, but also all the other members of the team and everyone associated with it. Finally, the estimated size of the event, number of personnel, and costs keep rising.

7/8/99

Major emphasis is now on ground search—campsites and portages. As agreed to at call up, Jim Hinds replaces Steve Jakala as Opts. Chief and Craig Scherfenberg replaces Pete Tentinger as Air Support. . . . Senator Grams in Ely. . . . Ordered a Type I crew but told there may not be any available. Continue to order needed resources—especially carded sawyers and first responder/EMT types personnel. Drove to Grand Marais to attend public meeting at Gunflint Lodge. . . . Approximately 90 people attended. . . . Phone service has generally been restored, but power may not be completely restored on Gunflint Trail for another 2–4 weeks. . . . Approximately 15% of portages and campsites checked to date. . . .

Estimate size of Incident: 250,000 + acres

Personnel on Incident: 181 including 38 overhead

Cost to date: $44,000

This summary notes key personnel changes as well as the first visit by an important public dignitary, U.S. Senator Rod Grams. It also notes that very few of the portages and campsites have been checked.

7/9/99

Hot shot crew order confirmed. . . . Set up meeting with Peterson, Wirt, Slover, Barnier, Sanders, Sletten, Berg and Schuldheisz to review incident status. . . . Concerns about crew working more than 12 hours a shift. . . . First injury today. Crew member sustains a muscle strain or tendon injury and is flown out for medical check up. . . . Approximately 25% of campsites and portages have been checked. . . .

Estimate size of Incident: 250,000 + acres

Personnel on Incident: 197 including 46 overhead

Cost to date: $160,000

A hotshot team consists of approximately twenty highly trained and experienced Forest Service employees. Teams are assembled and dispatched at the national level, so they can come from all over the United States. While their specialty is fighting wildland fires, they can also work on other disasters—in this case, the search and rescue, assessment, and cleanup resulting from a massive windstorm.

Over the next days, weeks, and months, many more of these kinds of national expert crews would be summoned to address the growing needs of this disaster. According to Tim Norman, the fire management officer for the east zone of the SNF, "It was a wet year, so there wasn't a lot going on nationally, fire-wise. We didn't have to compete for national resources, so we got hotshot crews and smoke jumpers to help out. They're some of the best sawyers in the country."

7/10/99

Added additional overhead help in Grand Marais—mainly deputy opts.—Mike Wurst and deputy logistics—Les Miller. . . . ETA for Sacramento Hot Shots now 2000. . . . Attended meeting at Isabella with Peterson, Wirt, Sletten, Schuldheisz, Berg, Wirt, Barnier, Slover, Sanders. General update. Notified Oberstar will be at Ely Airport approximately 1215 on 7/11. Bonde and Hinds to handle. . . .

Approximately 35% of campsites and portages have been ground checked. . . .

Estimate size of Incident: 250,000 + acres

Personnel on Incident: 222 including 53 overhead

Cost to date: $250,000

By July 10, it was becoming clear the eastern zone of the incident had incurred the most extensive damage. The entire forest was impacted, most of it severely, but maps were showing how much of the Gunflint Trail area was impacted. One of the big differences between the western and eastern zones of the incident was the amount of destruction that happened to populated areas. Most of the western zone destruction happened in wilderness, but the second half of the Gunflint Trail, replete with many cabins and resorts, was hit particularly hard. Consequently, more resources were being added to the Grand Marais area.

This report also notes a visit by another dignitary, U.S. Representative Jim Oberstar. He would be flying over the destruction to survey the damage with Ralph Bonde and Jim Hinds the next day, July 11.

Finally, while the estimated size of the incident hadn't appreciably increased (yet), the number of people working on it (222) and the costs ($250,000) kept rising.

7/11/99

Sacramento Hot Shot crew split up and assigned to BWCAW. . . . Spent an hour with Congressman Oberstar at Ely Airport. Gave hand outs and general briefing. Hinds then flew with Oberstar to look at incident from air. . . . Approximately 45% of campsites/portages checked. No additional injured parties. No known stranded parties.

Estimate size of Incident: 250,000 + acres

Personnel on Incident: 235 including 59 overhead

Cost to date: $310,000

7/12/99

Governor Ventura flies storm damaged area. . . . New information sets damage at approximately 487,000 acres, which includes 92,000 acres water (180,000 light, 158,000 medium, and 140,000 heavy damage). . . . Approximately 55% of campsites/portages checked. . . .

> Estimate size of Incident: 487,000 acres—includes 92,000 acres water
>
> Personnel on Incident: 233 including 66 overhead
>
> Cost to date: $350,000

The key developments on July 12 were a visit by Governor Jesse Ventura and a sizeable uptick in the estimated size of the incident. The costs kept climbing.

7/13/99

Three aircraft remain on incident. Sharon Karr scheduled to attend meeting in Grand Rapids with FEMA. . . . Drove to Grand Marais with Hinds. Asked Steve Schug to head up a small group to develop a rehab plan for campsites/portages. . . . Also discussed needs of next phase with Hinds, Schug, Wurst and Norman. Turn back planned for 7/18 or 7/19. Need new team in place when it happens. . . . Approximately 65% of campsites/portages checked.

> Estimate size of Incident: 487,000 acres
>
> Personnel on Incident: 237 including 73 overhead
>
> Cost to date: $410,000

Since the grid search and initial search-and-rescue efforts by air were largely finished by the end of the day on July 6, the only aircraft still engaged were those from the Forest Service—the Beaver planes from Ely. These were now primarily being used to shuttle work groups into and out of the wilderness. This summary documents, again, an intensification of the work being done on the east zone of the disaster, reflected in both the increased number of people working on the cleanup (most of whom were contractors) and the rising costs. Finally, for Ralph Bonde and other key members of the Type II team, there was light at the end of the tunnel. Even though the survey and assessment work was on-going (only 65 percent of campsites and portages had been checked), the team appeared to be ready to "turn back"—Ralph's term for disbanding the Type II team and turning the ongoing work over to the Forest Service and other agencies and organizations—on July 18 or 19.

7/14/99

GIS specialist demobed. . . . Worked on organization for turnover. Regional Forester OK's use of mechanized and motorized or me-chanical equipment to clear trails, portages and campsites only where use of non-motorized or mechanical equipment would be unsafe. Use of aircraft will not be allowed. . . . Nineteen contrac-tors/crews working on road clearing/repair . . . Good progress being made on campsites/portages. Approximately 80% have been checked. . . .

Estimate size of Incident: 487,000 acres

Personnel on Incident: 230 including 70 overhead

Cost to date: $496,000

These highlights from Ralph's summary of July 14 are interest-ing for a few reasons. First, the term "demobed," or demobilized. The GIS specialist who had been helping compile the daily BWCAW progress-tracking maps was returning to regular work. Ralph Bonde was also spending time contemplating what was needed for the eventual turnover of the team's work to the Forest Service and the other agen-cies who would be responsible for continuing the work on the forest. While the regional forester (SNF forest supervisor Jim Sanders's boss) had okayed the continued use of chainsaws, motorboats, and other pow-ered equipment, he signaled that it could not continue forever. Finally, for perhaps the first time, the total number of personnel on the incident decreased, including a drop in the number of people working on the disaster. Presumably other professionals and team members were being demobilized.

7/15/99

Attend 1100 meeting/briefing at Ely Tanker Base with Jerry Rose, Steve Morris, Brad Moore, Chuck Spoden, Wagner, Slover, Carlstrom and Sanow. Attended 1300 meeting at Kawishiwi Ranger District office to discuss progress to date and needed organization for turn over. Present were Wirt, Peterson, Slover, Chaney, Barnier, Nightengale, Berg, Schug, Malinowski, along with command and staff. Plan to have all campsites and portages checked by COB 7/18/99. Turn back meeting planned for 7/19/99, 1300 hours in room 28 of Kawishiwi Ranger District office. . . . Twelve crew/operators working on road cleanup/repair. . . . Approximately 85% of campsites/portages checked. . . . Demob increasing.

Estimate size of Incident: 487,000 acres

Personnel on Incident: 221 including 69 overhead

Cost to date: $550,000

Numerous meetings continued, beginning to lay the groundwork for ending the Type II team on July 19. The people mentioned in this report had played key roles in the incident and presumably would continue to do so after July 19. These included Sheriffs Dave Wirt and Steve Peterson of Lake and Cook Counties, SNF district rangers Jo Barnier and Bruce Slover for the east and west zones, assistant forester Tom Wagner, and Tofte District program manager Steve Schug. Perhaps most important, especially for incident commander Ralph Bonde (who had been working a string of twelve or more hours per day), was finalizing the date, time, and place for a "turn back meeting."

7/16/99

Slow demob. continues. Spent morning with command/staff developing proposed turn over organization. Once developed, it was run by Tom Wagner. Began filling positions needed for turn over, including new IC. . . . Mark Ringlever, Kawishiwi crew leader shows up on CBS TV. . . . Nine operators/crews working on road repair/clean up/blow down removal. Five BWCAW crews on R&R. . . . Approximately 90% of campsites/portages checked. No injured/stranded personnel found.

Estimate size of Incident: 487,000 acres

Personnel on Incident: 193 including 67 overhead

Cost to date: $675,000

The July 15 report concludes with the phrase "Demob increasing"; the July 16 report states, "Slow demob. continues." The summary statistics illustrate a demonstrable demobilization of personnel, from 221 on July 15 to 193 on July 16. Finally, several rangers and cleanup crews had been working in difficult conditions since July 5–6. Consequently, five crews were stepping back for some badly needed R&R. The cost of the event took its biggest jump to date, from $550,000 to $675,000.

7/17/99

Demob. continues. Confirming names/filing positions for turn over organization. Mark Carlstrom to become new IC at turn over. At turn over name of incident will change to 4th of July Storm Recovery. . . . Received confirmation on two hot shot and one burn crew that were ordered. Plan to release/demob. Sacramento Hot Shots on 7/21.

Estimate size of Incident: 487,000 acres

Personnel on Incident: 187 including 54 overhead

Cost to date: $750,000

Two days prior to the formal turnover of the IC2 team, there continued to be a marked changing of the guard. An exhausted Ralph Bonde and other members of his IC2 team were stepping down and would be replaced with fresh personnel. The IC name would change, signaling a more formal change in the purpose of the efforts moving forward. Now their work was about forest recovery, primarily the clearing and rehab of portages and campsites. Increasingly, they would be assisted by out-of-state hotshot crews. The first, the Sacramento Hotshots, were coming to the end of their tour of duty. They would be replaced by three new crews. Finally, the number of overhead personnel took the biggest drop since the start of the incident on July 5.

7/18/99

Two USFS Beavers and one DNR Beaver assigned to incident. Turn back planning in full gear. DNR Beaver to be demobed COB. First serious injury of the incident (third total) occurred today, (yesterday?). Hot shot crew member slipped and fell while portaging a canoe. Was taken out of BWCAW and sent to Duluth. Broken knee cap. Put in cast and demobed to New Mexico. . . . As of 1900 hours 100% of affected campsites and portages have been checked. No injured parties were found. Better yet, no fatalities. The last known injured party was evacuated on 7/5/99. The search and rescue portion of this task, the team's primary mission, is considered complete.

Estimate size of Incident: 487,000 acres

Personnel on Incident: 172 including 46 overhead

Cost to date: $800,000

Ralph Bonde must have been feeling an elation similar to that of a runner after the successful conclusion of a marathon. He had led this IC team since before its official inception, helping it achieve its remarkable goals without losing a single team member. No fatalities had been found—and "100% of affected campsites and portages have been checked."

7/19/99

1100—Overhead team meets at Kawishiwi RD office (room 28) to self critique operations the past sixteen days. 1300—Turn back meeting begins in room 28. Approximately thirty personnel present, including both county sheriffs, Forest Supervisor, three district rangers, reps from MIFC and others. Incident turned back to Forest at 1400 hours. Personnel not reassigned to turn over team are demobed. Turn over include a "TYPE 3" Team to manage the storm recovery phase of the incident (MN-SUP-99056) along with an Incident Action Plan for the operations period 7/19/99, a current status map, rehab plan, and list of resources being transferred to the Forest.

/ / /

Ralph Bonde's notes regarding the IC2 team's last official briefing barely capture what must have been a momentous meeting. Nearly everyone who had been present on July 5—when the first elements of the disaster were becoming known and Jim Sanders, the county sheriffs, and others decided to authorize the Type II incident management team—was present that day. Nothing in Ralph's words indicates anything more happening on July 19 than the official handoff of the IC2 team's duties to a new IC3 team. But one can imagine, reading between the lines, that he and the entire team might have marked the end of their duties with a standing ovation. It would have been a fitting conclusion to everyone's Herculean labors over the past fourteen days.

PART IV

—————

RECOVERY

37

BOW ECHOES, MESOSCALES, DERECHOS, AND MORE

West to East across Northern Minnesota

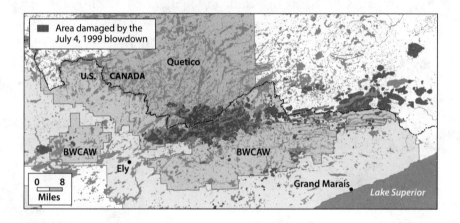

Area damaged by the July 4, 1999 blowdown

Quetico

U.S. CANADA

BWCAW

Ely

BWCAW

Grand Marais

Lake Superior

0 8 Miles

Historically, wind events happen across Minnesota every year. In the past, especially during the warm summer months, several have wreaked significant damage across the North Star State.

But there are wind events, and then there are derechos. This type of thunderstorm is long lasting and highly damaging. The NOAA/NWS Storm Prediction Center explains, "A storm is classified as a derecho if wind damage swath extends more than 240 miles and has wind gusts of at least 58 mph or greater along most of the length of the storm's path." Further, "'Derecho' is a Spanish word meaning 'right,' 'direct,' or 'straight ahead.' . . . . The word 'derecho' was coined in 1888 by Dr. Gustavus Hinrichs, a professor of physics at the University of Iowa. Hinrichs used the term in a paper published by the *American Meteorological Journal* to distinguish thunderstorm-induced straight-line winds from the damaging, rotary winds of tornadoes." The professor used the term to describe a significant wind event that crossed Iowa on July 31, 1877.

This origin is interesting for two reasons. First, the terrible storm that spawned the term happened in the Upper Midwest (Iowa). Second, it happened in July, a month that could be considered the most likely season for derechos. According to *About Derechos*, a NOAA paper that includes a list of thirty historic U.S. derechos, ten happened in July and five happened in the last half of June (most near the end). Notably, of the ten that happened in July, three of them occurred on July 4. But of the thirty derechos listed, only six came through Minnesota. Five of those were well south of northeastern Minnesota and the Boundary Waters. A derecho that happened July 12–13, 1995 (the "Right Turn Derecho"), was the only previous one to touch the BWCAW, along its southern border. And that was only the northern edge of the storm, so damage was minimal.

Clearly, derechos as far north as Minnesota's Arrowhead Region were unusual, which was just one of the reasons the storm that unfurled on July 4, 1999, was so unexpected.

/ / /

Even if there had been some way to forewarn Boundary Waters visitors about what the Duluth NWS office was predicting, those reports didn't predict the full extent of what eventually occurred. The Doppler radar and other meteorological tools were showing serious storm intensity, but the ingredients and climatological conditions required to foster a derecho of this intensity are so complex and multifarious that several meteorologists and scientists would subsequently study and write about the event.

In addition to the NWS report referenced in chapter 6, University of Wisconsin professor Madeline Sky Dierking published the paper "Factors Leading to the Development of the July 4, 1999 Boundary Waters Canoe Area Derecho" (May 5, 2009). Dierking was assisted in her effort by Professor Greg Tripoli and teaching assistant Dan Henz. Both reports are filled with meteorological jargon, making them practically incomprehensible to nonexperts. The Dierking report begins, in part, with the following abstract:

This storm developed due to interplay between synoptic forcing and mesoscale features which created a highly unstable environment and vertical forcing. In the early morning hours of July 4, 1999, thunderstorms that formed in South Dakota due to a cold front, merged into an MCS and linearly organized into a squall line near Fargo, North Dakota. Near Ely, Minnesota, this squall line encountered highly unstable air, due to abundant low-level moisture and heat, and additional vertical forcing due to the positioning downstream of a shortwave trough and location near the right entrance region of an upper level jet, causing the storm band to accelerate into a bow echo over the Boundary Waters Canoe Area Wilderness. This derecho event can be directly attributed to synoptic and mesoscale features, such as a vorticity max at mid levels, and density current that intensified the squall line's updraft. And a surface front south of the storms development that helped force stable frontal air into the updraft and get drawn past the level of inhibition and break into the convective available potential energy aloft, before the intensified downdraft lead stable air being held aloft to crash to the surface.

Understanding what this describes is best left to professionals with advanced degrees in climate science. Yet even a lay reader is struck by the meteorological complexity of what happened.

Peter Leschak, who for thirty years was chief of the French Township fire department in Side Lake, Minnesota, has long been a student of the weather, particularly in northern Minnesota. He has worked in a variety of wildfire-related capacities and held positions of leadership in the Minnesota Department of Natural Resources and the U.S. Forest Service. He has written ten books and countless journal, newspaper, and magazine articles. As someone who worked intensively on the July 4, 1999, blowdown cleanup, he recognizes the important role weather played in that event as well as many others.

Peter described what happened in the Boundary Waters the early afternoon of July 4 with less jargon than Professor Dierking's scientific paper. In part, when a warm front full of moisture meets a cold front, the warm air mass rises, is eventually cooled by the atmosphere, and condenses in precipitation. Typically, summer precipitation involves thunderstorms that, according to Peter, "anvil out. The top flattens out because it's reached the edge of the troposphere—49,000 to 50,000 feet. As you lift through the troposphere the temperature drops an average of 3.5 degrees per 1,000 feet. But the temperatures above the troposphere boundary, believe it or not, begin to rise." With a storm as strong as the one that happened on July 4, all of the various climatological ingredients—atmospheric pressures from a Canadian jet stream and a midlevel trough, as well as abundant moisture—were present to drive this storm's convection currents, forcing them to "bust through the troposphere/ stratosphere boundary," explained Peter. "I remember hearing that the derecho that hit that day . . . the top of the thunderhead was at 65,000 feet. The reason you get the violence in any thunderstorm, but especially in a derecho, is because what goes up must come down. As convection currents finally decay, they must come down. Crudely speaking, the higher up that the cell has gone, the more violent the downdrafts will be when it falls apart. And so, there it was . . . 100- to 110-mile straight-line winds."

/ / /

The derecho that spawned on that American holiday in 1999 continued storming for approximately 6,000 more miles. And while it left a serious path of destruction in its wake, the most intense part of the storm with the worst destruction unfolded in the early-afternoon hours of July 4 directly over the Boundary Waters Canoe Area Wilderness. The devastation and pain it wreaked was more severe than anything the region had ever seen.

EPILOGUE

The people referenced in this Epilogue either played a significant role in *Gunflint Falling* (and so readers might be interested to know what happened to them) or shared an interesting story about the blowdown that for one reason or another was not included in the book's narrative. For a list of everyone who assisted in the writing of this book, please see the Acknowledgments.

/ / /

Vicky Brockman recuperated in the Duluth hospital for ten days. "They were giving me IVs of painkillers," Vicky recalled. "I was on morphine."

After it was determined that the best course of treatment for Vicky was to keep her calm and let her body heal itself, she remained in bed for the first four days. She had a roommate her first night, but for the rest of her stay she had her own room. "It was nice to have my own room and a view of the lake," Vicky said with a laugh.

While she had several hairline fractures in her pelvis, the doctors were more concerned about "the humongous contusion on the side of my left leg where the tree had fallen," she said. "I had fluid going down my leg. No gash. It was a bruise. But it was the biggest bruise you've ever seen, and it swelled up 3 inches."

Vicky didn't walk until the day she left, though she eventually made a full recovery.

Approximately one year later she was contacted by the crew of *Storm Stories*, a documentary series produced by the Weather Channel. Vicky, Jan Fiola, and Sue Ann Martinson were all interviewed, and Vicky and Jan returned to Seagull Lake with a film crew. Others were also interviewed for their story. Vicky was hoping to return to their island campsite on Alpine Lake, "but they weren't interested in seeing the island."

Jan Fiola passed away in 2021. **Sue Ann Martinson** continues to work and thrive in South Minneapolis.

/ / /

Besides his own experience, **Bruce Kerfoot** shared others' harrowing blowdown stories, one involving another Gunflint Lodge guide who was camping on the end of a point near the Granite River. The point had several fully mature aspen trees. After making sure his guests were as safe as they could be, the guide had remained near the end of the point when the huge trees began to fall.

"They started coming down," Bruce recalled. "[The guide] stood there and he looked, and one came down to the right of him, just a couple feet. Then one came down to the left of him. Then he looked up and, holy smokes, here came another one right at him, and he was bunched in. He couldn't run either way because he was closed in with the trees on both sides of him. And there comes another tree right at him. I don't know if he said a prayer or whatever the hell he did, but it landed right on top of him."

Fortunately, the tree was an anomalous aspen. Normally aspens grow straight and tall, with their trunks nearly vertical all the way to their canopy. This one, however, split into a Y about 30 feet up. "When the tree fell," continued Bruce, "the Y was exactly oriented so that when it came down on top of him, it was exactly in the right axis, so that the two portions of the trunk were to the right and to the left of him by about a foot. I mean, this is a massive, big tree and it literally was the way it came down, and he was absolutely surrounded by downed aspen trees and he had to, you know, climb his way out of it eventually. He said it was the most religious moment he'd ever had."

In 2016, after more than eighty years of the Gunflint Lodge and Outfitters being under Kerfoot ownership, Bruce and Sue Kerfoot sold it. Bruce spent a little time dabbling in real estate before he and Sue bought a place in the Ozarks, where they spend their winters. When asked whether he was going to stay at the lodge during his 2023 visit to the

Gunflint area, Bruce said with a chuckle, "No. I can't afford one of their cabins for the summer." He and Sue worked out an arrangement with an old friend and cabin owner near the lodge to stay in the friend's guest cabin.

/ / /

Lisa Naas remained in the hospital for five days and was allowed to return home on Friday, July 9. While she was in the hospital she had other visitors besides her camping group, including her close colleagues from Cargill. One of them was her boss, who told her the acquisition she had been discussing with her friends at the campsite had happened. She would be going to Nebraska, if she wanted.

She did not want to leave Minneapolis. Earlier, around the campfire on Lake Polly, she had thought she would turn down the promotion and transfer. She loved her new Minneapolis home and being near her good friends.

And then in the wake of her tragedy, Cargill and her colleagues gave her their undivided attention and support. They worked with Lisa as she recuperated over the following days and weeks. In the end, she decided to take the transfer.

"From a career standpoint, it was a great move," Michelle said.

"Nebraska seemed like a good idea," Lisa said. "There weren't many trees."

"And then she also found her husband in Nebraska," Michelle added. "The man she's been married to for twenty-four years."

While Lisa's friends were sad to see her go, the Nebraska promotion lasted only four years, after which she returned to Cargill's headquarters in the Twin Cities. And her friends.

"But I have not done summer camping up there since," Lisa noted. "And it's not that I wouldn't. I just haven't."

In the aftermath of Lisa's ordeal, when people ask her whether she has any lasting problems from her near-death experience, "I tell them I used to be really smart. But . . ." She laughed. "The ones who knew me before say, 'Eh, you weren't really that smart.'"

Michelle and Ray Orieux and **Kristina and Mark Schwendinger** still live in the Twin Cities, not far from Lisa Naas Alsaker and her husband. They are all still good friends.

/ / /

Approximately one month after the blowdown, **Jen Nagel** left the Wilderness Canoe Base. "That was my last summer," Jen said. "I had other work the summer of 2000." She did not leave the base because of the blowdown—rather, it had been part of her plan all along. After nearly a decade off and on at the WCB, it was time to take the next step.

She had already obtained her bachelor's degree in religion and classics from Concordia College in Moorhead, Minnesota. "And then I got my master's of divinity from the University of Chicago Divinity School. Which is kind of like a seminary degree."

Eventually, she became the pastor at University Lutheran Church of Hope in Dinkytown, Minneapolis, near the University of Minnesota campus. She married, and she and her partner, whom she met at the WCB, now have two young children. They still like to canoe and camp in the Boundary Waters.

"It's really stuck with me," Jen said about her July 4 blowdown experience. "I was always someone who liked weather and thought about meteorology and thought that was interesting. And canoe guides are also people who watch the sky. [We are] more aware of that kind of thing than typical folks. That has very much continued to be my way of watching things. Over the years, many of us have talked about a strange PTSD-type phenomenon whenever the humidity rises and the sky greens. Twenty years later, it still takes us back to that moment."

/ / /

One of the things **Tim Norman** remembers from the storm is all the damaged cars. "The park east of Grand Marais, where Steve's Sports is now. The tow truck people would bring the vehicles down there. That was something to see, the whole parking lot full of smashed vehicles. Here in Tofte you'd see a minivan go by with some elaborate duct tape and blue tarp. There were a lot of ways people made their vehicles operational again. And then a lot of them didn't. They just waited until the insurance companies totaled them."

/ / /

On the northeast side of Gunflint Lake, **Christian Preus** and his family "couldn't see anything, because we don't have a clear view of the lake," Christian explained. "You literally had to crawl over trees to get to the lake."

Christian's mother and one of his sisters owned a cabin across the lake, on the U.S. side. When the storm finally eased enough, he went to check on them. "What was interesting," he said, "was that the lake was much rougher in the middle than on either shoreline. It was very odd. It's almost like when you have a small bowl and you tap it and it stays calm on the outside and the waves go to the middle. The weather wasn't windy in the middle, but the waves were sure a lot bigger in the middle than on the shores."

Over the first couple of days and nights after the storm, Christian recalled some other memorable incidents. "All you heard for the next few days were chainsaws. And of course we were working on it for days, weeks. That whole summer."

But on that first night, Christian recalled, "I went out and the lake was completely dark because there was no electricity. It was two weeks before they got the electricity back. We were the only ones with a generator." He laughed. "So that night we put our spotlight on just so everyone on the lake could see we had light."

In conclusion, Christian said, "The blowdown was like a pickup sticks configuration. You had one tree crossing over another, and another tree crossing over that. A couple days later our daughter Kristiana and her friend Addie and her parents were over. We were sitting around having a beer and we looked out and a hundred yards away we saw the two girls 20 to 25 feet off the ground, walking on these trees that are kind of parallel to the ground. It was like the biggest jungle gym in the world."

/ / /

With regard to the storm's aftermath, **Mike Prom** said, "It forced us to be ready for other things. Our business emergency plan." In addition to Voyageur Lodge and Canoe Outfitters, Mike is now also an owner/manager of Voyageur Brewing Company in Grand Marais. So perhaps first and foremost, he is a businessman. "After the blowdown it reinforced the need for an emergency plan. So over the next couple years we created one."

There were other wilderness changes wrought by the blowdown. Before the blowdown, the Department of Natural Resources had a plan to reintroduce woodland caribou to parts of the wilderness. But when the areas they were considering turned from old-growth forest into new-growth, the plan was abandoned.

"That storm was really a kind of decision point for a lot of things," Mike said. "Afterward everyone thought the whole place was going to burn." With all that blowdown fuel, it was considered only a matter of time before the forest went up in flame and smoke. "We eventually had fires."

The Cavity Lake fire happened in 2006 and burned approximately 32,000 acres. The Ham Lake fire happened the next year and burned approximately 76,000 acres. Much of those two fires was fueled by the downed trees leftover from the blowdown.

"But as resort owners," Mike continued, "it changed how we messaged about the wilderness." After the blowdown and those two large fires, some visitors would express disinterest in seeing an area that had suffered from the disasters. "But even with the biggest fires you can find places that are unaffected. And you don't always have to camp next to a two-hundred-year-old white pine or red cedar. You can experience all stages of the forest ecosystem."

"I am always amazed at how this Gunflint community comes together," continued Mike, who experienced it firsthand after the blowdown and in the wake of other disasters. "After the blowdown, the resort was fourteen days without power." The resort's refrigerated food began to spoil. "I remember pumping gas by hand for people needing fuel for their generators." But in a day or two "we had neighbors who brought us generators." They used the generators to power parts of the lodge and their fuel pump.

One of Voyageur's food providers is Upper Lakes Foods out of Cloquet.

When the owner of Upper Lakes Foods found out about the calamity at the end of the Gunflint Trail, he brought up a refrigerator truck that cabin and resort owners could use to keep their food from spoiling. "We ran it off two 55-gallon drums," Mike said.

Mike was on the north edge of the storm. He lost approximately thirty trees on his two acres, but many were left standing. Other nearby resort owners were not so lucky. Dan Baumann, the owner of Golden Eagle Lodge, was in the center of the storm and lost most of the trees on his property. "He got hammered," Mike recalled. After Mike and some of his employees cleared their property, they took their chainsaws and went down the Gunflint Trail to the Golden Eagle Lodge. There they worked side by side with Dan and his employees to help with the cleanup.

"And I tell that story because of the neighbor stuff," Mike concluded.

/ / /

After the blowdown, wilderness ranger **Nicole Selmer** transitioned to new U.S. Forest Service positions, some involving work on prescribed burns. In 2010 she was helping with a prescribed burn on and around Kekekabic Lake. After she was done, she chose to exit the area via the same route she had taken in 1999: Spoon Lake to Dix to Skoota and into Missionary. She had not visited the area in more than a decade.

"I didn't know what I would see," she recalled. "I had in my mind the memory of climbing a 10-foot wall of fallen trees like it was a ladder. The portage had been impassable, and there was no way to cross it. We cut our way through it, making a path just wide enough to haul our canoe and supplies to the other side."

Now Nicole saw almost no remnants of the blowdown. "The portage was open. If you looked to either side and you knew what you were looking for, you'd see some old fallen trees. But they were maybe 2 feet off the ground, not 10. And it was no longer a corridor bordered by fallen trees. To anyone else just traveling through, they never would have guessed it. Seeing the portages several years later, no one would know there had been a catastrophic wind event that leveled the forest. By 2010 the forest was filled with new growth—10- and 15-foot aspens had sprung up on the remnants of their ancestors. Mother Nature is amazing," concluded Nicole.

/ / /

"I spent until October working on the forest almost every day," wilderness ranger **Pete Weckman** said. "All of July, August, and September. I spent more than one hundred days using a chainsaw out in the bush. It was a heart-wrenching time of not getting any sleep and just go-go-go all the time. Quite the experience."

/ / /

"After the storm, it was an awful lot of chainsawing," remembered Wilderness Canoe Base director **Jim Wiinanen.** Half of Fishhook Island and all of Dominion reside outside the BWCAW, so the staff didn't need special approval to use chainsaws. Also, the only way to get around the islands is by foot, so all the footpaths, which were covered by fallen trees and debris, had to be cleared. "We were able to cut up what we needed for firewood, for winter and the sauna and whatever," Jim said. But they had many more downed trees and limbs and forest debris than they would ever need for firewood. "And we had an awful lot of old-growth jack pine and balsam fir."

Many people wondered why so much timber that had fallen in the BWCAW, especially mature old growth, wasn't harvested and used for lumber. But the laws and regulations governing the BWCAW don't permit harvesting trees, let alone building the infrastructure required to support that work. In order to use trees for lumber, you first need to be able to get to them, so they can be cut down. Then they need to be hauled out of the woods—placed on some sort of transport (typically a lumber truck) and hauled to a sawmill where they can be processed. Even if the Forest Service had relaxed the wilderness rules and allowed some rudimentary roads to be built into wilderness areas, it would have taken at least a year to build them. Once trees are on the ground and essentially dead, they begin to rot. If they lie on the ground for a year or more, they become unsuitable for use as lumber.

The preceding notwithstanding, in areas outside the BWCAW, logging was permitted, and in many cases loggers began a massive harvest. But it was very different from cutting down mature, healthy trees. Many trees were broken off at heights that made them unsuitable for turning into lumber.

At the WCB, Jim Wiinanen and others on the staff realized they had a massive lumber windfall if they could figure out how to take advantage of it. "Probably within a month of the storm, we were able to convince the administration to buy a small sawmill," Jim said. Eventually, they reached out to Wood-Mizer, a manufacturer of portable sawmills. Wood-Mizer had a philanthropic program that would provide organizations like the WCB with equipment. Unfortunately, the camp staff still needed to figure out how to ship the portable sawmill to the end of the Gunflint Trail. And then they had to find someone who knew, or could learn, how to operate it. Eventually, a former staffer who owned a trucking company facilitated the delivery. Another long-retired former staffer came to camp and started processing the logs on the mill.

In years past, the heavy lifting to build most of the camp facilities had been done by sheer human power. But salvaging logs for the mill was beyond what could be done by physical effort alone. "We made another plea for an ASV Posi-Track that had a bucket and a clam on the front that could grab and move logs around," Jim said. They waited until winter when the ice was thick enough to drive the loader to the island. "We were able to start stockpiling logs, and that got us into 2000. We were well on our way to creating 'lemonade out of lemons' and had over 10,000 board feet of lumber in the logs we had accumulated near the sawmill. The lumber our volunteer sawyer was producing was immediately put to use in repairs around camp, such as decks, steps, and boardwalks. Additional lumber was slated for camp enhancements such as improved signage, shelving, and smaller structures such as woodsheds and storage units."

While the camp was able to make excellent use of many of the fallen trees, not everyone shared the crew's enthusiasm for what they had accomplished. "As luck would have it," Jim concluded, "right at that time, the administration of the camp was leased to another organization that determined the machines unsafe and immediately sold the sawmill and ASV Posi-Track, bringing our operation to a halt with the remaining stockpiled logs turning into compost in the woods."

ADDENDUM
WIND, FIRE, AND WARMING

University of Minnesota, St. Paul Campus
Green Hall, Room 330F

T he August day is overcast and moderately cool for the second day of the second-hottest month in Minnesota. But that's according to historical averages. When Lee Frelich, the director of the Center for Forest Ecology at the University of Minnesota, discusses the changing climate, you begin to understand that we are entering uncharted territory. Climatological history is being forged anew, and what was true yesterday will not be true tomorrow. By averages we are talking about an increase of only a handful of degrees. But by resulting extreme weather events—especially wind (1999 blowdown), fires (Cavity Lake, Ham Lake, and Pagami Creek), and temperature rise (Ontario 2012)—and their resulting impact on the boreal forest, we are talking about something much more profound.

"If we had two springs in a row like 2012," Dr. Frelich begins, referencing a warm spell that drove March temperatures as far north as Ontario into the 80s, "it could wipe out the whole boreal forest in one fell swoop." Frelich supports his assertions with data, illustrating them with physical and visual evidence. In explaining what happened in that year, he points to an aerial photograph of a huge swath of Ontario spruce, fir, and jack pine. The photograph was taken in May 2012, after the unseasonably warm March temperatures triggered the trees' needles to come out of dormancy and start transpiring water, beginning the process of sprouting new needles. By May the typical gray-green healthy forest had been transformed into a solid plane of rust orange, appearing, for all intents and purposes, dead.

"They woke up too early and then froze later," Frelich explains. The trees lost most of their needles, which they use to convert sunlight into energy to survive. The typical spruce needle lives about six years. Eventually they were able to grow new ones. "They're just now fully recovered. But if it happened two springs in a row they would die, because they would not be able to make enough energy."

If current climatological trends continue, he concludes, "By 2090 an average spring will be like the spring of 2012. So sometime between now and then, if [the boreal forest] wasn't wiped out some other way, that will happen."

In spite of his predictions about a future in which the boreal forest might be wiped out "in one fell swoop," the professor is not given to hyperbole. Like Sergeant Joe Friday on the old TV police drama *Dragnet*, Frelich sticks to "just the facts." Also, unlike his dire predictions, his appearance is the antithesis of a modern-day Nostradamus. He wears a short-sleeved dark blue plaid shirt with a button-down collar, dark gray jeans, and matching dark gray tennis shoes. His demeanor is mild-mannered and Minnesota nice. His top corner office at the University of Minnesota's Green Hall is similarly modest, with a small circular fan in one of two windows, a long desk with overhead shelves filled with books, more shelves on a side wall filled with various papers, and a spartan table with two chairs.

While Nostradamus foretold a vague, distant cataclysmic future based on mysticism and the occult, Frelich predicts a shorter-term cataclysmic future based on scientific fact. Given his vitae, his prognostications should command our attention.

After acquiring his PhD in forest ecology from the University of Wisconsin–Madison in 1986, he wasted little time rising to the top of his class. According to his brief bio, he is "listed among the top 1% of all scientists in the world in the Web of Science, Ecology, and Environment Category." He has authored more than two hundred publications with 287 coauthors from twenty-six countries; his publishers include Cambridge University Press and Oxford University Press. When it comes to talking publicly about his research interests—including forest fires, wind, earthworm invasion, climate change, and related topics—he is frequently interviewed by and quoted in the popular media, including the *New York Times*, *Newsweek*, CBS Radio's *The Osgood Files*, and the *Washington Post*.

On this day, he is talking about the July 4, 1999, Boundary Waters blowdown and the Ham Lake fire of 2007, placing two of the state's most destructive disasters in historical context and explaining why they happened, what happened, and what they portend for our future.

All climate scientists predict a future in which extreme weather events happen more frequently. While the Ham Lake fire was started by a camper, the high winds that kindled and flared that flame were in part the result of one of the most tornadic days in midwestern history. On Friday, May 4, 2007, an EF5 tornado obliterated the town of Greensburg, Kansas. From May 4 to May 6 the supercell spawned 139 tornados across Oklahoma, Colorado, Kansas, and South Dakota and whipped up high winds as far north as the Boundary Waters. The moment the Ham Lake fire was sparked and began to grow, those winds immediately fanned it into a running crown fire. They continued to fan the fire through its first night. Most forest fires bed down at night, but on the evening of May 5, as the dark descended, the Ham Lake fire continued to burn, grow, and shift.

Frelich points out that some of the fuel that fed the Ham Lake fire was the result of one of the most anomalous climatological events in Boundary Waters history: the July 4, 1999, blowdown, when thirty million trees were knocked down by winds of more than 120 miles per hour.

Fires have been burning the world's boreal forests for millennia. Bud Heinselman, a U.S. Forest Service scientist, studied Boundary Waters trees during the second half of the twentieth century. Heinselman used the trees' fire scars and ages to chronicle and map forest fires in northern Minnesota from 1595 to 1976. Frelich uses a series of PowerPoint slides to demonstrate how Heinselman's nearly four-hundred-year fire history documents more than three-quarters of the Boundary Waters burning at one time or another. And those were only the parts of the vast 1-million-acre wilderness Heinselman was able to survey.

But while fires sometimes destroy vast tracts of trees, for the most part they have not changed the overall composition of the boreal forest.

Frelich explains that depending on frequency and intensity, fires almost always leave behind enough seeds to regrow the forest. "For fires like the work Heinselman chronicled, you get what you had. So if you had jack pine before the fire, you had jack pine after. If you had aspen before, you had aspen after. If you had red pine before, you had red pine after." Perhaps more typically, if a forest fire destroyed a mature mixed forest of jack pine, white pine, maybe some red pine, cedar, and aspen, for example, two to three decades after the fire had been extinguished you'd see the same mixed forest.

Heinselman found that this forest succession process largely holds, though not always. Because of the different ages at which different kinds of trees reach reproductive maturity, as well as the different ways in which they propagate, the frequency and intensity of forest fires can alter the typical forest succession path. In other words, if a jack pine and/or black spruce forest burns at 20- to 150-year intervals, it will be replaced with the same forest. If it burns more often than every 20 years, it will be replaced by aspen, birch, or both. And if there is no fire in a forest section for more than 150 years, the forest will typically consist of black spruce, balsam fir, paper birch, and white cedar.

When most people think about Minnesota's boreal forest, they think of majestic white pines and red pines. Generally these trees grow where forest fire intensity is diminished: on peninsulas, islands, and lakeshores.

Again, the "you get what you had" typical forest succession, as well as the periodic anomalies due to forest fire intensity and frequency, held true until the end of the twentieth century. At that point climate change began spawning more extreme climatological events that are today altering parts of Minnesota's boreal forest, possibly forever.

While fires rarely changed the overall face of the forest before the present era, windstorms are a different matter. Like forest fires, wind events have been knocking down Boundary Waters trees for millennia, but not to the extreme degree they did on July 4, 1999. During that famous blowdown, Frelich reports, "We lost thirty million trees. It was an anomalous Boundary Waters event, climatologically."

Lee Frelich narrates several presentation slides, explaining why the 1999 blowdown was so unusual. "It was partly because it was such a severe storm. Any trees more than thirty to forty years old would have been leveled. Winds were over 120 miles per hour," Frelich explains. "And its path really goes from Fargo to Maine. The worst damage was right in the Boundary Waters."

There are historical records of similar blowdown events, "but never at that latitude," Frelich continues. "I think we have much higher dew points now during the summer heat waves, and that's the energy that these storms feed on. It's all this tropical air that's getting further north than it used to. So a derecho—these big thunderstorms that are defined by having damage paths 250 miles in length—they need a feed of tropical air that goes into the storm. And that's in a low-level jet stream, not a high one. Those low-level jets are only a few thousand feet above the ground, and they come straight up the Mississippi River. If there's a low-level jet stream with tropical air from New Orleans feeding that air directly into a thunderstorm, it has unlimited energy."

During the 1999 derecho event, the thunderstorm was fed tropical air all the way from Fargo to Maine. It was, according to Frelich, *really extraordinary.* "There were six thousand cloud-to-ground lightning strikes per hour as it moved across the continent. One hundred per minute. . . . Some places had 7 inches of rain."

The event was devastating to the boreal forest. The felling of thirty million trees impacted the Boundary Waters and the surrounding boreal forest in several different ways. First, it created a sudden, huge quantity of burnable fuel.

The largest and most devastating forest fire in Minnesota history, the Hinckley fire of 1894, happened in large part because of a super-abundance of burnable fuel. Problematically, logging regulations in the late 1800s were nonexistent. Loggers would enter the woods, cut down trees, strip them of branches and bark, and haul out the trunks, leaving the forest detritus behind. After several years logging the entire area surrounding Hinckley (and nearby communities) and leaving behind the forest debris, the area was ripe for fire. Then in 1894 the summer was unseasonably hot and dry. When the area finally got a spark, Hinckley and eleven nearby towns blew up like a powder keg, killing 418 people and burning 350,000 acres.

Fortunately, the increase in burnable fuel in the immediate years after the 1999 blowdown didn't result in anything as devastating as the Hinckley fire, but it did feed and intensify small and large fires in the area during the next decade, most notably the Cavity Lake fire of 2006, the Ham Lake fire of 2007, and the Pagami Creek fire of 2011.

The blowdown was also devastating to the boreal forest because of its impact on forest propagation. Jack pine and black spruce, for example, have serotinous cones. Pine cones contain the seeds of the tree's next generation, but they are covered by a resin that must be melted to open and spread those seeds. When fires occur in healthy forests the intense heat opens the serotinous cones at the tops of these trees, releasing seeds that can then be spread by wind and gravity, regenerating the jack pine and spruce forest.

But blowdown events create no intense heat, felling jack pine and spruce without opening and spreading their seeds. A subsequent fire event may open the cones, but given the fire's location (on the ground) and intensity (significant, especially with abundant burnable fuel), they would also be quickly consumed.

Similarly, other tree species—such as red pine, white pine, white cedar, and balsam fir—that rely on more restrictive propagation methods may also be permanently affected.

At this point Frelich displays a progression map of the Ham Lake fire of 2007, comparing it to a map depicting areas where the forest was severely impacted by the 1999 blowdown. "So you can see part of the Ham Lake fire was not in the blowdown and part of it was," he continues. Given the different ways in which different boreal forest trees propagate, the resulting forest, at least in some areas, should be changed. "And that's exactly what we have observed. In the areas that have blown down and burned, you're only getting birch and aspen. While the areas unaffected by the blowdown are experiencing significant pine regeneration."

From Bud Heinselman's seminal forest research starting in the 1970s, moving forward to Frelich's research today, we now have a half century of boreal forest research. Some research is photographic, so Frelich can demonstrate in pictures the changes happening to the forest succession he describes.

"Here's a two-hundred-year-old red pine forest on Three Mile Island," he says, showing a slide containing two pictures of Seagull Lake.

The photograph on the left was taken before the 1999 blowdown and shows several beautiful, healthy red pines, telephone-pole thick and straight, their trunks rising above "an understory of black spruce and cedar." The photograph on the right shows the same scene after the 1999 blowdown. All but one of the red pines is horizontal. The rest of the pines lie fallen and scattered across the devastated landscape, as though Paul Bunyan and Babe the blue ox have been playing a game of pickup sticks.

The forest succession story continues on the next slide, which contains two more photographs of the same exact area. One shows the blown-down forest burned over by a U.S. Forest Service prescribed burn in 2002. The landscape appears postapocalyptic, with everything blackened and the earth covered with ash. A couple of trunks are still standing, with several more lying horizontally, but the dead trees and debris fueled an intense fire, and all of them have been severely burned.

To the right is a photograph of the same forest five years later. There are still fallen and standing dead red pines, their trunks bearing scars from the previous fire. The ground is now thick and green, but the only tree species growing is birch. "The pine forest was wiped out," Frelich concludes. "It started like that"—he flips back to the photograph of the forest thriving with two-hundred-year old red pines—"and now it's like that"—he flips back to the area covered in birch saplings.

Bringing his discussion back full circle, Frelich summarizes this part of his research: "If it was in the 1999 blowdown and it burned in the Ham Lake fire, it's coming back as birch and aspen. The blowdown destroyed the red, white, and jack pines. It blew them down and their cones were on the ground and were consumed by the fire instead of being briefly scorched like they would have if they were up in the canopy."

/ / /

Professor Lee Frelich enumerates other factors that, when combined with wind, fire, and rising temperatures, will—if our continued carbon emissions remain on their current trajectory—very likely alter the boreal forest in dramatic ways. Given the totality of threats, it makes a nonscientific observer wonder whether today's boreal forest could be wiped out over the next seventy-five to one hundred years.

"Oh, absolutely," affirms Frelich. "In some places it will be supplanted with maple and oak. But in other places it could become prairie."

As if the information he has already provided doesn't paint a complete enough picture, Frelich pulls out another document: *Report on Forest Vegetation Analyses Portion of "Climate Change Adaptation Planning for Northern Forest Ecosystems in the Great Lakes National Parks (PMIS 157471)"* from June 30, 2018. Frelich authored this report for the National Park Service (NPS) "with substantial collaborative efforts from Ryan Toot, graduate student, Natural Resource Science and Management Graduate Program; Ming Chen, postdoctoral associate, Department of Forest Resources; Ethan Butler, postdoctoral associate, Department of Forest Resources; and Peter B. Reich, Regents Professor and Hubachek Chair, Department of Forest Resources.

He quickly pages through the document until he comes to the section discussing Voyageurs National Park. Most people consider Voyageurs a Minnesota and NPS jewel, one of the finest examples of boreal forest in the world. However, Frelich's report reads, in part, "Although it has historically been thought of as a boreal forest park, and there is indeed heavy dominance of boreal species, nevertheless there is a significant and increasing representation of temperate tree species such as red maple due to the warming that has already occurred."

Will that trend continue? And if so, what does it portend? The report uses several different models to explain what the park's future could be. "Predictions show that by 2050, mixed forest will remain only for the coolest scenario . . . whereas the warmest of the nine scenarios would bring the prairie–forest border into the park."

A prairie in Voyageurs National Park?

This section of the report concludes that depending on whether the coolest or the warmest of the most extreme temperature and carbon emission scenarios prevail, "by 2070 the park could return to its current mixed forest status . . . or become mostly prairie."

The idea of seeing majestic stands of white and red pine replaced, by 2070, with prairie is a troubling perspective to consider.

ACKNOWLEDGMENTS

When you set out to write a book about a major catastrophe like the July 4, 1999, blowdown or the Ham Lake fire of 2007 (chronicled in my book *Gunflint Burning*), you have no idea how many people you're going to contact and interview. At first, you ask everyone for the names of others—anyone with whom you should speak. That process is exponential, and soon you have a long list of people to contact. In the case of this book, I spoke with more than one hundred people, and more than half are listed here. I tried to list everyone who assisted with the book, but I am certain I missed some; please accept my apology in advance. The majority of the people listed are retired, and some are deceased. In most but not all instances I've provided their title or position as of July 4, 1999.

Many thanks to these individuals, who shared their numerous perspectives and stories about the events surrounding the BWCAW blowdown. Although some of these people do not appear in *Gunflint Falling*, the information they gave me was indispensable in telling a complex and comprehensive story.

Terry Bergstrom, forestry technician
Ralph Bonde, forest management officer
Vicky Brockman, professor of sociology
Rob Bryers, Vermilion fishing guide
Carol Christensen, National Weather Service meteorologist
Constance Cummins, forest supervisor
Chip Elkins, law enforcement officer
Wayne Erickson, U.S. Forest Service pilot
Jan Fiola, voyageur

Dana Frame, area forest supervisor

Lee Frelich, forestry professor

Erica Hahn, EZ-GIS coordinator

Jim Hinds, forest management officer

Patti Hines, public information officer

Booker Hodges, Wilderness Canoe Base guide

Eric Humphrey, proprietor, Lake Superior Trading Post

Steve Jakala, National Park Service

Tom Kaffine, wilderness ranger

Stan Kegel, lieutenant colonel, Civil Air Patrol

Bruce Kerfoot, owner, Gunflint Lodge and Outfitters

Jody Leidholm, air attack supervisor

Peter Leschak, writer

Pat Loe, U.S. Forest Service pilot

Mike Magnuson, area forester, Minnesota Department of Natural
    Resources

Sue Ann Martinson, writer

David Meier, communications director, Friends of the BWCA

Lisa Naas Alsaker, accountant

Jen Nagel, pastor

Tim Norman, forest management officer

Maren Olson, pediatrician

Michelle Orieux, friend of Lisa Naas

Ray Orieux, friend of Lisa Naas

Roger Pekuri, engineer

John Pierce, wilderness ranger

Christian Preus, lawyer

Erika Preus, Christian Preus's daughter

Mike Prom, proprietor, Voyageur Lodge and Canoe Outfitters

Jennifer Rabuck, public information officer

Kris Reichenbach, Forest Service

Joel Rogness, Wilderness Canoe Base guide

Jim Sanders, forest supervisor

Craig Scherfenberg, air attack supervisor

Bonnie Schudy, Voyageur Canoe Outfitters employee

Steve Schug, wilderness ranger supervisor

Kristina Schwendinger, accountant
Mark Schwendinger, friend
Nicole Selmer, wilderness ranger
Bruce Slover, Kawishiwi District ranger
Mike Stewart, meteorologist
Ron Stoffel, DNR Forestry
Pete Tentinger, air attack supervisor
Kara Varberg, swamper
Pete Weckman, wilderness ranger
Jim Wiinanen, Wilderness Canoe Base director
Mike Wurst, operations section chief

While interviews with people directly impacted by the storm were important, so were many other sources. Near the end of the Gunflint Trail resides Chik-Wauk Museum and Nature Center, which is managed by the Gunflint Trail Historical Society (GTHS). Many of the preceding interviewees are, like me, GTHS members. During the writing of this book, I made several visits to Chik-Wauk, where I found extensive materials and viewed presentations about the blowdown. Chik-Wauk and the GTHS were indispensable resources.

Among the hundreds of news articles I read and reviewed, perhaps the most helpful printed resource was Jim Cordes's *Our Wounded Wilderness: The Great Boundary Waters Canoe Area Wilderness Storm* (2000). In the immediate aftermath of the storm, Jim, editor Tom Fiero, and designer Karen Hoeft gathered a plethora of eyewitness accounts, news articles, and photographs and self-published them in an invaluable compendium. Like the GTHS, Jim's book was an invaluable resource and was the first place I learned about many of the people featured in this book.

In 2003, the Weather Channel launched *Storm Stories*, a series that showcased extreme weather events. One of the first programs featured the July 4, 1999, blowdown. For that episode the Weather Channel reached out to Vicky Brockman, Jan Fiola, and Sue Ann Martinson, among others, and featured their harrowing story of storm survival. It was helpful to see the interview comments of the survivors when the event was still fresh in everyone's mind.

Minnesota Public Radio and its Grand Marais affiliate, WTIP, have periodically covered interesting blowdown programs and stories. When I was first undertaking research on this book, WTIP produced *The 1999 Blowdown Storm: Looking Back after Twenty Years*. This excellent program conveys many interesting and riveting firsthand accounts of what happened during the blowdown and its aftermath.

Other informative resource materials included:

Dierking, Madeline Sky. "Factors Leading to the Development of the July 4, 1999, Boundary Waters Canoe Area Derecho." Madison: University of Wisconsin, 2009.

Moser, W. Keith, et al. *After the Blowdown: A Resource Assessment of the Boundary Waters Canoe Area Wilderness, 1999–2003*. Newtown Square, Penn.: U.S. Forestry Service, 2007.

Muus, Pastor Ham. *Wilderness Witness*. Minnetonka, Minn.: self-published, 2006.

NWS Storm Prediction Center. "July 4–5, 1999, Derecho: 'The Boundary Waters—Canadian Derecho.'" 2014.

Parke, Peter S., and Norvan J. Larson. *Boundary Waters Windstorm: The Blowdown of July 4th, 1999*. Duluth, Minn.: Duluth Weather Forecast Office, National Weather Service, September 28, 2009.

Cary J. Griffith is the author of several books. His nonfiction includes *Lost in the Wild, Opening Goliath* (winner of a Minnesota Book Award), and *Gunflint Burning: Fire in the Boundary Waters* (Minnesota, 2018). His novels are *Wolf Kill, Cougar Claw,* and *Killing Monarchs.*